The Definitive Guide to Linux Network Programming

KEIR DAVIS, JOHN W. TURNER, AND NATHAN YOCOM

Apress®

The Definitive Guide to Linux Network Programming
Copyright © 2004 by Keir Davis, John W. Turner, Nathan Yocom

ISBN (pbk): 1-59059-322-7

Printed and bound in the United States of America 9 8 7 6 5 4 3 2 1

Trademarked names may appear in this book. Rather than use a trademark symbol with every occurrence of a trademarked name, we use the names only in an editorial fashion and to the benefit of the trademark owner, with no intention of infringement of the trademark.

Lead Editor: Jim Sumser

Technical Reviewer: Kirk Bauer

Editorial Board: Steve Anglin, Dan Appleman, Ewan Buckingham, Gary Cornell, Tony Davis, John Franklin, Jason Gilmore, Chris Mills, Steve Rycroft, Dominic Shakeshaft, Jim Sumser, Karen Watterson, Gavin Wray, John Zukowski

Project Manager: Laura Cheu

Copy Edit Manager and Copy Editor: Nicole LeClerc

Production Manager: Kari Brooks

Production Editor: Janet Vail

Compositor: Molly Sharp, ContentWorks

Proofreader: Linda Seifert

Indexer: James Minkin

Artist: Kinetic Publishing Services, LLC

Cover Designer: Kurt Krames

Manufacturing Manager: Tom Debolski

Distributed to the book trade in the United States by Springer-Verlag New York, Inc., 175 Fifth Avenue, New York, NY 10010 and outside the United States by Springer-Verlag GmbH & Co. KG, Tiergartenstr. 17, 69112 Heidelberg, Germany.

In the United States: phone 1-800-SPRINGER, email orders@springer-ny.com, or visit http://www.springer-ny.com. Outside the United States: fax +49 6221 345229, email orders@springer.de, or visit http://www.springer.de.

For information on translations, please contact Apress directly at 2560 Ninth Street, Suite 219, Berkeley, CA 94710. Phone 510-549-5930, fax 510-549-5939, email info@apress.com, or visit http://www.apress.com.

The information in this book is distributed on an "as is" basis, without warranty. Although every precaution has been taken in the preparation of this work, neither the author(s) nor Apress shall have any liability to any person or entity with respect to any loss or damage caused or alleged to be caused directly or indirectly by the information contained in this work.

The source code for this book is available to readers at http://www.apress.com in the Downloads section.

To the loving memory of my mother, Nancy. And to my lovely wife, Jennifer, who put up with me throughout this process. Yes, honey, the book is finished.
—Keir

My participation in this project would not have been possible without the love, encouragement, and support of my family and friends, particularly my parents. I was encouraged to learn, explore, and question from my earliest days, and my parents never shied away from providing me the opportunity to do just that. My contributions to this project are dedicated to my father, William Turner, to the memory of my mother, Susan Turner, and to my sister, Becki.
—John

For my wonderful wife, Katie, who never loses faith in me; my family for supporting me; and my daughter, who makes me smile every day.
—Nate

Contents at a Glance

Contents

About the Authors

Keir Davis was first exposed to programming at the age of 12, when his father brought home a Texas Instruments TI-99/4A. Keir has been programming ever since and now holds a master's degree in computer science from the University of North Carolina at Greensboro. Today, Keir is the owner of Xtern Software (http://www.xternsoftware.com), a provider of custom software development services to manufacturers around the world.

Recently married, Keir and his wife, Jennifer, live with their two dogs, Tess and Maggie, in North Carolina. When not sitting in front of a computer, Keir enjoys playing racquetball.

John Turner is an application developer and systems administrator in Detroit, Michigan, supporting the advertising and marketing campaigns of Fortune 50 clients. With over two decades of computer experience, John has designed and administered high-availability and fault-tolerant systems for the automotive, health care, and advertising industries. He coauthored the *Apache Tomcat Security Handbook* and is an Apache Group committer. He holds a bachelor's degree in information systems.

John's industry interests include vintage hardware, open source, mobile computing, and wireless networking. His outside interests include farming, DIY projects, dogs, history, recycling, tattoos, travel, and music composition.

Nathan Yocom has worn many hats in the IT industry over the years. He currently works as a software engineer for Bynari, Inc., specializing in messaging and groupware software. With a bachelor's degree in computer science from Pacific Lutheran University, Nathan is also the cofounder of XPA Systems (http://www.xpasystems.com) and author of pGina, an open source program that simplifies the Windows logon process by providing for the authentication of a user via many different methods.

In his spare time, in addition to playing the guitar and an occasional round of golf, Nathan enjoys spending time with his wife, Katie.

About the Technical Reviewer

Kirk Bauer has been involved in computer programming since 1985. He has been using and administering UNIX systems since 1994. Although his personal favorite UNIX variant is Linux, he has administered and developed on everything from FreeBSD to Solaris, AIX, and IRIX. He is the author of various open-source system administration programs such as AutoRPM and Logwatch.

Bauer has been involved with software development and system/network administration since his first year at Georgia Tech. He has done work for the Georgia Tech Residential Network, the Georgia Tech Research Institute, and the Fermi National Accelerator Laboratory. Bauer was one of the founders and the CTO of TogetherWeb in 2000, which was purchased in 2003 by Proficient Systems. He is currently a software architect with Proficient Systems, and continues to support and develop the collaborative browsing software and Linux-based network appliance created by TogetherWeb, including C++ server software that provides high scalability, high efficiency, and high reliability.

Kirk graduated from Georgia Tech in 2001 with a bachelor's degree in computer engineering. Shortly thereafter, he began work on his first book, *Automating UNIX and Linux Administration*, which was published by Apress in September 2003. He currently lives in Peoria, Arizona, with his wife, Amber, and their two dogs and four cats.

Acknowledgments

I wish to thank the wonderful people at Apress for believing in the book and seeing it through to publication. It's been a long time coming, but I think that it's been worth it. Thanks also to Jim Sumser, our editor. Jim, your positive outlook and encouragement made all the difference. To Kirk Bauer, our technical editor, your insight made this a better book. Finally, I wish to thank my wife, Jennifer. I can't wait to put this book in your hands so that you can see what I've been working on all this time.

—Keir

I'd like to thank my aunts, Mary Pryde and Ann Turner; my friends Peter, Clarissa, Carla, Rich, Jessica, Jerry, and Debbie; and especially TreachRS in Boston for their constant support and for helping me keep it real. Trevor Deason and Sophia Colpean reminded me of what's important when it counted. I must also thank my coauthors, Nate and Keir, who put up with my bad jokes and choppy schedule, and made it amazingly easy to be a part of this project. The writing portion is only the beginning. There's a lot more involved in delivering a book than the writing, and the team Apress put together for this project rocked the house. Kirk's reviews were insightful, concise, and improved every chapter. Jim, Laura, Nicole, and Janet kept us all focused, organized, and happy, and took care of the myriad tasks required to actually put a book on the shelf with speed and enthusiastic aplomb. Thanks, everyone!

—John

I would like to acknowledge the help and support from Apress, whose determination to publish quality books on great subjects has helped us to make this book everything we knew it could be. Specifically, I would like to thank Jim Sumser (editorial director) and Laura Cheu (project manager) for making the DTY team complete. I would also like to thank the faculty at Pacific Lutheran University's Computer Science department for their continual excellence in education and their unwavering support of their students. Lastly, but most important, my thanks to my fellow authors and our technical reviewer, whose professionalism and ability lend great compliment to their character.

—Nathan

Introduction

As DEVELOPERS, WE FIND ourselves challenged by the ubiquity of the Internet on a daily basis as we often need or want to provide some level of network service within our applications. Whether our goal is to allow remote monitoring of an application's health, enable multiple users to access a centralized service, or even authenticate a user's identity prior to giving him access to an application, network programming is a seemingly dark art practiced by only the most experienced developers. We have written this text to help you meet the challenge, and to show you that network programming can be both enjoyable and easy to learn.

From exploring the basics of networking, to creating complex multithreaded servers, to securing network communications, we present you with precise definitions, clear explanations, and easy-to-read examples. For the inexperienced network developer familiar with the C language, as well as the expert looking to pick up some extra tips, we provide information on and insight into a topic that is so often ignored, and yet sorely in need of attention.

What You Should Read

Depending on your experience with network programming and your reading style, you may find that a different approach to this text is in order. We have endeavored to write in a modular manner that presents as much independent information about each topic as possible without requiring you to have read the topics before it. However, it is impossible be completely modular, as with any programming paradigm there are foundational concepts you must understand before moving along to more advanced topics. What follows is an explanation of the book's structure and suggestions as to where you might start to get the most out of the book.

We have organized the book into three parts and an appendix. The first part covers the fundamentals of networks and network programming. The second part discusses different approaches to the design of a network application, and walks through protocol and advanced application design. The last part details methods of securing a network application, programming with the OpenSSL toolkit, and authentication, and discusses a methodology for reducing a network application's susceptibility to attack.

The Beginner: If you do not have any prior experience with networking concepts, how computers communicate on a local area network, or what abbreviations such as DNS stand for, then reading from the beginning of the book to the end is highly recommended.

The Novice: If you are familiar with networking concepts but have never encountered network programming before, then you can probably skip the first chapter. Starting with the second chapter, you will be introduced to the basic functions used in network programming and can continue through the book building concepts on top of each other.

The Experienced: Given that you have some experience with network programming, or you have even written a network application in the past, starting with the Part Two is highly recommended. Although much of this information may seem familiar to you, it is important to fully understand the different approaches to design to make the best decisions when it comes to choosing an architecture that fits your needs.

The Expert: Although it is probably not required, we recommend that even the most experienced network developer read from Chapter 7 on. While much of this material may be familiar to an expert, it is vitally important that you understand the advanced approaches to defensive programming, security, and methodology.

The Others: We fully recognize that every reader is different. If you don't like to read parts, or topics only, we encourage you to read the whole text, from start to finish. This book is packed with useful information from cover to cover, and we would like to think that there is something for everyone, regardless of experience level or learning style.

Chapter Summaries

The following sections detail the topics covered in each chapter.

Part One: Fundamentals

In this part, we will explore and practice the fundamentals of networks and network programming.

Chapter 1: Networks and Protocols

This chapter provides an introduction to the world of networking. We discuss how packets of information flow between computers on a network, and how those packets are created, controlled, and interpreted. We look at the protocols used, how DNS works, how addresses are assigned, and what approaches are often used in network design.

Chapter 2: Functions

Here you will learn the basic functions used in network programming. We examine the concept of sockets and how they are used in creating networked applications. We also present an example of a client-server program to highlight the use of these basic functions in communicating data from one machine to another.

Chapter 3: Socket Programming

This chapter discusses more real-world applications of what you learned in Chapter 2. It is in this chapter that we look at our first UDP client-server program example. We also detail the creation of a TCP client-server program for simple file transfers, highlighting the ease with which just a few basic network functions allow us to provide network services and applications.

Chapter 4: Protocols, Sessions, and State

This final chapter of Part One takes you through a thorough explanation of the various methods by which network applications can maintain state. We also walk through both a stateless (HTTP) and a stateful (POP3) protocol to see how they differ and where each is beneficial.

Part Two: Design and Architecture

This part covers the different approaches to network application design, and provides you with a thorough grounding in protocol and advanced application design.

Chapter 5: Client-Server Architecture

In this chapter, you will look at the different ways you can handle multiple, simultaneous clients. We cover the concepts and applications of multiplexing, multiprocessing servers, and the single-process-per-client approach versus the process-pool approach. Multithreaded servers are introduced and we look at an interesting approach used by the Apache 2 Web Server. We also demonstrate how to handle sending and receiving large amounts of data by using nonblocking sockets and the select system call.

Chapter 6: Implementing Custom Protocols

This chapter walks you through the creation of a custom protocol. As an example, we examine the creation of a protocol for a networked chat application similar to the popular IRC. We also detail registering a custom protocol with the operating system.

Chapter 7: Design Decisions

Here we discuss the many considerations a developer must take into account when creating a network application. There are many decisions to be made, from whether to use TCP or UDP to choices relating to protocol creation, server design, scalability, and security. These decisions are discussed in detail, and we highlight the pros and cons of each to help you make informed decisions.

Chapter 8: Debugging and Development Cycle

This chapter takes you through the many tools and methods that are useful when creating and maintaining a network application. With coverage of protocol analysis tools and code analysis tools, this is an important chapter for the new developer and the "old hand" alike.

Chapter 9: Case Study: A Networked Application

This chapter presents the first of two case studies in the book. This case study takes you through the creation of a real-world chat application from the ground up, resulting in an application that implements the protocol discussed in Chapter 6 and allows many users to chat in a method very similar to the popular IRC used for Internet chatting today.

Part Three: Security

This part details methods of securing a network application, programming with the OpenSSL toolkit, and authentication. We also present a secure programming methodology that you can use to reduce a network application's susceptibility to attack.

Chapter 10: Securing Network Communication

This chapter introduces the concepts of tunneling and public key cryptography. Discussion of the OpenSSL toolkit leads into examples using OpenSSL to secure a client-server application with the TLS protocol.

Chapter 11: Authentication and Data Signing

Here you will learn how you can use the PAM stack on your Linux machines to authenticate users of your applications transparently. We then look at identity verification through PKI and data signing, including example code for managing keys on disk and over the network.

Chapter 12: Common Security Problems

This chapter moves away from the API level for a look at the common methods by which network programs are attacked and what you can do about it. We detail each method of attack, and then examine ways to approach program design and implementation to avoid successful attacks.

Chapter 13: Case Study: A Secure Networked Application

This final chapter presents the second of our two case studies. This case study takes you through the creation of a secure networked application intended for user authentication first by password, and then using the passwordless data signing method. We bring the information presented in the entire part together into an example that has application in the real world.

Appendix: IPv6

The appendix discusses the future of network programming and the move from the current-day IPv4 to the coming IPv6. It addresses why the move is necessary and how can you write your code to be capable of using both protocols.

Conventions

Throughout this book, we have used several typographical conventions to help you better understand our intent. Here are some of the most common:

 TIP *Tips give you additional information relating to the topic at hand.*

 NOTE *Notes indicate a piece of information that is important to understand or know regarding the topic at hand.*

 CAUTION *These indicate a piece of information that it is important you understand in order to prevent security problems, errors, or common mistakes.*

We have also adopted a special font for code and user commands. Code appears as follows:

```
If ( value == true ) { // do something }
```

When we provide user commands or command output, we use a similar font, where bold text indicates what you should type. In the following example, you type the text "ping 127.0.0.1" at a prompt.

```
user@host$> ping 127.0.0.1
```

Feedback

We have made every effort to keep mistakes, typos, and other errors out of this book, but we are all only human. We would love to hear what you think, where we could be clearer, or if you find mistakes or misprints. Please feel free to drop us an e-mail at DTY@apress.com. You can also go to the Downloads area of the Apress site at http://www.apress.com to download the code from the book.

Part One

Fundamentals

CHAPTER 1

Networks and Protocols

NETWORKS CAME INTO EXISTENCE AS SOON as there was two of something: two cells, two animals and, obviously, two computers. While the overwhelming popularity of the Internet leads people to think of networks only in a computer context, a network exists anytime there is communication between two or more parties. The differences between various networks are matters of implementation, as the intent is the same: communication. Whether it is two people talking or two computers sharing information, a network exists. The implementations are defined by such aspects as medium and protocol. The network medium is the substance used to transmit the information; the protocol is the common system that defines how the information is transmitted.

In this chapter, we discuss the types of networks, the methods for connecting networks, how network data is moved from network to network, and the protocols used on today's popular networks. Network design, network administration, and routing algorithms are topics suitable for an entire book of their own, so out of necessity we'll present only overviews here. With that in mind, let's begin.

Circuits vs. Packets

In general, there are two basic types of network communications: *circuit-switched* and *packet-switched*. Circuit-switched networks are networks that use a dedicated link between two nodes, or points. Probably the most familiar example of a circuit-switched network is the legacy telephone system. If you wished to make a call from New York to Los Angeles, a circuit would be created between point A (New York) and point B (Los Angeles). This circuit would be dedicated—that is, there would be no other devices or nodes transmitting information on that network and the resources needed to make the call possible, such as copper wiring, modulators, and more would be used for your call and your call only. The only nodes transmitting would be the two parties on each end.

One advantage of a circuit-switched network is the guaranteed capacity. Because the connection is dedicated, the two parties are guaranteed a certain amount of transmission capacity is available, even though that amount has an upper limit. A big disadvantage of circuit-switched networks, however, is cost. Dedicating resources to facilitate a single call across thousands of miles is a costly proposition, especially since the cost is incurred whether or not anything is transmitted. For example, consider making the same call to Los Angeles and getting an answering machine instead of the person you were trying to reach. On a circuit-switched network, the resources are committed to the network connection and the costs are incurred even though the only thing transmitted is a message of unavailability.

A packet-switched network uses a different approach from a circuit-switched network. Commonly used to connect computers, a packet-switched network takes the information communicated on the network and breaks it into a series of packets, or pieces. These packets are then transmitted on a common network. Each packet consists of identification information as well as its share of the larger piece of information. The identification information on each packet allows a node on the network to determine whether the information is destined for it or the packet should be passed along to the next node in the chain. Once the packet arrives at its destination, the receiver uses the identification portion of the packet to reassemble the pieces and create the complete version of the original information. For example, consider copying a file from one computer in your office to another. On a packet-switched network, the file would be split into a number of packets. Each packet would have specific identification information as well as a portion of the file. The packets would be sent out onto the network, and once they arrived at their destination, they would be reassembled into the original file.

Unlike circuit-switched networks, the big advantage of packet-switched networks is the ability to share resources. On a packet-switched network, many nodes can exist on the network, and all nodes can use the same network resources as all of the others, sharing in the cost. The disadvantage of packet-switched networks, however, is the inability to guarantee capacity. As more and more nodes sharing the resources try to communicate, the portion of the resources available to each node decreases.

Despite their disadvantages, packet-switched networks have become the de facto standard whenever the term "network" is used. Recent developments in networking technologies have decreased the price point for capacity significantly, making a network where many nodes or machines can share the same resources cost-effective. For the purposes of discussion in this book, the word "network" will mean a packet-switched network.

Internetworking

A number of different technologies exist for creating networks between computers. The terms can be confusing and in many cases can mean different things depending on the context in which they're used. The most common network technology is the concept of a *local area network*, or LAN. A LAN consists of a number of computers connected together on a network such that each can communicate with any of the others. A LAN typically takes the form of two or more computers joined together via a hub or switch, though in its simplest form two computers connected directly to each other can be called a LAN as well. When using a hub or switch, the ability to add computers to the network becomes trivial, requiring only the addition of another cable connecting the new node to the hub or switch. That's the beauty of a packet-switched network, for if the network were circuit-switched, we would have to connect every node on the network to every other node, and then figure out a way for each node to determine which connection to use at any given time.

LANs are great, and in many cases they can be all that's needed to solve a particular problem. However, the advantages of a network really become apparent when you start to connect one network to another. This is called *internetworking*, and it forms the basis for one of the largest known networks: the Internet. Consider the following diagrams. Figure 1-1 shows a typical LAN.

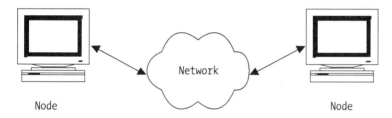

Figure 1-1. A single network

You can see there are a number of computers, or nodes, connected to a common point. In networking parlance, this is known as a *star configuration*. This type of LAN can be found just about anywhere, from your home to your office, and it's responsible for a significant portion of communication activity every day. But what happens if you want to connect one LAN to another?

As shown in Figure 1-2, connecting two LANs together forms yet another network, this one consisting of two smaller networks connected together so that information can be shared not only between nodes on a particular LAN, but also between nodes on separate LANs via the larger network.

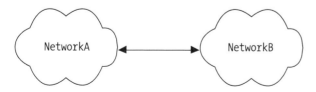

Figure 1-2. Two connected networks

Because the network is packet-switched, you can keep connecting networks together forever or until the total number of nodes on the network creates too much traffic and clogs the network. Past a certain point, however, more involved network technologies beyond the scope of this book are used to limit the traffic problems on interconnected networks and improve network efficiency. By using routers, network addressing schemes, and long-haul transmission technologies such as dense wavelength division multiplexing (DWDM) and long-haul network protocols such as asynchronous transfer mode (ATM), it becomes feasible to connect an unlimited number of LANs to each other and allow nodes on these LANs to communicate with nodes on remote networks as if they were on the same local network, limiting packet traffic problems and making network inter-connection independent of the supporting long-distance systems and hardware. The key concept in linking networks together is that each local network takes advantage of its packet-switched nature to allow communication with any number of other networks without requiring a dedicated connection to each of those other networks.

Ethernets

Regardless of whether we're talking about one network or hundreds of networks connected together, the most popular type of packet-switched network is the *Ethernet*. Developed 30 years ago by Xerox PARC and later standardized by Xerox, Intel, and Digital Equipment Corporation, Ethernets originally consisted of a single cable connecting the nodes on a network. As the Internet exploded, client-server computing became the norm, and more and more computers were linked together, a simpler, cheaper technology known as *twisted pair* gained acceptance. Using copper conductors much like traditional phone system wiring, twisted pair cabling made it even cheaper and easier to connect computers together in a LAN. A big advantage to twisted pair cabling is that, unlike early Ethernet cabling, a node can be added or removed from the network without causing transmission problems for the other nodes on the network.

A more recent innovation is the concept of *broadband*. Typically used in connection with Internet access via cable TV systems, broadband works by mul-tiplexing multiple network signals on one cable by assigning each network signal a unique frequency. The receivers at each node of the network are tuned to the correct frequency and receive communications on that frequency while ignoring communications on all the others.

A number of alternatives to Ethernet for local area networking exist. Some of these include IBM's Token Ring, ARCNet, and DECNet. You might encounter one of these technologies, as Linux supports all of them, but in general the most common is Ethernet.

Ethernet Frames

On your packet-switched Ethernet, each packet of data can be considered a *frame*. An Ethernet frame has a specific structure, though the length of the frame or packet is variable, with the minimum length being 64 bytes and the maximum length being 1518 bytes, although proprietary implementations can extend the upper limit to 4096 bytes or higher. A recent Ethernet specification called Jumbo Frames even allows frame sizes as high as 9000 bytes, and newer technologies such as version 6 of the Internet Protocol (discussed later) allow frames as large as 4GB. In practice, though, Ethernet frames use the traditional size in order to maintain compatibility between different architectures.

Because the network is packet-based, each frame must contain a source address and destination address. In addition to the addresses, a typical frame contains a *preamble*, a *type* indicator, the *data payload*, and a *cyclic redundancy checksum* (CRC). The preamble is 64 bits long and typically consists of alternating 0s and 1s to help network nodes synchronize transmissions. The type indicator is 16 bits long, and the CRC is 32 bits. The remaining bits in the packet consist of the actual packet data being sent (see Figure 1-3).

Figure 1-3. An Ethernet frame

The type field is used to identify the type of data being carried by the packet. Because Ethernet frames have this type indicator, they are known as *self-identifying*. The receiving node can use the type field to determine the data contained in the packet and take appropriate action. This allows the use of multiple protocols on the same node and the same network segment. If you wanted to create your own protocol, you could use a frame type that did not conflict with any others being used, and your network nodes could communicate freely without interrupting any of the existing communications.

The CRC field is used by the receiving node to verify that the packet of data has been received intact. The sender computes the CRC value and adds it to the packet before sending the packet. On the receiving end, the receiver recalculates the CRC value for the packet and compares it to the value sent by the sender to confirm the packet was received intact.

Addressing

We've discussed the concept of two or more computers communicating over a network, and we've discussed the concept of abstracting the low-level concerns of internetworking so that as far as one computer is concerned, the other computer could be located nearby or on the other side of the world. Because every packet contains the address of the source and the destination, the actual physical distance between two network nodes really doesn't matter, as long as a transmission path can be found between them. Sounds good, but how does one computer find the other? How does one node on the network "call" another node?

For communication to occur, each node on the network must have its own *address*. This address must be unique, just as someone's phone number is unique. For example, while two or more people might have 555-9999 as their phone number, only one person will have that phone number within a certain area code, and that area code will exist only once within a certain country code. This accomplishes two things: it ensures that within a certain scope each number is unique, and it allows each person with a phone to have a unique number.

Ethernet Addresses

Ethernets are no different. On an Ethernet, each node has its own address. This address must be unique to avoid conflicts between nodes. Because Ethernet resources are shared, every node on the network receives all of the communications on the network. It is up to each node to determine whether the communication it receives should be ignored or answered based on the destination address. It is important not to confuse an Ethernet address with a TCP/IP or Internet address, as they are not the same. Ethernet addresses are physical addresses tied directly to the hardware interfaces connected via the Ethernet cable running to each node.

An Ethernet address is an integer with a size of 48 bits. Ethernet hardware manufacturers are assigned blocks of Ethernet addresses and assign a unique address to each hardware interface in sequence as they are manufactured. The Ethernet address space is managed by the Institute of Electrical and Electronics Engineers (IEEE). Assuming the hardware manufacturers don't make a mistake, this addressing scheme ensures that every hardware device with an Ethernet interface can be addressed uniquely. Moving an Ethernet interface from one node to another or changing the Ethernet hardware interface on a node changes the Ethernet address for that node. Thus, Ethernet addresses are tied to the Ethernet device itself, not the node hosting the interface. If you purchase a network card at your local computer store, that network card has a unique Ethernet address on it that will remain the same no matter which computer has the card installed.

Let's look at an example using a computer running Linux.

```
[user@host user]$ /sbin/ifconfig eth0
eth0      Link encap:Ethernet  HWaddr 00:E0:29:5E:FC:BE
          inet addr:192.168.2.1  Bcast:192.168.2.255  Mask:255.255.255.0
          UP BROADCAST RUNNING MULTICAST  MTU:1500  Metric:1
          RX packets:35772 errors:0 dropped:0 overruns:0 frame:0
          TX packets:24414 errors:0 dropped:0 overruns:0 carrier:0
          collisions:0 txqueuelen:100
          RX bytes:36335701 (34.6 Mb)  TX bytes:3089090 (2.9 Mb)
          Interrupt:5 Base address:0x6000
```

Using the /sbin/ifconfig command, we can get a listing of the configuration of our eth0 interface on our Linux machine. Your network interface might have a different name than eth0, which is fine. Just use the appropriate value, or use the –a option to ifconfig to get a listing of all of the configured interfaces if you don't know the name of yours. The key part of the output, though, is the first line. Notice the parameter labeled HWaddr. In our example, it has a value of 00:E0:29:5E:FC:BE, which is the physical Ethernet address of this node. Remember that we said an Ethernet address is 48 bits. Our example address has six hex values. Each hex value has a maximum of 8 bits, or a value range from 00 to FF.

But what does this tell us? As mentioned previously, each hardware manufacturer is assigned a 24-bit value by the IEEE. This 24-bit value (3 octets) must remain consistent across all hardware devices produced by this manufacturer. The manufacturer uses the remaining 3 octets as a sequential number to create a unique, 48-bit Ethernet address. Let's see what we can find out about our address.

Open a web browser and go to this address: http://standards.ieee.org/regauth/oui/index.shtml. In the field provided, enter the first 3 octets of our example address, in this case 00-e0-29 (substitute a hyphen [-] for the colon [:]). Click Search, and you'll see a reply that looks like this:

```
00-E0-29   (hex)            STANDARD MICROSYSTEMS CORP.
00E029     (base 16)        STANDARD MICROSYSTEMS CORP.
                            6 HUGHES
                            IRVINE CA 92718
                            UNITED STATES
```

That's pretty descriptive. It tells us that the hardware manufacturer of our network interface is Standard Microsystems, also known as SMC. Using the same form, you can also search by company name. To illustrate how important it is that these numbers be managed, try searching with a value similar to 00-e0-29, such as 00-e0-27. Using 27, you'll find that the manufacturer is Dux, Inc. Thus, as each manufacturer is creating their products, they'll increase the second half of the Ethernet address sequentially to ensure that each device has a unique value. In our case, the second half of our address is 5E-FC-BE, which is our hardware interface's unique identifier. If the results of your search don't match the vendor of your network card, keep in mind that many companies resell products produced by another or subcontract their manufacturing to someone else.

The Ethernet address can also take on two other special values. In addition to being the unique address of a single physical interface, it can be a broadcast address for the network itself as well as a multicast address. The broadcast address is reserved for sending to all nodes on a network simultaneously. Multicast addresses allow a limited form of broadcasting, where a subset of network nodes agrees to respond to the multicast address.

The Ethernet address is also known as the MAC address. MAC stands for *Media Access Control*. Because our Ethernet is a shared network, only one node can "talk" at any one time using the network. Before a node transmits information, it first "listens" to the network to see if any other node is using the network. If so, it waits a randomly chosen amount of time and then tries to communicate again. If no other node is using the network, our node sends its message and awaits a reply. If two nodes "talk" at the same time, a collision occurs. Collisions on shared networks are normal and are handled by the network itself so as not to cause problems, provided the ratio of collisions to communications does not get too high. In the case of Ethernets, a collision rate higher than 60 percent is typically cause for concern. Each MAC address must be unique, so a node about to transmit can compare addresses to check whether another node is already transmitting. Thus, the MAC address (Ethernet address) helps control the collision rate and allows nodes to determine if the network is free to use.

Gateways

We've discussed that the Internet is a network built by physically connecting other networks. To connect our networks together, we use a special device called a *gateway*. Any Ethernet node can conceivably act as a gateway, though many do not. Gateways have two or more physical network interfaces and do a particular job, just as their name implies: they relay packets destined for other networks, and they receive packets destined for nodes on one of their own networks. Building on our earlier diagram, here's how it looks when you connect two networks together with a gateway (see Figure 1-4).

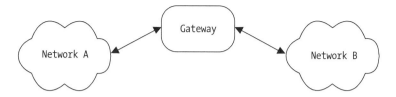

Figure 1-4. Two connected networks with a gateway

Gateways can also be called *routers*, since they *route* packets from one network to another. If you consider that all networks are equal, then the notion of
transmitting packets from one to the other becomes a little easier. No longer is
it necessary for our network nodes to understand how to find every other node
on remote networks. Maintaining that amount of ever-changing information on
every computer connected to every network would be impossible. Instead, nodes
on our local network only need to know the address of the gateway. That is, local
nodes only need to know which node is the "exit" or "gate" to all other networks.
The gateway takes on the task of correctly routing packets with foreign destina-
tions to either the remote network itself or *another gateway*. For example,
consider Figure 1-5, which shows three interconnected networks.

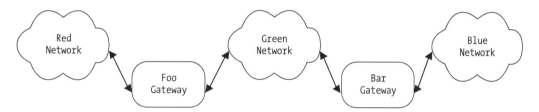

Figure 1-5. Multiple networks, multiple gateways

In this diagram, we have three networks: Red, Green, and Blue. There are
two gateways, Foo and Bar. If a node on the Red network wants to send a packet
to a node on the Green or Blue network, it does not need to keep track of the
addresses on either network. It only needs to know that its gateway to any other
network besides its own is Foo. The packets destined for the remote network are
sent to Foo, which then determines whether the packet is destined for the Green
network or the Blue network. If Green, the packet is sent to the appropriate node
on the Green network. If Blue, however, the packet is sent to Bar, because Foo

only knows about the Red and Green networks. Any packet for any other network needs to be sent to the next gateway, in this case Bar. This scenario is multiplied over and over and over in today's network environment, and it significantly decreases the amount of information that each network node and gateway has to manage.

Likewise, the reverse is true. When the receiver accepts the packet and replies, the same decision process occurs. The sender determines if the packet is destined for its own network or a remote network. If remote, then the packet is sent to the network's gateway, and from there to either the receiver or yet another gateway. Thus, a *gateway* is a device that transmits packets from one network to another.

Gateways seem simple, but as we've mentioned, asking one device to keep track of the information for every network that's connected to every other network is impossible. So how do our gateways do their job without becoming hopelessly buried by information? The gateway rule is critical: *network gateways route packets based on destination networks, not destination nodes.*

Thus, our gateways aren't required to know how to reach every node on all the networks that might be connected. A particular set of networks might have thousands of nodes on it, but the gateway doesn't need to keep track of all of them. Gateways only need to know which node on their own network will move packets from their network to some other network. Eventually, the packets reach their destination network. Since all devices on a particular network check all packets to see if the packets are meant for them, the packets sent by the gateway will automatically get picked up by the destination host without the sender needing to know any specifics except the address of its own gateway. In short, a node sending data needs to decide one thing: whether the data is destined for a local network node or remote network node. If local, the data is sent between the two nodes directly. If remote, the data is sent to the gateway, which in turn makes the same decision until the data eventually gets picked up by the recipient.

Internet Addresses

So far, you've seen that on a particular network, every device must have a unique address, and you can connect many networks together to form a larger network using gateways. Before a node on your network "talks," it checks to see if anyone else is "talking," and if not, it goes ahead with its communication. Your networks are interconnected, though! What happens if the nodes on your office LAN have to wait for some node on a LAN in Antarctica to finish talking before they can talk? Nothing would ever be sent—the result would be gridlock! How do you handle the need to identify a node with a unique address on interconnected networks while at the same time isolating your own network from every other network? Unless one of your nodes has a communication for another node on another network, there should be no communication between networks and no need for one to know of the existence of the other until the need to communicate exists. You handle the need for a unique address by assigning protocol addresses to physical addresses in conjunction with your gateways. In our scenario, these protocol addresses are known as *Internet Protocol* (IP) addresses.

IP addresses are virtual. That is, there is no required correlation between a particular IP address and its physical interface. An IP address can be moved from one node to another at will, without requiring anything but a software configuration change, whereas changing a node's physical address requires changing the network hardware. Thus, any node on an internet has both a physical Ethernet address (MAC address) and an IP address.

Unlike an Ethernet address, an IP address is 32 bits long and consists of both a network identifier and a host identifier. The network identifier bits of the IP addresses for all nodes on a given network are the same. The common format for listing IP addresses is known as *dotted quad notation* because it divides the IP address into four parts (see Table 1-1). The network bits of an IP address are the leading octets, and the address space is divided into three classes: Class A, Class B, and Class C. Class A addresses use just 8 bits for the network portion, while Class B addresses use 16 bits and Class C addresses use 24 bits.

Table 1-1. Internet Protocol Address Classes

CLASS	DESCRIPTION	NETWORK BITS	HOST BITS
A	Networks 1.0.0.0 through 127.0.0.0	8	24
B	Networks 128.0.0.0 through 191.255.0.0	16	16
C	Networks 192.0.0.0 through 223.255.255.0	24	8
D	Multicast (reserved)		
E	Reserved for future use		

Let's look at an example. Consider the IP address 192.168.2.1. From Table 1-1, you can tell that this is a Class C address. Since it is a Class C address, you know that the network identifier is 24 bits long and the host identifier is 8 bits long. This translates to "the node with address 1 on the network with address 192.168.2." Adding a host to the same Class C network would require a second address with the same network identifier, but a different host identifier, such as 192.168.2.10, since every host on a given network must have a unique address.

You may have noticed that the table doesn't include every possible value. This is because the octets 0 and 255 are reserved for special use. The octet 0 (all 0s) is the address of the network itself, while the octet 255 (all 1s) is called the *broadcast address* because it refers to all hosts on a network simultaneously. Thus, in our Class C example, the network address would be 192.168.2.0, and the broadcast address would be 192.168.2.255. Because every address range needs both a network address and a broadcast address, the number of usable addresses in a given range is always 2 less than the total. For example, you would expect that on a Class C network you could have 256 unique hosts, but you cannot have more than 254, since one address is needed for the network and another for the broadcast.

In addition to the reserved network and broadcast addresses, a portion of each public address range has been set aside for private use. These address ranges can be used on internal networks without fear of conflicts. This helps alleviate the problem of address conflicts and shortages when public networks are connected together. The address ranges reserved for private use are shown in Table 1-2.

Table 1-2. Internet Address Ranges Reserved for Private Use

CLASS	RANGE
A	10.0.0.0 through 10.255.255.255
B	172.16.0.0 through 172.31.0.0
C	192.168.0.0 through 192.168.255.0

If you know your particular network will not be connected publicly, you are allowed to use any of the addresses in the private, reserved ranges as you wish. If you do this, however, you must use software address translation to connect your private network to a public network. For example, if your office LAN uses 192.168.2 as its network, your company's web server or mail server cannot use one of those addresses, since they are private. To connect your private network to a public network such as the Internet, you would need a public address for your web server or mail server. The private addresses can be "hidden" behind a single public address using a technique called *Network Address Translation* (NAT), where an entire range of addresses is translated into a single public address by the private network's gateway. When packets are received by the gateway on its public interface, the destination address of each packet is converted back to the private address. The public address used in this scenario could be one assigned dynamically by your service provider, or it could be from a range of addresses *delegated* to your network, also by your service provider. When a network address range is delegated, it means that your gateway takes responsibility for routing that address range and receiving packets addressed to the network.

Another IP address is considered special. This IP address is known as the *loopback* address, and it's typically denoted as 127.0.0.1. The loopback address is used to specify the local machine, also known as *localhost*. For example, if you were to open a connection to the address `127.0.0.1`, you would be opening a network connection to yourself. Thus, when using the loopback address, the sender is the receiver and vice versa. In fact, the entire `127.0.0.0` network is considered a reserved network for loopback use, though anything other than `127.0.0.1` is rarely used.

Ports

The final component of IP addressing is the *port*. Ports are virtual destination "points" and allow a node to conduct multiple network communications simultaneously. They also provide a standard way to designate the point where a node can send or receive information. Conceptually, think of ports as "doors" where information can come and go from a network node.

On Linux systems, the number of ports is limited to 65,535, and many of the lower port numbers are reserved, such as port 80 for web servers, port 25 for sending mail, and port 23 for telnet servers. Ports are designated with a colon when describing an IP address and port pair. For example, the address `10.0.0.2:80` can be read as "port 80 on the address `10.0.0.2`," which would also mean "the web server on `10.0.0.2`" since port 80 is typically used by and reserved for web services. Which port is used is up to the discretion of the developer, provided the ports are not already in use or reserved. A list of reserved ports and the names of the services that use them can be found on your Linux system in the `/etc/services` file, or at the Internet Assigned Numbers Authority (IANA) site listed here: `http://www.iana.org/assignments/port-numbers`. Table 1-3 contains a list of commonly used (and reserved) ports.

Table 1-3. Commonly Used Ports

PORT	SERVICE
21	File Transfer Protocol (FTP)
22	Secure Shell (SSH)
23	Telnet
25	Simple Mail Transfer Protocol (SMTP)
53	Domain Name System (DNS)
80	Hypertext Transfer Protocol (HTTP)
110	Post Office Protocol 3 (POP3)
143	Internet Message Access Protocol (IMAP)
443	Hypertext Transfer Protocol Secure (HTTPS)

Without ports, a network host would be allowed to provide only one network service at a time. By allowing the use of ports, a host can conceivably provide more than 65,000 services at any time using a given IP address, assuming each service is offered on a different port. We cover using ports in practice when writing code first in Chapter 2 and then extensively in later chapters.

This version of IP addressing is known as *version 4*, or *IPv4*. Because the number of available public addresses has been diminishing with the explosive growth of the Internet, a newer addressing scheme has been developed and is slowly being implemented. The new scheme is known as *version 6*, or *IPv6*. IPv6 addresses are 128 bits long instead of the traditional 32 bits, allowing for 2^96 more network nodes than IPv4 addresses. For more on IPv6, consult Appendix A.

Network Byte Order

One final note on IP addressing. Because each hardware manufacturer can develop its own hardware architecture, it becomes necessary to define a standard data representation for data. For example, some platforms store integers in what is known as *Little Endian* format, which means the lowest memory address contains the lowest order byte of the integer (remember that addresses are 32-bit integers). Other platforms store integers in what is known as *Big Endian* format, where the lowest memory address holds the highest order byte of the integer. Still other platforms can store integers in any number of ways. Without standardization, it becomes impossible to copy bytes from one machine to another directly, since doing so might change the value of the number.

In an internet, packets can carry numbers such as the source address, destination address, and packet length. If those numbers were to be corrupted, network communications would fail. The Internet protocols solve this byte-order problem by defining a standard way of representing integers called *network byte order* that must be used by all nodes on the network when describing binary fields within packets. Each host platform makes the conversion from its local byte representation to the standard network byte order before sending a packet. On receipt of a packet, the conversion is reversed. Since the data payload within a packet often contains more than just numbers, it is not converted.

The standard network byte order specifies that the most significant byte of an integer is sent first (Big Endian). From a developer's perspective, each platform defines a set of conversion functions that can be used by an application to handle the conversion transparently, so it is not necessary to understand the intricacies of integer storage on each platform. These conversion functions, as well as many other standard network programming functions, are covered in Chapter 2.

Internet Protocol

So far, we've discussed building a network based on Ethernet. We've also discussed connecting two or more networks together via a gateway, called an internet, and we've covered the basic issues surrounding network and host addressing that allow network nodes to communicate with each other without conflicts. Yet how are all of these dissimilar networks expected to communicate efficiently without problems? What is it that lets one network look the same as any other network?

A protocol exists that enables packet exchanges between networks as if the connected networks were a single, homogenous network. This protocol is known as the *Internet Protocol*, or *IP*, and was defined by RFC 791 in September 1981. These interconnected networks are known as *internets*, not to be confused with *the* Internet. The Internet is just one example of a global internet, albeit the most popular and the most well known. However, this does not preclude the existence of other internets that use the same technologies, such as IP.

Because IP is hardware independent, it requires a hardware-independent method of addressing nodes on a network, which is the IP addressing system already discussed. In addition to being hardware independent and being a packet-switching technology, IP is also *connectionless*. IP performs three key functions in an internet:

- It defines the basic unit of data transfer.

- It performs the routing function used by gateways and routers to determine which path a packet will take.

- It uses a set of rules that allow unreliable packet delivery.

These rules determine how hosts and gateways on connected networks should handle packets, whether a packet can be discarded, and what should happen if things go wrong.

Like the physical Ethernet frame that contains data as well as header information, the basic unit of packet transfer used by IP is called the *Internet datagram*. This datagram also consists of both a header portion and a data portion. Table 1-4 lists the format of the IP datagram header, along with the size of each field within the header.

Table 1-4. IP Datagram Header Format

FIELD	SIZE	DESCRIPTION
VERS	4 bits	The version of IP used to create this datagram
HLEN	4 bits	The length of the datagram header, measured in 32-bit words
SERVICE TYPE	8 bits	Specifies how the datagram should be handled
TOTAL LENGTH	16 bits	The total length of the datagram, measured in octets
IDENTIFICATION	16 bits	A unique integer generated by the sender that allows accurate datagram reassembly
FLAGS	3 bits	Various control flags, such as whether the datagram may be fragmented
FRAGMENT OFFSET	13 bits	Indicates where in the datagram this fragment belongs
TIME TO LIVE	8 bits	Specifies how long, in seconds, the datagram is allowed to exist
PROTOCOL	8 bits	Specifies which higher-level protocol was used to create the data in the data portion of the datagram
HEADER CHECKSUM	16 bits	Checksum for the header, recomputed and verified at each point where the datagram is processed
SOURCE ADDRESS	32 bits	IP address of the sender
DESTINATION ADDRESS	32 bits	IP address of the recipient
OPTIONS	Variable	Any number of various options, typically used for testing and debugging
PADDING	Variable	Contains the number of zero bits needed to ensure the header size is an exact multiple of 32 bits

Most of these fields look pretty similar to the description of an Ethernet frame. What is the relationship between Ethernet frames, or packets, and IP datagrams? Remember that IP is hardware independent and that Ethernet is hardware. Thus, the IP datagram format must be independent of the Ethernet frame specification. In practice, the most efficient design would be to carry one IP datagram in every Ethernet frame. This concept of carrying a datagram inside a lower-level network frame is called *encapsulation*. When an IP datagram is encapsulated within an Ethernet frame, it means the entire IP datagram, including header, is carried within the *data* portion of the Ethernet frame, as shown in Figure 1-6.

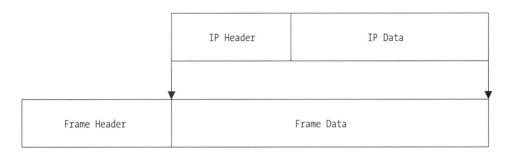

Figure 1-6. IP datagram encapsulation in an Ethernet frame

We've said that an Ethernet frame has a maximum size of 1500 octets. Yet an IP datagram has a maximum total length of 16 bits. A 16-bit number can represent a data size of up to 65,535 octets and could potentially be much higher. How do we cram 65,535 octets into a network frame that maxes out at 1500? By using a technique called *fragmentation*.

Fragmentation is necessary in network protocols because the goal should be to hide the underlying hardware used to create the network. In our case, it's Ethernet, but in practice it could be any number of different systems, past or future. It wouldn't make sense to require changes to higher-level protocols every time someone invented a new hardware network technology, so to be universally compatible, the designers of IP incorporated the ability to split IP datagrams into fragments, assigning one fragment per network frame in the most efficient way possible.

The IP protocol does not guarantee that large datagrams will be delivered without fragmentation, nor does it limit datagrams to some smaller size. The sending node determines the appropriate datagram size and performs the fragmentation, while the receiving node performs the reassembly. The reassembly is made possible by the *fragment offset* field of the datagram header, which tells the receiver where this particular fragment should go. When the datagram is fragmented, each fragment carries a header that is essentially a duplicate of the original datagram header, with some minor changes. The fragment's header differs because, if there are more fragments, the "more fragments" flag is set, and the fragment offset will change on each fragment to prevent overwriting.

Thus, an IP datagram of 4000 octets might get fragmented into three Ethernet frames, two containing the maximum data size and the third containing what's left. On the receiving end, these fragments would be reassembled into the original datagram and would be processed. If our physical network had a smaller frame size than Ethernet, we would get more fragments, and less fragments (or no fragments at all) with a larger frame size.

 NOTE *Gateways are responsible for converting packets from one frame size to another.*

Every network has a *maximum transfer unit*, or MTU. The MTU can be any size. If your packets are sent from a network with a large MTU value to a network with a smaller value (or vice versa), the gateway between the two is responsible for reformatting the packets to comply with each network's specifications. For example, say you had a gateway with an Ethernet interface and a Token Ring interface. The MTU on one network is 1500 octets, while the MTU on the Token Ring network might be larger or smaller. It is the gateway's responsibility to reformat and fragment the packets again when moving from one network to another. The downside to this is that once fragmented to accommodate the smaller MTU, the packets aren't reassembled until they reach their destination. Thus, the receiving node will receive datagrams that are fragmented according to the network with the smallest MTU used in the transfer. This can be somewhat inefficient, since after traversing a network with a small MTU, the packets might traverse a network with a much larger MTU without being reformatted to take advantage of the larger frame size. This minor inefficiency is a good trade-off, however, because the gateways don't need to store or rebuild packet fragments, and the packets can be sent using the best path without concern for reassembly problems for the destination node.

Protocol Layering

So far we've discussed the underlying physical hardware of a network, and in the case of an internet, the protocol used to ensure compatibility between different networks. More than one protocol exists, however. For example, take the acronym "TCP/IP." You already know what "IP" stands for: Internet Protocol. But what about "TCP"? What about other protocols we use on our networks, such as HTTP or FTP? How do these protocols relate to each other if they're not all the same?

It's practically impossible to create a single protocol that can handle every issue that might be encountered on a network. Consider security, packet loss, hardware failure, network congestion, and data corruption. These issues and more need to be addressed in any networked system, but it can't be done with just a single "super" protocol. The solution, then, is to develop a system in which complementary protocols, each handling a specific task, work together in a standardized fashion. This solution is known as *protocol layering*.

Imagine the different protocols involved in network communications stacked on top of each other in *layers*. This is also known as a *protocol stack* or *stack*. Each layer in a stack takes responsibility for a particular aspect of sending and receiving information on a network, with each layer in the stack working in concert with the other layers (see Figure 1-7).

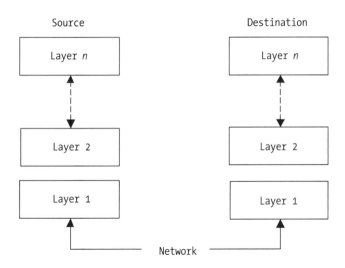

Figure 1-7. Protocol layers

As shown in Figure 1-7, sending information to another computer means sending the information "down" through a stack, over the network, and then "up" through the stack on the receiving node. When the receiving node wishes to send a response, the roles are reversed: it becomes a sender and the process is repeated. Each layer on each node is the same. That is, the protocol in layer 3 on the sender is the same protocol in layer 3 on the receiver. Thus, a protocol layer is designed so that layer *n* at the destination receives essentially the same datagram or packet sent by layer *n* at the source. We say "essentially" because datagrams have components like *time to live* fields that will be changed by each node involved in the transfer, even though the core data payload should remain identical from sender to receiver.

Protocol Layer Models

The dominating standard for a protocol layer is from the International Organization for Standardization (ISO) and is known as the *Open Systems Interconnection reference model*, or simply the OSI model. The OSI model describes seven specific layers: Application, Presentation, Session, Transport, Network, Data Link, and Physical Hardware. A description of each layer is shown in Table 1-5.

Table 1-5. OSI Seven-Layer Reference Model

LAYER	NAME	DESCRIPTION
7	Application	Application programs such as web browsers and file transfer programs
6	Presentation	Standard routines such as compression functions used by layer 7
5	Session	Establishes transmission control between two nodes, regulating which node can transmit and how long it can transmit
4	Transport	Provides additional reliability checks to those performed by lower layers
3	Network	Defines the basic unit of communication across a network, including addressing and routing
2	Data Link	Controls how data is sent between nodes, such as defining frames and frame boundaries
1	Physical Hardware	Controls the physical aspects of a network connection, such as voltage

Figure 1-8 shows the result of applying the OSI model to our earlier layer diagram.

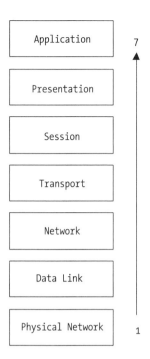

Figure 1-8. The OSI model

In practice, though, the typical protocol stack found in most networked environments today is known as a *TCP/IP stack* and, while perfectly compatible with the OSI model, it is conceptually different. The "TCP" in TCP/IP means *Transmission Control Protocol* and will be discussed later in this chapter. Just by the name alone, you can see that today's networks require multiple protocols working together to function.

In a TCP/IP environment, the network transport is relatively simple, while the nodes on the network are relatively complex. TCP/IP requires all hosts to involve themselves in almost every network function, unlike some other networking protocols. TCP/IP hosts are responsible for end-to-end error checking and recovery, and also make routing decisions since they must choose the appropriate gateway when sending packets.

Using our OSI diagram as a basis, a corresponding diagram describing a TCP/IP stack would look like Figure 1-9.

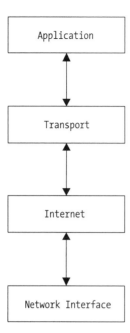

Figure 1-9. The TCP/IP layer model

This diagram shows a TCP/IP stack as having four layers versus the seven layers in an OSI model. There are fewer layers because the TCP/IP model doesn't need to describe requirements that are needed by older networking protocols like X.25, such as the Session layer. Looking at our TCP/IP stack, we can see that Ethernet is our Network Interface, IP is our Internet layer, and TCP is our Transport layer. The Application layer, then, consists of the applications that use the network, such as a web browser, file transfer client, or other network-enabled applications.

There are two boundaries in our TCP/IP stack that describe the division of information among the application, the operating system, and the network. These boundaries correspond directly to the addressing schemes already discussed. In the Application layer, the application needs to know nothing other than the IP address (and port) of the receiver. Specifics such as datagram fragmentation, checksum calculations, and delivery verification are handled in the operating system by the Transport and Internet layers. Once the packets move from the Internet layer to the Network layer, only physical addresses are used.

At first it would seem like a lookup must be performed to get the physical address of the receiver when starting communications, but this would be incorrect. Remembering the gateway rule, the only physical address that needs to be known by the sender is the physical address of the destination if the destination is on the same network, or the physical address of the *gateway* if the destination is on a remote network.

User Datagram Protocol

At the Internet layer in our TCP/IP protocol stack, the only information available is the address of the remote node. No other information is available to the protocol, and none is needed. However, without additional information like a port number, your receiving node is limited to conducting a single network communication at any one time. Since modern operating systems allow multiple applications to run simultaneously, you must be able to address multiple applications on the receiving node simultaneously, instead of just one. If you consider that each networked application can "listen" on one or more ports, you can see that by using an IP address and a port, you can communicate with multiple applications simultaneously, up to any limits imposed by the operating system and protocol stack.

In the TCP/IP protocol stack, there are two protocols that provide a mechanism that allows applications to communicate with other applications using ports. One is the Transmission Control Protocol (TCP), which we will discuss in the next section, and the other is the *User Datagram Protocol* (UDP). UDP makes no guarantee of packet delivery. UDP datagrams can be lost, can arrive out of sequence, can be copied many times, and can be sent faster than the receiving node can process them. Thus, an application that uses UDP takes full responsibility for controlling message loss, reliability, sequencing, and loss of connection. This can be both an advantage and a disadvantage to developers, for while UDP is a lightweight protocol that can be used quickly, the additional application overhead needed to thoroughly manage packet transfer is often overlooked or poorly implemented.

TIP *When using UDP for an application, make sure to thoroughly test your applications in real environments beyond a low-latency LAN. Many developers choose UDP and test in a LAN environment, only to find their applications are unusable when used over a larger TCP/IP network with higher latencies.*

UDP datagrams have a simple format. Like other datagrams, UDP datagrams consist of a header and a data payload. The header is divided into four fields, each 16 bits in size. These fields specify the source port, the destination port, the length of the datagram, and a checksum. Following the header is the data area, as shown in Figure 1-10.

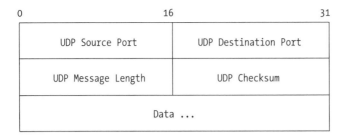

Figure 1-10. The UDP datagram format

The source port is optional. If used, it specifies the port to which replies should be sent. If unused, it should be set to zero. The length field is the total number of octets in the datagram itself, header and data. The minimum value for length is 8, which is the length of the header by itself.

The checksum value is also optional, and if unused should be set to zero. Even though it's optional, however, it should be used, since IP doesn't compute a checksum on the data portion of its own datagram. Thus, without a UDP checksum, there's no other way to check for header integrity on the receiving node. To compute the checksum, UDP uses a *pseudo-header*, which is prepended to the datagram, followed by an octet of zeros, which is appended, to get an exact multiple of 16 bits. The entire object, pseudo-header and all, is then used to compute the checksum. The pseudo-header format is shown in Figure 1-11.

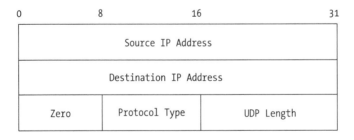

Figure 1-11. The UDP pseudo-header

The octet used for padding is *not* transmitted with the UDP datagram, nor is the pseudo-header, and neither is counted when computing the length of the datagram.

A number of network services use UDP and have reserved ports. A list of some of the more popular services is shown in Table 1-6.

Table 1-6. Popular UDP Services

PORT	NAME
7	echo
13	daytime
37	time
43	whois
53	domain (DNS)
69	tftp
161	snmp

Transmission Control Protocol

The main difference between UDP and TCP is that, like IP, UDP provides no guarantee of delivery and does not use any method to ensure datagrams are received in a certain order or are transmitted at a certain rate. TCP, on the other hand, provides a mechanism known as *reliable stream delivery*. Reliable stream delivery guarantees delivery of a stream of information from one network node to another without duplication or data loss. TCP has a number of features that describe the interface between it and the application programs that use it:

- **Virtual circuit**: Using TCP is much like making a phone call. The sender requests a connection with the receiver. Both ends negotiate the parameters of the connection and agree on various details defining the connection. Once the connection is finalized, the applications are allowed to proceed. As far as the applications are concerned, a dedicated, reliable connection exists between the sender and the receiver, but this is an illusion. The underlying transfer mechanism is IP, which provides no delivery guarantee, but the applications are removed from dealing with IP by the TCP layer.

- **Buffered transfer**: The TCP layer, independent of the application, determines the optimal way to package the data being sent, using whatever packet sizes are appropriate. To increase efficiency and decrease network traffic, TCP typically waits, if possible, until it has a relatively large amount of data to send before sending the packet, even if the application is generating data 1 byte at a time. The receiving TCP layer delivers data to the receiving application exactly the way it was sent, so a buffer may exist at each end, independent of the application.

- **Stream orientation**: The receiving node delivers data to the receiving application in exactly the same sequence as it was sent.

- **Full duplex**: Connections provided by TCP over IP are *full duplex*, which means that data can be transmitted in both directions simultaneously via two independent packet streams. The streams can be used to transfer data or to send control information or commands back to the sender, and either stream can be terminated without harming the other.

- **Unstructured stream**: TCP does not guarantee the structure of the data stream, even though delivery is guaranteed. For example, TCP does not honor markers that might exist in a record set sent to or from a database. It is up to the applications to determine stream content and assemble or disassemble the stream accordingly on each end of the connection. Applications do this by buffering incoming packets when necessary and assembling them in an order that the applications recognize.

The method that TCP uses to guarantee reliable delivery can be described as *confirmation and retransmission*. The sender keeps track of every packet that is sent and waits for confirmation of successful delivery from the receiver before sending the next packet. The sender also sets an internal timer when each packet is sent and automatically resends the packet should the timer expire before getting confirmation from the receiver. TCP uses a *sequence number* to determine whether every packet has been received. This sequence number is sent on the confirmation message as well as the packet itself, allowing the sender to match confirmations to packets sent, in case network delays cause the transmission of unnecessary duplicates.

Even with full duplex, though, having to wait for a confirmation on every packet before sending the next can be horribly slow. TCP solves this by using a mechanism called a *sliding window*. The easiest way to imagine a TCP sliding window is to consider a number of packets that needs to be sent. TCP considers a certain number of packets to be a *window* and transmits all packets in that window without waiting for confirmation on each one. Once the confirmation is received for the first packet in the window, the window "slides" to contain the next packet to be sent, and it is sent. For example, if the window size was 8, then packets 1 through 8 would be sent. When the confirmation for packet 1 was received, the window would "slide" so that it covered packets 2 through 9, and the ninth packet would be sent. A packet that has been transmitted without confirmation is called an *unacknowledged* packet. Thus, the total number of unacknowledged packets allowed is equal to the window size. The advantage to a sliding window protocol is that it keeps the network saturated with packets as much as possible, minimizing the time spent waiting for confirmation. The window is matched on the receiving end, so that the receiver "slides" its own window according to which confirmation messages have been sent.

We noted earlier that TCP connections use what is known as a virtual circuit. Taking that abstraction further, TCP defines connections as a pair of endpoints, each endpoint consisting of an integer pair, consisting of the 32-bit integer IP address and the 16-bit integer port number. This is important, because by defining an endpoint as an integer pair, a TCP service on a given port number can be used by multiple connections at the same time. For example, even though a mail server has only one port 25 on which to receive mail, each sender making a connection offers a different integer pair because the source IP address and source port are different, allowing multiple concurrent connections on the same receiving port.

The TCP datagram is also known as a *segment*. Segments do all of the work: establishing and closing connections, advertising window sizes, transferring data, and sending acknowledgments. Figure 1-12 shows a diagram of a TCP segment.

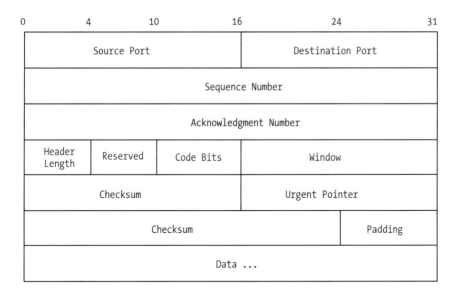

Figure 1-12. The TCP segment format

As with other datagrams, a TCP segment consists of two parts: header and data. A description of each header field is listed in Table 1-7.

Table 1-7. TCP Header Fields

NAME	SIZE	DESCRIPTION
Source port	16 bits	The port number of the sending connection endpoint
Destination port	16 bits	The port number of the receiving connection endpoint
Sequence number	32 bits	The position of this segment's payload in the sender's stream
Acknowledgment number	32 bits	The octet that the source expects to receive next
Header length	4 bits	The length of the header, in 32-bit multiples
Reserved	6 bits	Reserved for future use
Code bits	6 bits	Defines the purpose and content of this segment (see Table 1-8)
Window	16 bits	Specifies the maximum amount of data that can be accepted
Checksum	16 bits	Verifies the integrity of the header
Urgent pointer	16 bits	Flag notifying the receiver that the segment should be handled immediately
Options	24 bits	Various options used to negotiate between endpoints
Padding	8 bits	Needed to accommodate an OPTIONS value of varying length to ensure header and data end on a 32-bit boundary

Much like the UDP header, the TCP header has fields such as checksum, source port, destination port, and length. However, the TCP header goes much farther due primarily to the need to guarantee delivery. The *sequence number* is used to indicate the position of the data in a particular segment within the overall byte stream being sent. If a byte stream had 100 packets in it, the sequence number field would be where each segment was numbered, so the receiver would know how to reassemble the stream.

The *acknowledgment number*, on the other hand, is used by the sender to identify which acknowledgment the sender expects to receive next. Thus, the sequence number refers to the byte stream flowing in the same direction as the segment, while the acknowledgment number refers to the byte stream flowing in the opposite direction as the segment. This two-way synchronization system helps ensure that both connection endpoints are receiving the bytes they expect to receive and that no data is lost in transit.

The *code bits* field is a special header field used to define the purpose of this particular segment. These bits instruct the endpoint how to interpret other fields in the header. Each bit can be either 0 or 1, and they're counted from left to right. A value of 111111, then, means that all options are "on." Table 1-8 contains a list and description of the possible values for the code bits field.

Table 1-8. Possible Values for Code Bits Header Field

NAME (LEFT TO RIGHT)	MEANING
URG	Urgent pointer field is valid.
ACK	Acknowledgment field is valid.
PSH	Push requested.
RST	Reset the connection.
SYN	Synchronize sequence numbers.
FIN	Sender has completed its byte stream.

Even though TCP is a stream-oriented protocol, situations arise when data must be transmitted *out of band*. Out-of-band data is sent so that the application at the other end of the connection processes it immediately instead of waiting to complete the entire stream. This is where the *urgent* header field comes into play. Consider a connection a user wishes to abort, such as a file transfer that occurs slower than expected. For the abort signal to be processed, the signal must be sent in a segment out of band. Otherwise, the abort signal would not be processed until the file transfer was complete. By sending the segment marked urgent, the receiver is instructed to handle the segment immediately.

The Client-Server Model

Let's recap. We've discussed circuits versus packets; the concept of connecting one or many networks together via gateways; physical addresses; virtual addresses; and the IP, UDP, and TCP protocols. We've also used the terms "sender," "source," "receiver," and "destination." These terms can be confusing, because as you've seen already, a TCP connection is a connection of equals, and in a virtual circuit, the roles of sender, source, receiver, and destination are interchangeable depending on what sort of data is being sent. Regardless of which term is used, the key concept to remember is that applications are present at both endpoints of a TCP connection. Without compatible applications at both ends, the data sent doesn't end up anywhere, nor can it be processed and utilized. Nevertheless, changing the terminology between "source" and "destination" to describe every communication between two endpoints can be pretty confusing. A better model is to designate roles for each endpoint for the duration of the communication. The model of interaction on a TCP connection, then, is known as the *client-server model*.

In the client-server model, the term "server" describes the application that offers a service that can be utilized by any other application over the network. Servers accept connections over a network, perform their service, and respond with the result. The simplest servers are those that accept a single packet and respond with a single packet, though in many cases servers are more complex. Some features common to servers include the ability to accept more than one request at a time (multiple connections) and the ability to service requests independently of other operating system processes such as user sessions.

A "client" is the application sending the request to the server and waiting for the response. Client applications typically make only one request to a particular server at any given time, though there is no restriction preventing them from making simultaneous requests, or even multiple requests to different servers.

There are many different types of client-server applications. The simplest of them use UDP to communicate, while others use TCP/IP with higher-level application protocols such as *File Transfer Protocol* (FTP), *Hypertext Transfer Protocol* (HTTP), and *Simple Mail Transfer Protocol* (SMTP). The specifics of a client-server system are fairly simple. On the server, the application is started, after which it negotiates with the operating system for permission to use a particular port number for accepting requests. Assuming that the application is allowed to start on the given port, it begins to *listen* for incoming requests. The specifics of how to write an application that will listen on a port are covered in Chapter 2. Once listening, the server executes an endless loop until stopped: receive request, process request, assemble response, send response, repeat. In the process, the server reverses the source and destination addresses and port numbers, so that the server knows where to send the response and the client also knows that the server has responded.

The client, unlike the server, typically stops sending requests once the server has responded. At this point, the client itself may terminate, or it may simply go into a wait state until another request must be sent. Ports are handled differently on clients than on servers, however. While the server typically uses a reserved port, clients do not. This is because every client must know how to reach the server, but the server does not need to know in advance how to reach every client, since that information is contained in the packets it receives from the client, in the source address and source port fields. This allows clients to use any port they wish as their endpoint in the TCP connection with the server. For example, a web page server is usually found on port 80. Even though the client must send its requests to the server's port 80, it can use any available port as its own endpoint, such as port number 9999, 12345, 64400, or anything in between, as long as it isn't one of the reserved ports mentioned earlier or a port already in use by another application. Thus, the two endpoints involved in a web page request might be `192.168.2.1:80` for the server endpoint and `10.0.0.4:11908` for the client endpoint. The main requirement for a client is that it knows, through configuration or some other method, the address and port of the server, since all other information needed will be sent within the packets.

The Domain Name System

We've discussed how it isn't necessary for every node on every network to store information about how to reach all of the other nodes on the network. Because of the gateway rule, a node only needs to know how to reach nodes on its own network or a gateway. With IP addresses 32 bits long, there are plenty of addresses to go around (and when we run out, there's always IPv6, which is covered in Appendix A). We still have a problem, though. While computers can take advantage of the gateway rule, people can't. It's not enough to instruct our computers to make a connection—we have to specify the other end of the connection, even if we don't have to specify exactly how our packets will get there. We still need a system people can use to point computers to the other endpoint of our connections, without requiring them to remember nearly endless lists of numbers.

A system exists that lets us assign easily remembered names to their corresponding IP addresses, without having to remember the addresses themselves. This system is called the *Domain Name System* (DNS). You can think of DNS as a type of phone book for computers. Rather than remember the addresses of every network node you may want to reach, you instead can assign meaningful names to those nodes, and use DNS to translate the names that people like to use into the numbers that computers must use. To contact the other computer, your computer performs a *DNS lookup*, the result of which is the address of the other computer. Once the address is known, a connection can be made. Performing a DNS lookup is much like using a phone book. You know the name of the other computer, and you want to find the number, or address. You "look up" the name, and the phone book tells you the number that has been assigned to that name. From there, you make your call, or in our case, your connection.

How often do new phone books come out? What happens if someone changes his or her phone number before the new phone book is printed? Just like people change their phone numbers, computers change their addresses all the time. Some, in the case of dial-up networks, might change their addresses every day, or even several times a day. If our name-to-number system required that we all pass a new phone book around every day, our networks would come to a standstill overnight, since managing such a database of names and numbers and keeping it current for the number of computers connected together on today's networks is impossible. DNS was designed to be easily updateable, redundant, efficient and, above all, distributed, by using a hierarchical format and a method of *delegation*. Just like the gateway rule, a DNS server isn't required to know the names and addresses of every node on our networks. Instead, it's only necessary for a DNS server to know the names and addresses of the nodes it's managing, and the names and addresses of the *authoritative* servers in the rest of the hierarchy. Thus, a particular DNS server is delegated the responsibility for a particular set of addresses and is given the names and addresses of other DNS servers that it can use if it can't resolve the name using its own information.

The hierarchical nature of DNS can be seen in the names commonly used on the Internet. You often hear the phrase *dot-com* and routinely use *domain names* when making connections. The first level of our hierarchy contains what are known as the *top-level domains* (TLDs). Table 1-9 contains a list of the more popular TLDs and their purpose.

Table 1-9. Popular Top-Level Domains

TLD	PURPOSE
.com	Commercial use
.net	Commercial use, though originally for use only by network service providers
.org	Noncommercial use by organizations and individuals
.mil	Military use
.edu	Educational institution use
.gov	Government use

The six domains in Table 1-9 are the original TLDs. In recent years, as the Internet became more and more popular, other TLDs were created, such as .biz, .name, .info, .pro, .coop, .aero, and .museum. In addition, every country in the world is assigned its own TLD, which is a two-letter English designation related to the country name. For example, the country TLD for the United Stated is .us, while the country TLD for Ireland is .ie and the country TLD for China is .cn. Each TLD is managed by a *registrar*, an organization that handles registration of domain names within a particular TLD. For some TLDs, such as .com, .net, and .org, there are many registrars. For others, such as .gov or .mil, there is only one.

A registrar is responsible for managing domain registrations. This means keeping them current, including accepting new registration requests as well as expiring those domains that are no longer valid. An example of a domain would be "apress.com". Domain names are read right to left, with the leftmost name typically being the *host name* or name of a specific network node. Thus, a name such as www.apress.com would be translated as "the network node known as **www** within the domain **apress** within the TLD **.com**." Another node within the same domain might have a name such as www2.apress.com. The actual names used are up to the discretion of the owner, with the following restrictions:

- Names are restricted to letters and numbers, as well as a hyphen.

- Names cannot begin or end with a hyphen.

- Not including the TLD, names cannot exceed 63 characters.

The TLDs are managed by special domain name servers known as *root servers*. The root servers are special servers set up in redundant fashion and spread out across the Internet. The root servers are updated twice daily by the registrars. As of this writing, there are 13 root servers. You can see a list of their names, and the organizations responsible for them, at http://www.root-servers.org. Even though there are 13 root servers, there are actually more than 13 physical servers. The root servers are typically set up redundantly in diverse locations to spread out the load, and in general the closest one to the node making the request is the one that answers the request. Each root server has a list of the active domains and the name servers that are responsible for those domains. Remember that DNS is hierarchical and delegated. The root servers have a list of subordinate domain name servers, each one responsible for one or many domains such as apress.com or yahoo.com or google.com. Thus, the root servers for .com have a list of the servers handling a particular domain. A request for that particular name is handled by the server responsible, not by the root servers. Further delegation is possible, because a company or other organization can have its own domain name servers.

Let's look at an example. You would like to visit the Apress website to download the source code used in this book. Putting everything we've discussed so far in this chapter together, that means your web browser is the client application, and the web server at Apress is the server application. You know that to make a successful connection, you need four pieces of information: source address, source port, destination address, and destination port. You know from your list of reserved ports that web servers are typically available on port 80, and you know that your client application can use any port it likes as the source port for the request, as long as the port isn't already in use on your own computer. You also know your own address. Thus, the only thing you need to determine before making your TCP/IP connection and web page request is the address of the web server that is accepting requests for the Apress website.

To get the address, you'll perform a DNS lookup on www.apress.com. Note that the lookup happens transparently to the user and is performed by the client application, or the application "making the call." The goal is to translate the name www.apress.com into an address that your web browser can use to make its network connection. In this case, the name lookup happens in a series of steps:

1. The browser queries one of the root servers for .com and asks for the IP addresses of the domain name servers (there are usually two, a primary and a backup) managing the domain named "apress".

2. The root server consults its database for a name matching "apress" and, if found, replies with the list of IP addresses of the domain name servers delegated to handle those requests.

3. The browser queries one of the servers in that list and asks it for the IP address of the network node with the name of "www".

4. The domain name server managing the domain named "apress" consults its database for the name "www" and, if found, returns the IP address associated with that name.

5. If the browser receives an answer from the domain name server with the IP address for www.apress.com, the browser makes a connection to port 80 at that IP address and requests the web page.

The domain name system is transparent and public. You can make DNS queries in a number of different ways, from using the host and whois commands on your Linux system to using any of the web-based query sites. Let's walk through the query process for apress.com that we just described, using the command line. To query the root name servers for information, you use whois:

```
[user@host user]$ whois apress.com
```

After the whois command executes, you'll see output that looks like this:

```
Domain Name: APRESS.COM
Registrar: NETWORK SOLUTIONS, INC.
Whois Server: whois.networksolutions.com
Referral URL: http://www.networksolutions.com
Name Server: AUTH111.NS.UU.NET
Name Server: AUTH120.NS.UU.NET
Status: ACTIVE
Updated Date: 19-apr-2002
Creation Date: 23-feb-1998
Expiration Date: 22-feb-2007
Registrant:
Apress (APRESS-DOM)
```

```
2560 Ninth Street
Suite 219
Berkeley, CA 94710
US


Domain Name: APRESS.COM

Administrative Contact, Technical Contact:
    Apress  (235763350)                wanshun_tam@apress.com
    2560 Ninth Street
    Suite 219
    Berkeley, CA 94710
    US
    510-549-5930 fax: 123 123 1234


Record expires on 22-Feb-2007.
Record created on 23-Feb-1998.
Database last updated on 18-Jan-2004 22:43:05 EST.


Domain servers in listed order:

AUTH111.NS.UU.NET              198.6.1.115
AUTH120.NS.UU.NET              198.6.1.154
```

The information is self-explanatory. You see that the registrar used to register the domain name is Network Solutions, and you see that the domain was registered in 1998 and is paid up through 2007. This is the information held at the TLD level—it still doesn't tell you the IP address of the web server, which is what you need. The information you do have, though, includes the names and IP addresses of the name servers delegated to handle further information for apress.com, namely auth111.ns.uu.net and auth120.ns.uu.net, with addresses of 198.6.1.115 and 198.6.1.154, respectively. Either one of those name servers can help you find the address of the web server.

The next step is to use the host command to make a specific request of one of the name servers. You want the IP address of the machine with the name www.apress.com:

```
[user@host user]$ host www.apress.com auth111.ns.uu.net
Using domain server:
Name: auth111.ns.uu.net
Address: 198.6.1.115#53
Aliases:
www.apress.com has address 65.215.221.149
```

The host command takes two parameters: the name you want to translate into an IP address and the name (or address) of the server you want to use to make the translation. Using one of the name servers returned by the whois query, you ask for the IP address of the web server, and the name server responds with the IP address 65.215.221.149. At this point, your web browser would have the four pieces of information it needs to make a successful TCP/IP connection. Incidentally, you can see the port information for DNS in the name server's reply shown previously. Note the #53 tacked onto the end of the name server's IP address. As shown earlier in Table 1-3, the port used by DNS is port 53. The host command can also be used without specifying the name server as a parameter. If you just use the name that you want to translate, you'll get an abbreviated response with just the IP address, without the other information.

You can use the host command to make all sorts of domain name queries by using command-line parameters such as -t for type. For example, using a type of "MX" will return the IP addresses of the machines handling mail for a given domain name. Using a type of "NS" will return an abbreviated version of the whois information, listing the name servers themselves. Let's see which machines handle mail and name serving for linux.org:

```
[user@host user]$ host -t mx linux.org
linux.org mail is handled by 10 mail.linux.org.
[user@host user]$ host -t ns linux.org
linux.org name server ns.invlogic.com.
linux.org name server ns0.aitcom.net.
```

The two queries tell you that mail for addresses in the linux.org domain is handled by a machine named mail.linux.org. Likewise, the name servers for linux.org are listed. If you wanted to send mail to someone at linux.org, you would use the name server information to resolve the name mail.linux.org into an IP address and make your connection from there. A list of common DNS record types and their purpose is shown in Table 1-10.

Table 1-10. Common DNS Record Types

TYPE	NAME	PURPOSE
A	Host Address	A 32-bit IP address identifying a specific host.
CNAME	Canonical Name	A name used as an alias for an A record.
MX	Mail Exchanger	The name of the host acting as a mail exchanger for the domain.
NS	Name Server	The name of an authoritative domain name server for this domain.

Table 1-10. Common DNS Record Types (continued)

TYPE	NAME	PURPOSE
PTR	Pointer	A record that points an IP address to a name. This is the reverse of an A record.
SOA	Start of Authority	A multiple-field record specifying particulars for this domain, such as timeouts.

As you can see, DNS information is public information, and you can easily obtain it once you know what to look for and which commands to use. On your Linux system, use the man command to get more information on host and whois. Older systems use a utility called nslookup, which performs essentially the same functions as host. It's also possible to have private DNS information, since any Linux system is capable of acting as a name server. Many companies and organizations use both private, or internal, DNS and public, or external, DNS. Internal DNS is used for those machines that aren't available to the public.

Summary

In this chapter, we discussed the basic ingredients for today's popular networking technologies. Here's a summary of what we covered:

- In general, networks are either *packet-switched* or *circuit-switched*, with the Internet being an example of a packet-switched network.

- All networks need a common, physical medium to use for communications, the most popular of which is Ethernet. Ethernet uses a system of *frames* containing *header* and *data* portions.

- Networks require the use of addressing so that one network node can find another network node. Addressing takes different forms, from MAC addresses used to identify physical network hardware interfaces to IP addresses used to identify virtual software addresses used by the TCP and IP network protocols.

- The *gateway rule* means that a node does not need to know how to reach every other node on a network. It only needs to know how to reach the nodes on its own network, and how to reach the *gateway* between its own network and all other networks.

- Using a system of *protocol layering* and *encapsulation*, IP and TCP "wrap" and "unwrap" each packet of header and data information as it travels up or down the *protocol stack* at each endpoint of the connection.

- TCP/IP networks use the *client-server model*, in which the source of the communication is known as the client, and the server is the destination. The server is the network node providing services consumed by the client. Depending on whether the communication is a request or a response, the roles of client and server may change back and forth.

- Because people find it easier to remember names instead of numbers, networks use name translation systems to translate familiar names into the actual IP addresses of the other network nodes. The most popular naming system is the *Domain Name System* (DNS), which is a collaborative, distributed, hierarchical system of managing namespaces where specific responsibilities for certain domains are delegated from root servers to subordinate servers.

CHAPTER 2

Functions

APPROXIMATELY 20 YEARS AGO, the Advanced Research Projects Agency (ARPA) tasked a group at the University of California, Berkeley (UC Berkeley), to port TCP/IP software to the UNIX operating system. A significant part of the project was creating the interface between the TCP/IP-based network and the networked applications that used it. The group decided that wherever possible, the interface should use existing UNIX system calls and algorithms, and add new functions only when absolutely necessary. The interface that resulted from this project became known as the *socket interface*, sometimes called the *Berkeley socket interface*. The system became known as Berkeley UNIX or BSD UNIX.

While other network interfaces exist, the Berkeley socket interface is considered the de facto standard and is widely supported and accepted. The Berkeley socket interface is the interface used by Linux.

What Is a Socket?

Essentially, a *socket* is an abstraction for network communication, just as a file is an abstraction for file system communication. Let's consider the basic network I/O functions for a Linux system. In general, an application that performs network input and output needs to perform the five basic functions described in Table 2-1: open, close, read, write, and control.

Table 2-1. Primary Socket Functions

OPERATION	EXPLANATION
Open	Prepare for input or output operations.
Close	Stop previous operations and return resources.
Read	Get data and place in application memory.
Write	Put data from application memory and send control.
Control (ioctl)	Set options such as buffer sizes and connection behavior.

In a non-networked application, I/O functions are performed on files. A file is opened, data is read from or written to the file (or both), and then the file is closed. These functions work by using what is known as a *file descriptor*. A file descriptor is a small integer returned by a function that an application can use for subsequent operations. The system maintains a file descriptor table for each process. When the process opens a file, a pointer to the internal data structures for that file is placed in the file descriptor table and the index to the pointer is returned to the calling function. The application only needs to work with the descriptor; the operating system will handle the underlying operations by following the pointer in the descriptor table and getting the information it needs. Thus, when a file is opened, a file descriptor is returned. Other functions use this file descriptor to perform reads and writes, change file options, and close the file when finished.

The Berkeley socket interface extends the concept of a file descriptor to that of a *socket descriptor*. Like a file, an active socket is identified by an integer known as its socket descriptor. These descriptors are allocated in the same way as file descriptors, in the same descriptor table, by process. An application cannot have a file descriptor and a socket descriptor with the same value.

Let's continue with the file analogy. When an application creates a file or begins to work with an existing file, a file descriptor is created. This descriptor is a pointer to the data structure that describes the file. This data structure might include the name of the file, the file's actual location on disk or in memory, whether the file is read-only or read-write, and the file's size. Likewise, when an application creates a socket, a socket descriptor is created that points to a data structure holding information about that socket. The information, while similar to that of a file, is network oriented. The socket data structure will include information such as the socket type, the local address and port being used by the socket, and the remote address and port that will receive communications from the socket. Some of this information may be available immediately, and some of it may be filled in later by other function calls. If the terms *address* and *port* are unfamiliar to you, don't worry—we'll cover those in a moment.

By extending the file/file descriptor concept, the UC Berkeley team made it easy to visualize communicating across a network. To communicate across a network, a connection (socket) to the network must be opened. Once it's opened, data is read from or written to the socket. When communication is finished, the connection to the network is closed and the resources used by the socket are released.

Sockets can be used in two ways. Once created, a socket can wait for an incoming connection, or it can initiate a connection to another socket on a remote host, or even its own local host in some cases. A socket used by a client program to initiate a connection to a server is known as an *active socket*. A socket that acts as a server and waits for an incoming connection is known as a *passive socket*. Both active and passive sockets are created the same way. The only difference is how a networked application uses them.

Using Sockets

Let's take a look at the two ways a socket can be used. Figure 2-1 shows the sequence of function calls for two simple socket applications: a client and a server. For the purposes of describing the application flow, the function calls shown in the diagram are generic. We'll get into specific uses of the functions, the parameters used for each one, and other details later.

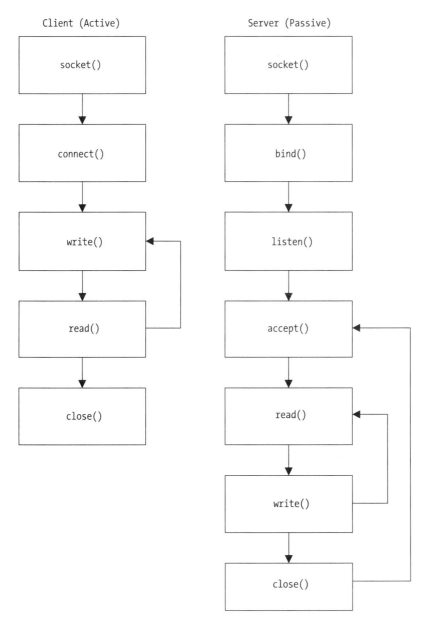

Figure 2-1. Function call flow

On the client side, the application creates the socket with `socket()`, calls `connect()` to connect to the server, and then interacts with the server by using `write()` to send requests to the server and `read()` to read responses from the server. When the client is finished, it calls `close()`.

On the server side, the application creates the socket with `socket()`, and then calls `bind()` to specify which local address and port to use, and then proceeds to call `listen()` to set the length of the connection queue. The *connection queue* is the number of requests that the application should hold while waiting for the server to process any current request. Once the connection queue is set, the server calls `accept()` and waits until the next connection request arrives from the client. When the request arrives, the server uses `read()` and `write()` to read the request and write the response. When finished, the server calls `close()` to terminate the connection to the client and returns to the `accept()` function, where it waits for the next connection request from a client.

Socket Constants

Like any other application programming interface (API), the socket interface uses a set of predefined symbolic constants and data structure declarations. These constants and structures help applications specify function parameters and declare data structures in a consistent way. This increases portability and eases application maintenance by not requiring a developer to do things a different way for each environment. There are two primary sets of constants used in the Berkeley socket interface: *protocol type constants* and *address family constants*. In addition, a number of standard data structure declarations are available, as are the function prototypes themselves. These constants, function prototypes, and data structures are typically available in header files that can be incorporated into a program using the #include C preprocessor directive. The two files that should be included are `types.h` and `socket.h`, which are found in the /usr/include directory. The include statements in your application's code would look like this:

```
#include <sys/types.h>
#include <sys/socket.h>
```

The #include directives are relative. That is, relative to the include directory, which in this case is /usr/include. That means the header files can be found in /usr/include/sys on a typical Linux system.

The protocol type and address family constants consist of two groups each. In the case of the protocol types, an application can use several different types of sockets. Address family constants, also known as protocol families, belong to the Internet address family for all TCP/IP communications, including UDP. This address family is known as `AF_INET`. Another option for an address constant is

AF_UNIX, which is used when the socket communications will be internal to the local machine only, not across a network. As you do more network programming, you will probably run into constants known as *protocol family* constants, denoted by PF_ instead of AF_. For our purposes, the protocol family constants and address family constants are the same. That is, wherever you see AF_INET, you can also use PF_INET, though the AF_ version is preferred and is the one used by recent versions of the Berkeley socket interface library. In fact, if you review /usr/include/bits/socket.h, you will see the protocol family constants defined, and later the address family constants declared as aliases to the protocol family constants, like this:

```
#define PF_INET        2      /* IP protocol family.  */
#define PF_INET6       10     /* IP version 6.  */
#define PF_IPX         4      /* Novell Internet Protocol.  */
#define PF_APPLETALK   5      /* Appletalk DDP.  */
#define PF_X25         9      /* Reserved for X.25 project.  */


#define AF_INET        PF_INET
#define AF_INET6       PF_INET6
#define AF_IPX         PF_IPX
#define AF_APPLETALK   PF_APPLETALK
#define AF_X25         PF_X25
```

Table 2-2 contains the more commonly used address family constants, also known as domains, as used with socket().

Table 2-2. Address Family Constants

ADDRESS FAMILY	DESCRIPTION
AF_UNIX, AF_LOCAL	Communications local to same host
AF_INET	IPv4 Internet protocols
AF_INET6	IPv6 Internet protocols
AF_IPX	IPX–Novell protocols
AF_NETLINK	Kernel user interface
AF_X25	X.25 protocols
AF_AX25	Amateur radio AX.25 protocols
AF_ATMPVC	ATM Private Virtual Circuits (PVCs)
AF_APPLETALK	AppleTalk protocols
AF_PACKET	Low-level packet communications

A number of other constants are also available. You can find their definitions in /usr/include/bits/socket.h.

In addition to the protocol family, a call to socket() takes another constant, known as the *type*. There are a number of different type constants that can be used, as shown in Table 2-3, though the most common are SOCK_STREAM and SOCK_DGRAM, or TCP and UDP, respectively. UDP connections are *connectionless*— that is, UDP packets do not offer any sort of transmission guarantees and do not arrive in any sort of sequence. TCP connections are *connection based*, which means that TCP packets provide transmission guarantees, are assembled in a certain sequence once they arrive at their destination, and are typically more reliable than UDP packets.

Table 2-3. Socket Type Constants

TYPE	DESCRIPTION
SOCK_STREAM	Communications are connection-based, sequenced, reliable, and two-way.
SOCK_DGRAM	Connectionless, unreliable message-type communications using a fixed length.
SOCK_SEQPACKET	Message-type communications with fixed-length packets, but sequenced and more reliable.
SOCK_RAW	Access to raw network protocols.
SOCK_RDM	Connectionless but reliable communications, without using a particular packet order.
SOCK_PACKET	Obsolete and should not be used.

Thus, three arguments are needed to use the socket() function call to create a socket, as shown in Table 2-4.

Table 2-4. Socket Function Arguments

ARGUMENT	EXPLANATION
Family	Protocol or address family (AF_INET for TCP/IP; AF_UNIX for internal)
Type	Type of service (SOCK_STREAM for TCP; SOCK_DGRAM for UDP)
Protocol	The protocol number to use, typically a zero (0) to use the default for a given family and type

A call to socket(), then, for the purposes of opening a connection to another host and communicating with TCP, would look like this:

```
mySocket = socket(PF_INET, SOCK_STREAM, 0);
```

We'll look at the socket function call in detail later in the chapter.

Address Structure

Before we discuss functions, we should take a look at some building blocks provided by the socket interface to make network application development a little easier and a little more standard. The Berkeley socket interface provides a set of defined C structures that helps you handle different endpoint addresses and other socket programming duties. Probably the most important structure you will work with is the sockaddr_in structure. Its purpose is to provide a standard way of handling endpoint addresses for network communications. The sockaddr_in structure contains both an IP address and a protocol port number. The structure looks like this:

```
struct sockaddr_in {
    short    sin_family;   /* type of address              */
    u_short  sin_port;     /* protocol port number         */
                           /* network byte ordered         */
    u_long   sin_addr;     /* net address for the remote host */
                           /* network byte ordered         */
    char     sin_zero[8];  /* unused, set to zero          */
};
```

In sockaddr_in, there is a 2-byte field that identifies the address type or family such as PF_INET, then a 2-byte field for the port number, and finally a 4-byte IP address field. The last field in the structure is unused, and is typically set to 0.

Another structure that you'll use with your sockets is the linger structure. linger is a parameter that determines whether a socket waits to see that all data is read once the other end of the communication closes. The linger structure, which can be found in socket.h, looks like this:

```
{
int l_onoff;               /* Nonzero to linger on close.  */
int l_linger;              /* Time to linger.              */
};
```

It's a simple structure, but using it correctly can ensure that your network communications are completed. The first structure member is an integer that determines whether the socket should linger. A zero value for l_onoff will keep the socket from lingering. To keep the socket open until all data is read, set l_onoff to any nonzero value. The other member of the structure, l_linger, is an integer that defines the length of time, in seconds, that the socket should linger before closing.

Last but not least is the servent structure. This structure is important, because without it you will find it difficult to connect to a server. Many of the standard TCP/IP services such as FTP, NTP, DNS, and others use standard ports, regardless of host operating system. These ports are defined in a file called /etc/services. For example, if you were to look up HTTP in /etc/services, you would see the following entries:

```
http            80/tcp        www www-http    # WorldWideWeb HTTP
http            80/udp        www www-http    # HyperText Transfer Protocol
```

If you were developing a web browser, for instance, you could always hard-code the server's IP address and port number into your connect() call, but that wouldn't be much help. By using specific addresses and ports in your code, you lock your applications to a certain set of parameters, requiring you to recompile them should those parameters change. A better programming practice is to use runtime resources such as DNS and the /etc/services file, allowing your application to use dynamic parameters without recompiling. We'll cover getting the IP address for a host using the gethostbyname() function later in the chapter. Using the /etc/services file is done with the servent structure and a function called getservbyname(). The servent structure, typically found in the netdb.h header file, looks like this:

```
struct servent
{
  char *s_name;             /* Official service name.  */
  char **s_aliases;         /* Alias list.  */
  int s_port;               /* Port number, in network byte order.  */
  char *s_proto;            /* Protocol to use.  */
};
```

Calling getservbyname() with a service name will perform a lookup in /etc/services and populate the servent structure for you, and allow you to use the values such as port number elsewhere in your application. We'll discuss getservbyname() and several other similar functions later in this chapter.

Byte Order Functions

Another problem addressed by the Berkeley socket interface team is number representation. The TCP/IP protocol specifies the way to represent the binary integers found in the protocol headers. Binary integers must be specified with the most significant byte first. This is called *network byte order*.

Why is this a problem? The TCP/IP specification is for network communications. It has no bearing on how a particular node on the network represents numbers internally. Over the years, different operating systems and hardware platforms have chosen different ways to represent numbers. For example, *Big Endian* and *Little Endian* were explained in the previous chapter. Both are different ways to represent numbers. If you try to store a TCP/IP number in network byte order on a local host whose method of storing integers is different from network byte order, you will run into problems because the values you store will be scrambled.

The TCP/IP protocol is Big Endian, but it's not important to understand the details of the different ways to represent numbers. What's important is understanding that the Berkeley team already took care of this for you by incorporating several conversion functions into the socket interface. These functions automatically convert short and long integers from network byte order to the local host's native byte order, whatever that may be, and back again. These functions operate on 16-bit and 32-bit integers. The functions are called `htons()`, `ntohs()`, `htonl()`, and `ntohl()`.

Which function to use should be fairly clear. The functions called "hton" will convert integers from local host's native byte order to network byte order. The functions called "ntoh" will convert integers from network byte order to the local host's native byte order, whatever that may be. The functions ending in "s" are for short integers; the functions ending in "l" are for longs. In some cases, calling these functions is unnecessary. If you take a look at the `servent` structure earlier in this chapter, you'll note that the U member is already in network byte order, eliminating the need for calling `htons()` before using the value. Some functions and structures will handle the network-to-local byte transformation for you without the need for the conversion functions, so if you experience problems with garbled values, take a quick look and confirm that the values are being returned the way that's needed by your application.

Using Socket Functions

Depending on your needs, your application might use only a few of the following functions, all of them, or even some that aren't listed here. A number of platform-specific and third-party libraries are available for working with socket interfaces, but they all can't be addressed here. We'll show you the functions that you'll find on a typical Linux system, define how they're used, cover the parameters they take, explain the values they return, and provide example code.

Core Functions

You can't have a client without having a server first, so we'll take a look at the common functions used to implement a server application.

socket()

socket() is a critical function. Without it, your application cannot communicate with a network. socket() is used to create a network endpoint, and it returns a socket descriptor that is used later by other functions.

```
int socket(int domain, int type, int protocol);
```

As discussed in previous sections, the domain is one of the values shown in Table 2-1, such as AF_INET. The type is one of the values shown in Table 2-2, such as SOCK_STREAM. The protocol can be 0 to use the default that matches the other two parameters, or you can use IPPROTO_TCP for SOCK_STREAM and IPPROTO_UDP for SOCK_DGRAM.

socket() returns a –1 if there is an error. Otherwise, the value returned is the descriptor to the socket.

```
#include <stdio.h>
#include <sys/types.h>
#include <sys/socket.h>
#include <netdb.h>

const char APRESSMESSAGE[] = "APRESS - For Professionals, by Professionals!\n";

int main(int argc, char *argv[]) {

    int simpleSocket = 0;
    int simplePort = 0;

    /* make sure we have a port number    */
    if (2 != argc) {

        fprintf(stderr, "Usage: %s <port>\n", argv[0]);
        exit(1);

    }
```

```
/* create a streaming socket   */
simpleSocket = socket(AF_INET, SOCK_STREAM, IPPROTO_TCP);

if (simpleSocket == -1) {

    fprintf(stderr, "Could not create a socket!\n");
    exit(1);

}
else {
    fprintf(stderr, "Socket created!\n");
}

}
```

The preceding code example doesn't do much beyond creating a socket, but we'll add to it as we progress. The goal is to create a simple server application that listens on a given port for a connection and sends a text string to the client when the connection is received. We'll do the server first, then the client.

bind()

Now that we've created our socket, we need to bind it to an address. Simply creating a socket doesn't do anything—you have to give it a place to go, much like creating a file doesn't do much unless you save it to disk somewhere. The bind() function is used to bind the socket to a given address once the socket is created.

```
int bind(int sockfd, struct sockaddr *my_addr, socklen_t addrlen);
```

The first value bind() needs is our socket descriptor. The second parameter is a pointer to the sockaddr structure we discussed earlier, while the third parameter is the length of the sockaddr structure. In this example, we'll use the constant INADDR_ANY to signal that we want to bind to all of our local host's addresses. Let's add some more to our server:

```
/* retrieve the port number for listening       */
simplePort = atoi(argv[1]);

/* set up the address structure                  */
/* use INADDR_ANY to bind to all local addresses */
/* note use of htonl() and htons()               */
bzero(&simpleServer, sizeof(simpleServer));
simpleServer.sin_family = AF_INET;
simpleServer.sin_addr.s_addr = htonl(INADDR_ANY);
```

```
        simpleServer.sin_port = htons(simplePort);

        /*  bind to the address and port with our socket  */
        returnStatus = bind(simpleSocket,
                            (struct sockaddr *)&simpleServer,
                            sizeof(simpleServer));

        if (returnStatus == 0) {
                fprintf(stderr, "Bind completed!\n");
        }
        else {
            fprintf(stderr, "Could not bind to address!\n");
            close(simpleSocket);
            exit(1);
        }
```

We've created a socket, and we've taken that socket and bound it to an address and a port. Our program still doesn't do much, so let's take a look at listen() and accept() to keep moving.

listen()

The next function we need is listen(). This function tells our socket that we're ready to accept connections, and it also specifies a maximum number of connections that can be queued before connections are refused.

```
int listen(int s, int backlog);
```

backlog is the value that determines the connection queue. A typical value for backlog is 5, though it can be larger as needed. Some systems, however, such as BSD-based systems, limit the value at 5, so if you're going to port your application to other environments besides Linux, don't rely on backlog being greater than 5. Note that with Linux versions after 2.2, only completely established sockets are counted in the queue, instead of incomplete connection requests.

We'll add our call to listen() to our program, which is very easy to do. If our call to listen() is successful, a value of 0 is returned:

```
/*  tell the socket we are ready to accept connections */
returnStatus = listen(simpleSocket, 5);

if (returnStatus == -1) {
    fprintf(stderr, "Cannot listen on socket!\n");
    close(simpleSocket);
    exit(1);
}
```

accept()

So far, we've created our socket, bound it to an address and port, and told our socket that we're ready to receive connection requests. Now we need to actually accept and handle those connection requests, and we do that using the accept() function.

```
int accept(int s, struct sockaddr *addr, socklen_t *addrlen);
```

accept() takes our socket descriptor, a pointer to the address structure, and the length of the address structure as its parameters. The key thing to remember with this function is that it will typically run in an endless loop. The only time you want a network server to stop listening is when you shut it down manually. Otherwise, your application should be listening and accepting connections constantly. Here's how this can be done:

```
while (1) {

    /* set up variables to handle client connections */
    struct sockaddr_in clientName = { 0 };
    int simpleClient = 0;
    int clientNameLength = sizeof(clientName);

    /* block on accept function call */
    simpleChildSocket = accept(simpleSocket,
                    (struct sockaddr *)&clientName, &clientNameLength);

    if (simpleClient == -1) {
        fprintf(stderr, "Cannot accept connections!\n");
        close(simpleSocket);
        exit(1);
    }

}
```

Is not socklen_t *

Compared to the functions we've already discussed, accept() is slightly different. The first difference is that accept() is a *blocking* function. That means your application will wait at the accept() function call until a connection request is received from a client. This behavior is configurable, but the default blocking behavior is typically the desired behavior.

The second difference is that the structures passed to accept() are client related, not server related. As you can see in the preceding example, the second and third parameters passed to accept() are locations for storing information about the client, not about the server. When started, the value for the client name is set to 0, as is the length of the name. When a call from accept() returns, both of the structures should be populated with correct information. On success, accept() returns a new socket descriptor for the new connection. In the preceding listing, the new socket descriptor is named simpleChildSocket. The original socket descriptor is unchanged and still able to listen for more connection requests. Keep in mind that a server can typically handle more than one connection at a time.

write()

Now that we have our new socket descriptor for our new client connection, it's time to do something with it. In this example, we'll simply send a string of characters back to the client. We'll do this using the write() function.

```
ssize_t write(int fd, const void *buf, size_t count);
```

write() writes up to *count* bytes of the contents of *buf* to the designated descriptor, in this case our child socket.

```
/* handle the new connection request   */
/* write out our message to the client */
write(simpleChildSocket, APRESSMESSAGE, strlen(APRESSMESSAGE));
```

close()

Lastly, we need to do some cleanup. Use the close() function to close your sockets:

```
int close(int fd)
```

The first thing to do is close our child socket as soon as the write to the client is done.

```
        close(simpleChildSocket);
    }
```

Remember that even though we're closing this socket, our accept() function is a blocking function and is in a loop. As soon as this child socket is closed, our program will loop back around and wait for another connection. Lastly, assuming our program is done, we close our primary socket:

```
    close(simpleSocket);
    return 0;

}
```

Listing 2-1 is the complete listing for our simple server.

Listing 2-1. Simple Server

```
#include <stdio.h>
#include <sys/types.h>
#include <sys/socket.h>
#include <netdb.h>

const char APRESSMESSAGE[] = "APRESS - For Professionals, By Professionals!\n";

int main(int argc, char *argv[]) {

    int simpleSocket = 0;
    int simplePort = 0;
    int returnStatus = 0;
    struct sockaddr_in simpleServer;

    if (2 != argc) {

        fprintf(stderr, "Usage: %s <port>\n", argv[0]);
        exit(1);

    }

    simpleSocket = socket(AF_INET, SOCK_STREAM, IPPROTO_TCP);

    if (simpleSocket == -1) {

        fprintf(stderr, "Could not create a socket!\n");
        exit(1);

    }
    else {
        fprintf(stderr, "Socket created!\n");
    }
```

[handwritten annotation: also #include <unistd.h> as of gcc 4.7.? <string.h> for strlen()]

```
/* retrieve the port number for listening */
simplePort = atoi(argv[1]);

/* set up the address structure */
/* use INADDR_ANY to bind to all local addresses  */
bzero(&simpleServer, sizeof(simpleServer));
simpleServer.sin_family = AF_INET;
simpleServer.sin_addr.s_addr = htonl(INADDR_ANY);
simpleServer.sin_port = htons(simplePort);

/*  bind to the address and port with our socket  */
returnStatus = bind(simpleSocket,
                    (struct sockaddr *)&simpleServer,
                    sizeof(simpleServer));

if (returnStatus == 0) {
    fprintf(stderr, "Bind completed!\n");
}
else {
    fprintf(stderr, "Could not bind to address!\n");
    close(simpleSocket);
    exit(1);
}

/* let's listen on the socket for connections      */
returnStatus = listen(simpleSocket, 5);

if (returnStatus == -1) {
    fprintf(stderr, "Cannot listen on socket!\n");
    close(simpleSocket);
    exit(1);
}

while (1)

{

    struct sockaddr_in clientName = { 0 };
    int simpleChildSocket = 0;
    int clientNameLength = sizeof(clientName);

    /* wait here */
```

```
    simpleChildSocket = accept(simpleSocket,
                               (struct sockaddr *)&clientName,
                               &clientNameLength);

    if (simpleChildSocket == -1) {
        fprintf(stderr, "Cannot accept connections!\n");
        close(simpleSocket);
        exit(1);

    }

    /* handle the new connection request  */
    /* write out our message to the client */
    write(simpleChildSocket, APRESSMESSAGE, strlen(APRESSMESSAGE));
    close(simpleChildSocket);

  }

  close(simpleSocket);
  return 0;

}
```

More Socket Functions

A number of other functions can be used with sockets in server-type applications, as well as two functions used in clients that we haven't discussed yet. The functions you'll find in client applications are the connect() function and the read() function. We'll discuss those in this section, and then convert our server application into a client.

connect()

The connect() function is very similar to the bind() function. It takes a socket descriptor, a pointer to an address structure, and the size of the address structure as parameters.

```
int connect(int sockfd, const struct sockaddr *serv_addr, socklen_t addrlen);
```

The difference with connect() is that the address used in the second parameter is the address of the server, not the address of the host running the client program, as is the case with a server and bind(). If successful, connect() returns 0. Otherwise, –1 is returned.

read()

The other client function we'll need is read(). The opposite of write(), read() will accept what is sent by the server after our successful connection request.

```
ssize_t read(int d, void *buf, size_t nbytes);
```

Using our socket descriptor, read() will accept *nbytes* of data and store it in the buffer *buf*. If the call to read is successful, the actual number of bytes read will be returned. If end of communication is encountered, 0 is returned. Otherwise, –1 is returned.

Converting Our Server Application into a Client

Let's convert our server program to be a client instead, as shown in Listing 2-2. The two programs will be very similar, the key differences will be the use of connect(), the use of read(), and the need to call the program with an additional parameter, the IP address of the server. Note that the port number used as an argument for the client should match the port number used as an argument for the server.

Listing 2-2. Simple Client

```
#include <stdio.h>
#include <sys/types.h>
#include <sys/socket.h>
#include <netdb.h>

int main(int argc, char *argv[]) {

    int simpleSocket = 0;
    int simplePort = 0;
    int returnStatus = 0;
    char buffer[256] = "";
    struct sockaddr_in simpleServer;

    if (3 != argc) {

        fprintf(stderr, "Usage: %s <server> <port>\n", argv[0]);
        exit(1);
```

```
}

/* create a streaming socket     */
simpleSocket = socket(AF_INET, SOCK_STREAM, IPPROTO_TCP);

if (simpleSocket == -1) {

    fprintf(stderr, "Could not create a socket!\n");
    exit(1);

}
else {
        fprintf(stderr, "Socket created!\n");
}

/* retrieve the port number for connecting */
simplePort = atoi(argv[3]);

/* set up the address structure */
/* use the IP address argument for the server address  */
bzero(&simpleServer, sizeof(simpleServer));
simpleServer.sin_family = AF_INET;
inet_addr(argv[2], &simpleServer.sin_addr.s_addr);
simpleServer.sin_port = htons(simplePort);

/*  connect to the address and port with our socket  */
returnStatus = connect(simpleSocket,
                       (struct sockaddr *)&simpleServer,
                       sizeof(simpleServer));

if (returnStatus == 0) {
        fprintf(stderr, "Connect successful!\n");
}
else {
    fprintf(stderr, "Could not connect to address!\n");
    close(simpleSocket);
    exit(1);
}

/* get the message from the server    */
returnStatus = read(simpleSocket, buffer, sizeof(buffer));

if ( returnStatus > 0 ) {
    printf("%d: %s", returnStatus, buffer);
```

```
    } else {
        fprintf(stderr, "Return Status = %d \n", returnStatus);
    }

    close(simpleSocket);
    return 0;

}
```

Identification Functions

In addition to the core socket interface functions, there are a number of other functions that can be used to make things easier on the developer. You've already seen the integer conversion functions htons(), htonl(), ntohs(), and ntohl(). In the client example, we also took advantage of inet_addr(), which is a function that makes it easy to convert strings into IP addresses that are compatible with the sockaddr structure.

What follows are the functions typically used in a socket-oriented program, along with a description of what they do, how to call them, and what they return.

gethostbyaddr() and gethostbyname()

These two functions perform similar tasks. The first performs a lookup that returns a host name when given an address. The second does the reverse, performing a lookup that returns an address when given a name.

```
struct hostent *gethostbyaddr(const char *addr, int len, int type);
struct hostent *gethostbyname(const char *name);
```

Each function returns a pointer to a structure called the hostent structure. The hostent structure is similar to the servent structure we discussed earlier. hostent looks like this:

```
struct  hostent {
            char    *h_name;        /* official name of host          */
            char    **h_aliases;    /* NULL-terminated array of alternate */
                                    /* names                          */
            int     h_addrtype;     /* host address type, typically AF_INET */
            int     h_length;       /* length of address              */
            char    **h_addr_list;  /* NULL-terminated list of addresses */
                                    /* returned from name server in network */
                                    /* byte order                     */
};
```

The members of the structure are self-explanatory. Which functions you call will determine which members of the structure are populated. Calling gethostbyaddr() will populate h_name and h_aliases, while calling gethostbyname() will populate h_add_list and h_addrtype.

Depending on the system configuration, using either of these functions may or may not make a call to an external host for the information. If the request can be satisfied by a local file such as /etc/hosts, the hostent structure will be populated with the information without requiring the use of the network or a name server. In a Linux environment, this behavior is determined by the /etc/nsswitch.conf file. Using this file, you can configure name resolution to happen using a network service like DNS first, and then a local file, or the local file first, then the network. If your application is making repeated requests for information on the same host, it may be better to enter the host's information in /etc/hosts and configure /etc/nsswitch.conf to use local files for lookup information first.

gethostname() and sethostname()

gethostname() returns the name of the current local host where the function call originates, while sethostname() can be used to set the name of the host.

```
int gethostname(char *name, int namelen);
int sethostname(const char *name, int namelen);
```

Only the superuser is allowed to call sethostname(), which usually occurs during the server's boot sequence. Anyone can use gethostname(), which may come in handy if you want to know the name of the server without making a call to an external name server or other lookup table like the /etc/hosts file, as discussed previously. In both cases, a successful call returns 0. If an error occurs, –1 is returned.

getservbyname() and getservbyport()

As discussed earlier in this chapter, getservbyname() returns a pointer to the servent structure. getservbyport() is a companion function.

```
struct servent *getservbyname(const char *name, const char *proto);
struct servent *getservbyport(int port, const char *proto);
```

Which you use will determine which members of the servent structure are populated. Remember that the port number must be in network byte order. Both functions return 0 on success or –1 on error.

getsockopt() and setsockopt()

getsockopt() and setsockopt() manipulate a socket's options. A socket has a number of options that can be used to configure behavior, such keeping connections alive, setting timeout values, or setting the buffer size.

```
int getsockopt(int s, int level, int optname, void *optval, socklen_t *optlen);
int setsockopt(int s, int level, int optname,
               const void *optval, socklen_t optlen);
```

You've seen one option already, SO_LINGER, which is used with the linger structure discussed earlier to determine whether a socket should stay open or not. Depending on the function used, you can either set the socket's option to the given constant or you can retrieve the current value of the option for that socket. Table 2-5 presents a list of the socket options.

Table 2-5. Socket Options

NAME	DESCRIPTION
SO_DEBUG	Enables recording of debugging information
SO_REUSEADDR	Enables local address reuse
SO_REUSEPORT	Enables duplicate address and port bindings
SO_KEEPALIVE	Keeps connections alive
SO_DONTROUTE	Enables routing bypass for outgoing messages
SO_LINGER	Linger on close if data present
SO_BROADCAST	Enables permission to transmit broadcast messages
SO_OOBINLINE	Enables reception of out-of-band data in band
SO_SNDBUF	Sets buffer size for output
SO_RCVBUF	Sets buffer size for input
SO_SNDLOWAT	Sets minimum count for output
SO_RCVLOWAT	Sets minimum count for input
SO_SNDTIMEO	Sets timeout value for output
SO_RCVTIMEO	Sets timeout value for input
SO_ACCEPTFILTER	Sets accept filter on listening socket
SO_TYPE	Gets the type of the socket (get only)

Successful calls to either function return 0 or –1 if an error occurs.

Summary

The Berkeley socket interface provides application developers with a standard method of referencing network functions, information, and communications. In this chapter, we discussed the following topics:

- The definition of a socket and a socket descriptor, and the differences between an active socket and a passive socket

- Which files to include in your program to use the socket interface

- Constants and structures used by the main socket interface functions

- How to create, bind, listen, accept, and write using a socket in a server application

- How to create, connect, and read using a socket in a client application

- Helper functions that make it easier to deal with integer byte conversion, structure manipulation, and socket options

CHAPTER 3

Socket Programming

IN CHAPTER 2, WE COVERED THE BASIC functions used in socket programming, and demonstrated a simple socket server and a simple socket client. Yet while our server and client programs were functional, they didn't do all that much. In this chapter and the following chapters, we'll go through implementing the socket interface in real-world scenarios and creating more robust networked applications step by step.

You'll remember that in Chapter 1 we discussed two types of network communications: those that required a connection, and those that did not. Our simple server and simple client require a connection and use the Transmission Control Protocol (TCP). Thus, the server and client applications in Chapter 2 use *streaming sockets*—that is, sockets that require a connection. There are also *datagram sockets*, or sockets that don't require a connection and use the User Datagram Protocol (UDP). In this chapter, we'll step through a UDP server and a UDP client. We'll also take a look at transferring files back and forth, which is more involved than just sending strings. Finally, we'll discuss error handling and error checking as a key part of any applications you develop.

User Datagram Protocol

In Chapter 2, our client and server programs were based on streaming sockets and used TCP. There is an alternative to using TCP, and that is UDP, or what is otherwise known as datagram sockets. Remember from Chapter 1 that a UDP-based network communication has some particular qualities:

- UDP makes no guarantee of packet delivery.

- UDP datagrams can be lost and arrive out of sequence.

- UDP datagrams can be copied many times and can be sent faster than the receiving node can process them.

UDP sockets are generally used when the entire communication between the server and client can exist within a distinct network packet. Some examples of

UDP-based communications include the Domain Name Service (DNS), Network Time Protocol (NTP), and the Trivial File Transfer Protocol (TFTP). For example, a simple DNS lookup request essentially consists of just two pieces of information: the name or number in the request, and the corresponding answer from the DNS server in the response (which might even be an error). There's no need to incur the overhead of opening a streaming socket and maintaining a connection for such a simple communication. An NTP request is similar. It consists of a question ("What time is it?") and the server's answer. No ongoing communications are necessary. More information on when to use UDP over TCP, or vice versa, is covered in Chapter 7.

UDP Server

Like our streaming socket example in Chapter 2, you can't have a client without having a server first, so let's create a simple UDP server. To begin, we'll set up the #include statements for the header files that we'll need.

```
#include <sys/types.h>
#include <sys/socket.h>
#include <netdb.h>
#include <string.h>
#include <stdio.h>
```

Next, we define a constant that is 1KB in size. We'll use this constant to define the sizes of any message buffers we use.

```
#define MAXBUF 1024
```

Our server starts with standard declaration for main(), followed by the initialization of some variables we'll need. We define a character buffer of size MAXBUF to hold anything we need to send to or receive from our socket, and we set up two sockaddr_in structures: one for the server and one for the client. These structures will hold the metadata about the endpoints in our communication.

```
int main(int argc, char* argv[])
{

    int udpSocket;
    int returnStatus = 0;
    int addrlen = 0;
    struct sockaddr_in udpServer, udpClient;
    char buf[MAXBUF];
```

Before we continue, we check to make sure we have the right number of arguments. The only argument we need for our server is the number of the port that the server should listen on for client connections. This could easily be a constant like MAXBUF, but using a command-line argument means our server can listen on any unused port without recompiling it. If we don't have the right number of arguments, we exit.

```
/* check for the right number of arguments */
if (argc < 2)
{
    fprintf(stderr, "Usage: %s <port>\n", argv[0]);
    exit(1);
}
```

Assuming we are good to go, the first thing we should do is create our socket. Note that this process looks nearly identical to the socket we created in the simple server shown in Listing 2-1 in the previous chapter, except that in this case, we're using SOCK_DGRAM instead of SOCK_STREAM. By using SOCK_DGRAM, we're creating a UDP socket instead of a TCP socket.

```
/* create a socket */
udpSocket = socket(AF_INET, SOCK_DGRAM, 0);
if (udpSocket == -1)
{
    fprintf(stderr, "Could not create a socket!\n");
    exit(1);
}
else {
    printf("Socket created.\n");
}
```

Next, we populate the sockaddr_in structure reserved for our server with the information we have. We use INADDR_ANY so that our socket will bind to any of the local addresses that are configured, and we use the port number that was passed as an argument. Note the call to htons() when dealing with the port. This ensures that the integer used for the port number is stored correctly for our architecture.

```
/* set up the server address and port */
/* use INADDR_ANY to bind to all local addresses */
udpServer.sin_family = AF_INET;
udpServer.sin_addr.s_addr = htonl(INADDR_ANY);

/* use the port passed as argument */
udpServer.sin_port = htons(atoi(argv[1]));
```

Next, we bind to the socket and prepare to receive connections. Our call to bind() uses the UDP socket descriptor we created previously, as well as a pointer to our server's sockaddr_in structure and the size of the structure itself.

```
/* bind to the socket */
returnStatus = bind(udpSocket, (struct sockaddr*)&udpServer,
                    sizeof(udpServer));
if (returnStatus == 0) {
    fprintf(stderr, "Bind completed!\n");
}
else {
    fprintf(stderr, "Could not bind to address!\n");
    close(udpSocket);
    exit(1);
}
```

Now that our setup is complete, we use a while loop that will keep our server running until it receives a signal to terminate from the operating system. The main loop in our server will listen on its socket for communications from a client. Remember that UDP is connectionless, so the client will not be making a request to set up and maintain a connection. Rather, the client will simply transmit its request or its information, and the server will wait for it. Because UDP does not guarantee delivery, the server may or may not receive the client's information.

You'll notice that we use the recvfrom() function instead of the listen(), accept(), and read() functions. recvfrom() is a blocking function, much like accept(). The function will wait on the socket until communications are received. Because UDP is connectionless, our server has no idea which client will be sending information to it, and to reply, the server will need to store the client's information locally so that it can send a response to the client if necessary. We'll use the sockaddr_in structure reserved for our client to store that information.

```
while (1)
{
    addrlen = sizeof(udpClient);
    returnStatus = recvfrom(udpSocket, buf, MAXBUF, 0,
                            (struct sockaddr*)&udpClient, &addrlen);
```

recvfrom() takes our size constant as one of its arguments. This means that the maximum amount of information that can be received from a client is limited to the size of the buffer. Any extra bytes of information that are sent are discarded. The recvfrom() function returns the total number of bytes received from the client or −1 if there's an error.

```
    if (returnStatus == -1) {
        fprintf(stderr, "Could not receive message!\n");
    }
    else {

        printf("Received: %s\n", buf);
        /* a message was received so send a confirmation */
        strcpy(buf, "OK");
        returnStatus = sendto(udpSocket, buf, strlen(buf)+1, 0,
                            (struct sockaddr*)&udpClient,
                              sizeof(udpClient));

        if (returnStatus == -1) {
            fprintf(stderr, "Could not send confirmation!\n");
        }
        else {
            printf("Confirmation sent.\n");
        }
    }
}
```

After receiving information from a client and displaying the message to the console, our server resets the buffer and sends a confirmation message back. This way, our client knows that the server got the information and made a reply. Our response uses the complimentary function to recvfrom(), called sendto(). Much like recvfrom(), sendto() takes our socket descriptor, the message buffer, and a pointer to the sockaddr_in structure for our client as arguments. The return from sendto() is the number of bytes sent or –1 if there is an error.

```
/*cleanup */
close(udpSocket);
return 0;
}
```

If our server receives a termination signal from the operating system, the while loop terminates. Before exiting, we clean up our socket descriptor. As you can see, our UDP server is remarkably similar to our TCP server, except for a few major differences. First, the socket type is SOCK_DGRAM instead of SOCK_STREAM. Second, the server has to store information about the client locally to send a response, since a connection isn't maintained. Third, the server doesn't acknowledge receipt of the client's request unless we provide the code to do it.

To run our UDP server, compile it and then run it using a port number as the only argument. You should see output similar to this:

```
[user@host projects]$ cc -o simpleUDPServer simpleUDPServer.c
[user@host projects]$ ./simpleUDPServer 8888
Socket created.
Bind completed!
```

At this point, the server is waiting to receive communications from any clients that choose to send them.

UDP Client

Now that we have our UDP server, let's cover a simple UDP client. Like our server, we'll start out with the relevant #include directives and a corresponding constant declaration setting up the maximum size for any message buffers. This constant should obviously be the same for both the server and the client; otherwise, it's possible to lose data.

```
#include <sys/types.h>
#include <sys/socket.h>
#include <netdb.h>
#include <string.h>
#include <stdio.h>

#define MAXBUF 1024
```

We use the standard declaration for main and initialize the variables we need, just like we did for our server. We also check to make sure we have the right number of arguments. In this case, we need two: the IP address of the server and the port number that the server is using.

```
int main(int argc, char* argv[])
{

    int udpSocket;
    int returnStatus;
    int addrlen;
    struct sockaddr_in udpClient, udpServer;
    char buf[MAXBUF];
```

```
if (argc < 3)
{
    fprintf(stderr, "Usage: %s <ip address> <port>\n", argv[0]);
    exit(1);
}
```

We create our datagram socket and set up our client's sockaddr_in structure with the information we have. In this case, we don't need to declare a specific port number for our client. The operating system will assign one randomly that our client can use to send its request. Since the UDP packet the server receives contains a header field with the source IP address as well as the source port, the server will have plenty of information to use when sending its response. Once our information is ready, we bind to the socket and prepare to transmit.

```
/* create a socket */
udpSocket = socket(AF_INET, SOCK_DGRAM, 0);

if (udpSocket == -1)
{
    fprintf(stderr, "Could not create a socket!\n");
    exit(1);
}
else {
    printf("Socket created.\n");
}

/* client address */
/* use INADDR_ANY to use all local addresses */
udpClient.sin_family = AF_INET;
udpClient.sin_addr.s_addr = INADDR_ANY;
udpClient.sin_port = 0;

returnStatus = bind(udpSocket, (struct sockaddr*)&udpClient,
                    sizeof(udpClient));

if (returnStatus == 0) {
    fprintf(stderr, "Bind completed!\n");
}
else {
    fprintf(stderr, "Could not bind to address!\n");
    close(udpSocket);
    exit(1);
}
```

Before we transmit, we need to set up our message, which in this case is a simple string. We also need to populate the sockaddr_in structure that we'll use to represent the server we want to contact.

```
/* set up the message to be sent to the server */
strcpy(buf, "For Professionals, By Professionals.\n");

/* server address */
/* use the command-line arguments */
udpServer.sin_family = AF_INET;
udpServer.sin_addr.s_addr = inet_addr(argv[1]);
udpServer.sin_port = htons(atoi(argv[2]));
```

Everything is set up, so we use the sendto() function to send our request to the server.

```
returnStatus = sendto(udpSocket, buf, strlen(buf)+1, 0,
                      (struct sockaddr*)&udpServer, sizeof(udpServer));

if (returnStatus == -1) {
    fprintf(stderr, "Could not send message!\n");
}
else {

    printf("Message sent.\n");
```

If the value we get back from our call to sendto() tells us our request was sent, our client gets ready to receive the server's response using the recvfrom() function.

```
/* message sent: look for confirmation */
addrlen = sizeof(udpServer);

returnStatus = recvfrom(udpSocket, buf, MAXBUF, 0,
                        (struct sockaddr*)&udpServer, &addrlen);
if (returnStatus == -1) {
    fprintf(stderr, "Did not receive confirmation!\n");
}
else {
    buf[returnStatus] = 0;
    printf("Received: %s\n", buf);
}


}
```

Assuming we got some information from recvfrom(), we display it to the screen, clean up, and then exit.

```
/* cleanup */
close(udpSocket);
return 0;

}
```

The key difference between a UDP communication and a TCP communication is that neither the server nor the client has any guarantee that they will receive anything at all. In our example, we had the server send back a confirmation message, but in the real world, a UDP server wouldn't do anything but send back the result of the client's request. For example, in the case of a network time-server, a client would request the current time, and the server's reply would be the current time, provided no errors occurred. If the client didn't receive a reply within a certain time frame, it would typically issue the request again. No confirmation messages or other status messages would be sent, and the server would take no action if the client didn't receive the response. In a TCP communication, the TCP layer on the server would resend the response until the client acknowledged receipt. This is different from a UDP communication, where the client and server applications are wholly responsible for any necessary acknowledgments or retries.

File Transfer

So far, our socket examples have demonstrated the programming concepts involved, but haven't done anything but pass a few strings back and forth. That's fine for example purposes, but what about other kinds of data, such as binary data? As you'll see in this section, sending binary information is a little different than sending simple strings.

Now that you've seen both a TCP connection and a UDP connection in action, let's take a look at what it takes to transfer a file. For this example, we'll use TCP (or streaming) sockets. Our server will bind to a particular port and listen for connections. When a connection is created, the client will send the name of a file to the server, and then the server will read the name of the file, retrieve the file from disk, and send that file back to the client.

One key difference in this example from our earlier TCP server is the use of two sockets instead of one. Why two sockets? With two sockets, our server can handle the request from a client while still accepting more connections from other clients. The connections will be put into a queue on a first-come, first-served basis. If we didn't use two sockets and were busy handling a request, then a second client would be unable to connect and would get a "connection refused" error message. By using two sockets, we can let our server handle its response while lining up other connections to be handled as soon as it's done, without returning an error. Note that this is different than servers that can handle more than one connection at a time.

The Server

Our file transfer server starts out with the familiar #include directives, with one new one. Because we're going to be working with files, we need to include fcntl.h, which contains some constants and other definitions we may need.

```
#include <fcntl.h>
#include <sys/types.h>
#include <sys/socket.h>
#include <netdb.h>
#include <stdio.h>
```

In this example, we're going to hard-code the port number using a constant called SERVERPORT. We'll do the same on the client. This could easily be changed to use an argument from the command line. We'll also use the same constant called MAXBUF to define the maximum size of our transfer buffers. When we initialize our variables, we'll add a second socket descriptor, giving us two to work with: socket1 and socket2. We'll also define two sockaddr_in structures: one for the server and one for the client.

```
#define SERVERPORT    8888
#define MAXBUF        1024

int main()
{

    int socket1,socket2;
    int addrlen;
    struct sockaddr_in xferServer, xferClient;
    int returnStatus;
```

First, we create our socket using SOCK_STREAM. We'll use the first socket descriptor, socket1, for this. If for some reason we can't create our socket, we'll print an error message and exit.

```
/* create a socket */
socket1 = socket(AF_INET, SOCK_STREAM, 0);

if (socket1 == -1)
{
    fprintf(stderr, "Could not create socket!\n");
    exit(1);
}
```

Next, we set up our sockaddr structures, using INADDR_ANY to bind to all of the local IP addresses and setting the port number to our SERVERPORT constant. After we're set up, we make a call to bind() to bind our first socket descriptor to the IP address and port.

```
/* bind to a socket, use INADDR_ANY for all local addresses */
xferServer.sin_family = AF_INET;
xferServer.sin_addr.s_addr = INADDR_ANY;
xferServer.sin_port = htons(SERVERPORT);

returnStatus = bind(socket1,
                    (struct sockaddr*)&xferServer,
                    sizeof(xferServer));

if (returnStatus == -1)
{
    fprintf(stderr, "Could not bind to socket!\n");
    exit(1);
}
```

If our call to bind() is successful, our next step is to tell our program to listen for requests on the socket using the listen() function. For arguments, we'll pass our socket descriptor and the number 5. The second argument defines the *backlog* of pending connections that are allowed. In our case, we are telling our socket that we will allow five connections to be waiting in the queue.

NOTE *The behavior of the backlog argument changed with version 2.2 of the Linux kernel. Previously, the backlog argument represented the maximum number of connection* requests *allowed in the queue. With 2.2 and later, the behavior changed to represent the maximum number of* completed, *established sockets allowed in the queue, not just simple requests.*

```
returnStatus = listen(socket1, 5);

if (returnStatus == -1)
{
    fprintf(stderr, "Could not listen on socket!\n");
    exit(1);
}
```

At this point, our server is listening on the socket for connections. Our next step is to build the logic to handle requests. In this control loop, we'll initialize some new variables that we'll use to keep track of our file reads and writes, as well as a standard file descriptor and a buffer to hold the filename that we'll be retrieving for clients. The key part of the loop is the call to accept(). Notice that we call accept() and pass it our first socket. The value returned by accept(), though, is the descriptor to yet another socket, socket2. This lets our server queue up other connections on the first socket while it waits to complete the one it is handling, up to the maximum limit of the backlog argument (in this case, five).

```
for(;;)
{

    int fd;
    int i, readCounter, writeCounter;
    char* bufptr;
    char buf[MAXBUF];
    char filename[MAXBUF];

    /* wait for an incoming connection */
    addrlen = sizeof(xferClient);

    /* use accept() to handle incoming connection requests      */
    /* and free up the original socket for other requests       */
    socket2 = accept(socket1, (struct sockaddr*)&xferClient, &addrlen);

    if (socket2 == -1)
    {
        fprintf(stderr, "Could not accept connection!\n");
        exit(1);
    }
```

accept() is a function that will *block* on a socket if there is no current connection. This is handy for servers, because otherwise the server stops as soon as it started, since there wouldn't be any connections on the socket. By blocking, the server waits for connections to come in on the socket.

If we have a connection, the first thing our client will do is send the name of the file it wants the server to retrieve. So, our first order of business is to read the filename sent by the client from the socket and store it in the buffer we set aside for it.

```
/* get the filename from the client over the socket */
i = 0;

if ((readCounter = read(socket2, filename + i, MAXBUF)) > 0)
{
    i += readCounter;
}

if (readCounter == -1)
{
    fprintf(stderr, "Could not read filename from socket!\n");
    close(socket2);
    continue;
}
```

We set readCounter to the number of bytes read from the socket. This is the length of the filename. We initially set up the filename variable to be quite large, because there's no way for us to know ahead of time which file the client will request. We want to make sure the filename we receive is only as large as it needs to be, so we will null-terminate the filename, making the buffer holding the name the right size so that we can use it later. If we don't get a filename, we'll close the socket and continue listening for other connections. If we do get a filename, we'll print a status message to the console so that we can see which files the clients are requesting. Then we'll open the file for reading, making sure to set the O_RDONLY flag to prevent any mishaps, such as overwriting a file or creating an empty file by mistake. The return from the open() call is a file descriptor.

```
filename[i+1] = '\0';

printf("Reading file %s\n", filename);

/* open the file for reading */
fd = open(filename, O_RDONLY);

if (fd == -1)
{
    fprintf(stderr, "Could not open file for reading!\n");
```

```
        close(socket2);
        continue;
    }


    /* reset the read counter */
    readCounter = 0;
```

By now we've hopefully gotten a handle to the file that our client wants. If we can't find or read the file for some reason, our server will close the socket and go back to waiting for another connection. Next, we reset the readCounter, because we're going to use it to count how many bytes we read from the disk while retrieving the file. We'll send the file to the client in chunks, using our MAXBUF constant as the size of each chunk. Because our files can be of varying sizes, we'll use nested loops to keep track of where we are in the transfer. As long as the number of bytes sent is smaller than the total file size, we'll know to keep sending.

```
    /* read the file, and send it to the client in chunks of size MAXBUF */
    while((readCounter = read(fd, buf, MAXBUF)) > 0)
    {
        writeCounter = 0;
        bufptr = buf;

        while (writeCounter < readCounter)
        {

            readCounter -= writeCounter;
            bufptr += writeCounter;
            writeCounter = write(socket2, bufptr, readCounter);

            if (writeCounter == -1)
            {
                fprintf(stderr, "Could not write file to client!\n");
                close(socket2);
                continue;
            }
        }
    }
```

As before, if we run into any problems writing to the client, we close the socket and continue listening for other connections. Once our file has been sent, we'll clean up the file descriptor and close the second socket. Our server will loop back and check for more connections on socket1 until it receives a termination signal from the operating system.

```
        close(fd);
        close(socket2);


    }

  close (socket1);
  return 0;


}
```

Once the termination signal is received, we'll clean up by closing the original
socket (socket1), and exiting.

The Client

Our file transfer client is slightly less complicated than our server. We begin with
the standard #include directives and the same constant declarations that we
used in the server, namely MAXBUF and SERVERPORT.

```
#include <sys/types.h>
#include <sys/socket.h>
#include <netinet/in.h>
#include <arpa/inet.h>
#include <string.h>
#include <stdio.h>
#include <sys/stat.h>
#include <fcntl.h>


  #define SERVERPORT    8888
  #define MAXBUF        1024
```

Next we do the standard setup and initialization, including the creation of a
streaming socket and the population of a sockaddr_in structure for our server.

```
int main(int argc, char* argv[])
{
    int sockd;
    int counter;
    int fd;
    struct sockaddr_in xferServer;
    char buf[MAXBUF];
    int returnStatus;
```

```
if (argc < 3)
{
    fprintf(stderr, "Usage: %s <ip address> <filename> [dest filename]\n",
            argv[0]);
    exit(1);
}

/* create a socket */
sockd = socket(AF_INET, SOCK_STREAM, 0);

if (sockd == -1)
{
    fprintf(stderr, "Could not create socket!\n");
    exit(1);
}

/* set up the server information */
xferServer.sin_family = AF_INET;
xferServer.sin_addr.s_addr = inet_addr(argv[1]);
xferServer.sin_port = htons(SERVERPORT);

/* connect to the server */
returnStatus = connect(sockd,
                       (struct sockaddr*)&xferServer,
                       sizeof(xferServer));

if (returnStatus == -1)
{
    fprintf(stderr, "Could not connect to server!\n");
    exit(1);
}
```

Once we have a successful connection to our server, our first task is to send the name of the file we want the server to retrieve for us. This was passed to our client as a command-line argument.

```
/* send the name of the file we want to the server */
returnStatus = write(sockd, argv[2], strlen(argv[2])+1);

if (returnStatus == -1)
{
    fprintf(stderr, "Could not send filename to server!\n");
    exit(1);
}
```

Once our filename is sent to the server, we don't need to send anything else, so we call the shutdown() function to set our socket to read-only.

```
/* call shutdown to set our socket to read-only */
shutdown(sockd, SHUT_WR);
```

Next, we set up our destination file. If a destination filename was an argument on our command line, we use that and open it for writing. If no destination filename was given, we use stdout, denoted by a file descriptor of 1.

```
/* open up a handle to our destination file to receive the contents */
/* from the server    */
fd = open(argv[3], O_WRONLY | O_CREAT | O_APPEND);

if (fd == -1)
{
    fprintf(stderr, "Could not open destination file, using stdout.\n");
    fd = 1;
}
```

As long as the server is sending us chunks of the file, read them from the socket and write them out to the system. In this example, we are writing the chunks to standard out (stdout). This could be changed easily to use the filename we sent to the server.

```
/* read the file from the socket as long as there is data */
while ((counter = read(sockd, buf, MAXBUF)) > 0)
{
    /* send the contents to stdout */
    write(fd, buf, counter);
}

if (counter == -1)
{
    fprintf(stderr, "Could not read file from socket!\n");
    exit(1);
}

close(sockd);
return 0;

}
```

Once all of the chunks have been read from the server, clean up by closing the socket, and exit.

Example File Transfer Session

Let's run our file transfer client and server, and look at what the output would be. First, let's start the server.

```
[user@host projects]$ cc -o xferServer xferServer.c
[user@host projects]$ ./xferServer
```

At this point, the server is listening on all local IP addresses, on port 8888, which is the value of SERVERPORT. Feel free to change this to anything you like. Next, we compile and launch the client.

```
[user@host projects]$ cc -o xferClient xferClient.c
[user@host projects]$ ./xferClient 127.0.0.1 filename > new-filename
```

The client takes two arguments: the IP address of the server that will be sending the file and the filename to retrieve. Remember that our client uses standard out (stdout) to write the file it receives from the server. Because we're using stdout, we need to redirect stdout to a new location using our login shell's redirection operator, the ">" character. If we don't redirect stdout to a new location, one of two things will happen:

- The file contents that are retrieved will be displayed on the screen.

- The file we retrieve will actually overwrite the file we asked the server to read if we're operating in the same directory and our client and server are running on the same machine.

In our previous example, both programs are running on the same machine and in the same directory. We don't want our client's write process to compete with the server's read process, so we use the redirection operator to send the contents of the retrieved file to another filename altogether. Because our file might be a binary file, such as an image or executable instead of ASCII text, we also don't want the contents sent to the screen. Sending the contents of the file to the screen is fine if it's text, but not if it's a binary file.

Error Handling

In all of our examples so far, we've been fairly diligent about checking the results of our function calls. In general, systems return negative numbers when something goes wrong and positive numbers when something is all right. However, it is possible, especially in the case of sockets, for a function call to return an error that isn't a negative number. These error codes are defined in the errno.h file on your system. On most Linux systems, for example, this file can be found at /usr/include/asm/errno.h.

It's a good idea to check the return value after every single system call. You'll save yourself time and effort by checking the values and printing or logging a relevant message to a file or to the console screen. There are a number of built-in support features that you can use to do this. For example, in the code you've seen so far, we've been using the fprintf() function to print our messages to the standard error device, known as stderr. This device can be easily redirected using your shell's redirection operators so that the messages received by stderr go where you want them to go, such as to a log file or even to mail or an alphanumeric pager.

Another function that can be used for error logging is the perror() function. This function behaves more simply than the fprintf() function, because perror() always uses stderr for its output and doesn't let you do any formatting of the error message. With fprintf() and using stderr as the file descriptor, you can easily include formatted information, such as the values of any relevant variables that may have caused the problem. These values can be any of the data types supported by fprintf().

Not only will you save time and effort by checking your error codes, but you'll also give your applications a solid foundation for security. It's well known that some of the primary exploits used by crackers are basic things like buffer overflows and unexpected payloads. If you take care in your programs to check the sizes of buffers and verify the content of variables, and take extra checks to ensure that the data you send or receive is the data you expect to send or receive, your applications will be less susceptible to those types of attacks. If you're expecting a date, then check to make sure the date is valid before doing anything with it. If you're setting up a 5KB buffer to store something, make sure your applications don't try to store 6KB of information there, or even 5KB + 1 byte.

One important thing to remember is that not all errors are failure errors, especially in the case of socket programming. Just because your function call returned an error doesn't mean your program can't continue, whether it's a server or a client. Remember that when making network connections over distributed networks, just about anything can happen. Because just about anything can happen, it's normal for some errors to occur, and your programs should determine which errors can be handled without stopping and which are serious failures.

For example, if you develop a server application, and the server can't do required operations like creating, binding to, or listening on a socket, then there's no reason to continue. If, however, the error returned is something expected such as a transmission error, your program should continue operations. In some cases, like UDP, your program might not even know a transmission error occurred, whereas with TCP, your program will know.

Probably the most important thing to know about error handling is that there is no "right way." The right way is the way that works for you and your application, since only you can set the design parameters. However, even though there is no "right way," it doesn't mean that you can ignore error handling. Ignoring errors will leave your applications unstable and insecure, not to mention difficult to maintain.

Summary

In this chapter, we covered building a couple of different types of socket applications. We built both a UDP server and a UDP client, and demonstrated the difference between using datagram sockets and streaming sockets. Then, using streaming sockets, we built a server and client capable of transferring any file that the server could access. This demonstrated how to send binary data instead of simple strings and stepped through a sample session. Finally, we discussed error checking and error handling, and explained that good error checking will not only save you time and effort when developing your applications, but also help make your applications more stable and more secure.

CHAPTER 4

Protocols, Sessions, and State

IN CHAPTER 1, WE PRESENTED an introduction to the concept of protocols—in particular, protocol layering. Protocol layering lets us develop complementary protocols and use them together to handle a complex task, instead of trying to develop a single protocol that does everything everywhere. In this chapter, we'll discuss different protocol architectures and methods, and step through real-world examples to explain them.

As we noted previously, TCP is a connection-oriented protocol. A complementary protocol to TCP is UDP, which is *connectionless*. To recap, a connection-oriented protocol is like a phone call. A connection is made to another node on the network, and the connection is maintained for the duration of the conversation between the nodes, until one or the other disconnects or a network or system error occurs that prevents the conversation from continuing. A connectionless protocol, instead of being like a phone call, is like shouting down the street to your neighbor. Your neighbor might hear you, and might respond, but there are no guarantees. Even if your neighbor does hear you, she may hear only portions of your communication—the rest may be garbled because of poor conditions, noisy traffic, or other reasons.

State vs. Stateless

There is another aspect of protocol communications beyond whether the communication supports connections or not: the concept of *state*. Servers that maintain state are known as *stateful servers*, and those that do not are known as *stateless servers*. If a server maintains state, it means that the server maintains information about all of the current connections with its clients and the communications sent between them. A server typically needs to maintain state when the chosen transport protocol is one that does not guarantee delivery, like UDP. If the transport protocol does not guarantee delivery, it is up to the application protocol to do so by keeping track of each client's status and current operations. Otherwise, the server application has no method to determine if the client intends to communicate further, is done communicating, is waiting for a response, or has experienced an error.

Developing a server that maintains state has advantages. By keeping information about a client connection on the server, the size of the messages between server and client can be reduced, allowing the server to respond quickly to requests. The primary disadvantage of maintaining state on the server is the risk that the information will become out of sync or incorrect should communications from the client be lost or corrupted. Essentially, it comes down to how much control is given to each end of the communication. A centralized, server-heavy model would be a stateful server, while a decentralized, distributed model would be a stateless server, requiring clients to keep track of their own information, sending it back to the server each time a request was made.

As an example, consider a stateful file server. The client requests a file. The server begins to deliver the file to the client. However, the file is quite large. Since the server cannot deliver the file to the client in one transmission due to things like protocol frame sizes, buffer sizes, and other network restrictions, the file must be delivered in portions, or chunks, one after the other. The server must maintain information about which portions of the file have been sent to the client as well as which portions of the file have been received, to determine whether the connection to the client can be closed. Because the file resides on the server, the client does not know the actual size of the file—only the server can know that, and thus only the server can maintain the state of the file transfer.

In a stateless file server environment, it would be up to the client to manage the file transfer. The client application would be responsible for controlling which portions of the file were sent by the server by specifying the next location for reading from the disk. The client would also need to specify the filename with every request, as well as authenticate with every request, since the server would not be keeping track from request to request.

Some of the most widely used Internet protocols are stateless protocols. The Hypertext Transfer Protocol (HTTP) is probably the most obvious example of a stateless protocol. Web servers do not maintain state by default. Each request from a client over HTTP is considered an *atomic* request, meaning the request has to stand by itself and does not have any relation to any previous or future requests. As far as the web server is concerned, the client making the request has never made a request before and never will again.

Other Internet protocols are stateful protocols. The popular Post Office Protocol (POP3) used to retrieve e-mail is an example of a stateful protocol, as are File Transfer Protocol (FTP) and Simple Mail Transfer Protocol (SMTP). In these cases, the respective servers are responsible for maintaining the state of each client connection within the application's resource space. This is necessary for various reasons. In the case of POP3, a connection has different states, such as authentication and transaction status. Each state has a set of server instructions that are allowed, so if the server didn't keep track of each client's status, there would be no way to determine if a certain operation was valid or invalid.

Table 4-1 shows some of the more popular Internet protocols and their particular properties.

Table 4-1. Internet Protocols and Their Properties

PROTOCOL	CONNECTION	CONNECTIONLESS	STATEFUL	STATELESS
HTTP	Yes	No	No	Yes
FTP	Yes	No	Yes	No
POP3	Yes	No	Yes	No
IMAP	Yes	No	Yes	No
SMTP	Yes	No	Yes	No
Telnet	Yes	No	Yes	No
DNS	No	Yes	No	Yes
NTP	No	Yes	No	Yes

Keep in mind that these protocols are *application protocols*. That is, they are independent of network protocol. In nearly all cases where the protocol requires a connection, they use TCP over IP as the network protocol. Connectionless protocols like DNS or NTP typically use UDP.

SMTP and HTTP are probably the most popular protocols in use today. As you can see from Table 4-1, both require a connection, yet one is stateless and one is not. To illustrate the differences, we'll take a walk through both a stateless protocol and a stateful protocol later in the chapter. Before we do, though, we'll discuss different ways of maintaining state should it be needed.

Methods for Maintaining State

There are various methods for maintaining state within a server application. These methods usually involve keeping a data structure on the server for each connection and updating that structure as the client's connection changes state. For example, on initial connection the data structure is allocated and initialized, but it might have the authentication state set to false. Once the client authenticates itself, that particular property would be set to true. Depending on the protocol used, the mechanism used to keep the data structure updated varies.

Storing State on the Server

Stateful servers use the concept of *sessions* to store state. How the state is stored is dependent on the server. The important thing to remember is that when a client makes its first connection to the server, the server sets up a session for that particular client. Within the session context, the server can do any number of things, mainly storing values that may be needed across client requests. These values can take the form of information visible to the client (the user), such as the items in a shopping cart, as well as internal control information used by the server, such as a list of user preferences and application defaults. The information held in the client's session, such as the current state of the connection, is typically kept in memory for fast access, but there are servers out there that can store session data in files or in some other mechanism such as a database. Thus, one client connection equals one session, and no client request should be able to access the session of another.

When a stateful server starts a session for a client, the session is said to be in an *initial* state. It is up to the client to request a change to that state to issue commands and instructions to the server, and it is up to the server to determine if the client's commands and instructions are valid within the current state. If the commands are not valid within that particular state, the server sends an error message or code in reply. Examples of such commands might be instructions to get ready to accept data from the client, send data to the client, or even to provide a listing of commands that can be used in the current state. Figure 4-1 shows the flow of a stateful server session.

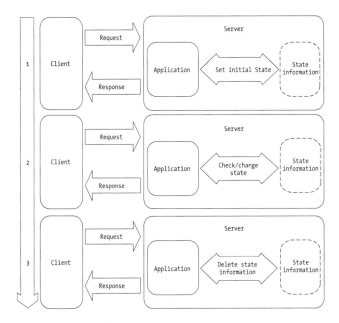

Figure 4-1. Stateful connection flow diagram

What happens to sessions, though, if the protocol and server used are stateless? Can a stateless server maintain a session? The answer is yes, but it requires an additional application layer. For example, HTTP has no concept of state, yet it's still possible to maintain sessions when communicating with a web server. In the case of HTTP, developers typically use an additional application server layer such as PHP, Active Server Pages (ASP), JavaServer Pages (JSP), Common Gateway Interface (CGI), or some other mechanism to track sessions. In this scenario, HTTP is stateless, but the application processing the request isn't the web server—it's some other application called by the web server. The web server merely passes the request to the application server where the request is processed and state is maintained in a session. After the response is assembled, it's sent back to the web server, which in turn sends the response on to the client. Figure 4-2 shows how an additional application layer can be used with a stateless server to maintain session state.

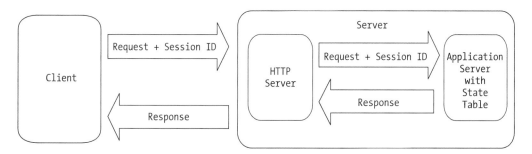

Figure 4-2. Using an additional layer to maintain state

Describing in detail how to use an additional application layer to store state during a session is beyond the scope of this chapter. Each of the technologies in use has extensive documentation available for the interested developer. For now, let's take a look at the fundamental requirement for maintaining state this way: the *session ID*. The session ID is the key to maintaining state when communicating with a stateless server if the requests are actually handled by an application other than the server itself.

> **NOTE** *Because a session ID is a key to more information on a server, it can be valuable. In a HTTP request, the session ID as well as the URL are transmitted in the clear. This makes it possible to* hijack *the user's session by monitoring the network and making requests using the stolen session ID. To help protect a session, use an encrypted protocol like HTTPS and store additional information as a session value on the server, such as the client's IP address. This extra information can be used to verify that each subsequent request is coming from the expected location.*

When each session is started, it is assigned a unique ID. This unique ID is sent with every request and serves as a key or pointer to the resource space allocated to that particular client where state is maintained. Depending on the application server's configuration, the session ID can be sent as a cookie or as a URL parameter. Both cookies and URL parameters are discussed in the next section. It's important to note that even though it is the client that sends the session ID to the server, the actual application state is maintained on the server, which also assigns the session ID.

Storing State on the Client

Of course, it is possible to maintain state using the client side of the transaction. This removes the burden of maintaining the session from the server, but it adds the burden to each request made by the client. In our stateless file server example, it would be up to the client to send additional parameters with each request (like a filename), how much of the file has already been sent, and which portions of the file to send next. The most prevalent example of maintaining state on a client is found in the HTTP protocol.

Figure 4-2 shows how developers can use additional server resources to maintain state when working with a stateless server. Developers can also maintain state on the client in a number of different ways, depending on the protocol. Let's consider HTTP. The client for a HTTP transaction is typically a web browser, in various forms. Some web browsers are automated, such as search engine robots, while others are text-only like lynx or wget, or graphical like Netscape or Mozilla. Depending on the client, methods of maintaining state include the following:

- **Using a cookie to store the value of a variable on the client**. Originally called "magic cookies," cookies reside on the client and are sent to the server with each request.

- **Using hidden form variables to hold values and information**. An additional application layer like PHP, CGI, or JSP can process these hidden form variables for information.

- **Using URL parameters to store variable information**. Like form variables, the information contained in a URL can be parsed and used by a server.

Which method is used is up to the developer, depending on the circumstances and the requirements of the application.

Cookies

Cookies are actually bits of information stored on a client, stored as a simple text file. In our HTTP example, then, a cookie would be stored and managed by the web browser. Each cookie is given a name, an expiration time limit, a domain, and a value. The rules of cookie handling dictate that only the cookies within a particular domain space are sent to a server. Thus, for the server whose name is www.apress.com, the only cookies sent by the browser are those within that domain. The server receives both the cookie's name and its value.

Cookies have some advantages. They use a minimum of resources, they're easy to manage, and they provide a clean interface for maintaining state. The main disadvantage to cookies is security. Since cookies are text files, they're visible to anyone with access to the computer and the right access permissions. All cookies and their values are visible regardless of the domain assigned to them—they can't be hidden, although one domain can't access the cookies of another. If you were to keep sensitive data in a cookie, that information could be compromised easily.

The default expiration value for a cookie is the current session. Thus, if the expiration date is not set, the cookie expires when the session ends. If the expiration date is set to the past, the cookie is deleted. If the expiration date is set to the future, the cookie is written from memory to disk when the session ends or the browser shuts down.

Form Variables

HTML forms have a type parameter that can be set to "hidden." A hidden form field looks like this:

```
<FORM NAME="MyForm" METHOD="POST">
    <INPUT TYPE="hidden" name="Field1" value="ABC123">
</FORM>
```

In this code snippet, the form variable Field1 is hidden. A developer can maintain state by setting the values of these hidden variables to whatever is expected by the server. Advantages to hidden form fields are that they do not require additional resources on the client like cookies do, and they are easy to set and work with. Like cookies, however, hidden form fields are not secure, and they are hidden only by default. By viewing the source of the HTML page, the values of the hidden form fields can be seen easily. Another disadvantage to form fields is the management overhead required. Every time the HTML page is sent to the browser, the developer must make sure all of the form fields required by the server on later requests are included into the form. Otherwise, the server will be unable to handle the requests properly.

URL Parameters

The third way to maintain state on the HTTP client is through the use of URL parameters. The HTTP standard allows you to append variable information called a *query string* to any HTTP URL. The information in the query string can be parsed and used to give your application server the information it needs to handle your request. Query string parameters, like cookies and form variables, use a name/value pattern to carry information. For example, to send the contents of two variables to our server, the URL might look like this:

```
http://host.domain.com/script.cgi?variable1=value1&variable2=value2
```

Each variable is separated by an ampersand (&) character, with the entire query string delimited by the question mark (?) character. On receipt, the server parses the query string and assigns the given values to the variables, using the information and then forming a response that is sent back to the client. Note that to maintain state across requests, the response generated by the server has to include links that are generated with the right state information. Otherwise, the state information would exist for only one request. For example, consider a scenario where a session ID is sent back and forth as a URL parameter. Since on the initial request the client has no idea what its session ID might be, and since the session still has to be initialized, it would be up to the server to rewrite any URLs contained within the response's HTML to append the session ID to any URLs.

So far, we've looked at some of the ways that state can be stored on a client, specifically a HTTP client or web browser. However, it's important to point out the difference between maintaining state using HTTP and maintaining state with an additional application layer. In our previous example, HTTP merely facilitates the transfer of state information, such as cookies or URL parameters. None of the state information is processed by the actual web server, but by an additional layer of software used by the web server. For example, in the URL parameter code snippet, the program handling the state information would be *script.cgi*, known as a CGI script. This script could be written in any number of languages, such as Perl, Python, or C. The HTTP server would call the CGI program and pass it the request string. After processing, the results would be sent back to the HTTP server and from there back to the HTTP client. Thus, as far as the web server is concerned, all of the requests are the same and there is no relationship between any of them.

Stateless Server Walk-through

In Chapter 1, we discussed the Domain Name System (DNS) as a way for network nodes to find the addresses of other network nodes. We stepped through an example request for the IP address of www.apress.com, and we also looked at how to query the domain name system for other information, such as the host responsible for handling mail for the linux.org domain. Before we step through an example stateful server session, let's expand our DNS example in Chapter 1 and take a look at what happens on the server when it receives a request.

Remember that whether an application maintains state or not does not determine whether it uses UDP or TCP. DNS is stateless, yet it can use either UDP or TCP, depending on the implementation. For reference, the DNS protocol is explained in several RFCs, mainly 1034 and 1035.

In a typical DNS request and response cycle, the information transferred between server and client is bundled into a single package called a *message*. That is, the client sends a query to the server, and then the server looks up the information, modifies the original message, and sends the message back to the client. A DNS message is composed of five pieces of information: a header, a question, an answer, a pointer to another server, and a section for additional information. Depending on the circumstances, some of these sections in the message will be empty.

The header section is always present. It contains fields that in turn specify which of the remaining message sections have information, and it also specifies whether the message is a query or a response. When a client makes a request, the only message section with information is the question, or query, section. The query section has three portions: the query type, the query class, and the query domain. For example, when we did a lookup on the mail exchanger for linux.org in Chapter 1, the query type was MX for "mail exchanger." The query class was IN for Internet, and the query domain was linux.org. The other message sections were empty.

On reply, the server sent us a message that had the requested information. In this case, the other message sections were filled in. Every section but the query section has the same format, which is a variable number of DNS resource records that match the original query. The number of resource records in each section is specified in the message header. It's important to remember that with DNS, a request can be successful even if a specific answer isn't received, since one of the message sections can contain a pointer to another domain name server.

Let's step through the communication. A DNS client assembles the message using query information, such as the requested type, the class, and the domain. In our Chapter 1 example, it was a type of MX and a class of IN, within the domain linux.org. These three pieces of information go in the query section, and the message is sent off to the domain name server. On receipt, the server checks to see if it can resolve the query for the client. If it can, it fills in the answer section, and if possible, the additional information section of the message, and sends the reply. If the server can't fulfill the request, it keeps the answer section empty and instead fills the pointer section with information on which domain servers can actually fill the request. Then the reply is sent to the client.

When the client receives the response message, it checks to see if there was an actual answer. If so, it uses the information in the answer section to continue operations however it was programmed. If not, it uses the information in the pointer section to make a second request using the same query type, class, and domain, this time from the server pointed to by the pointer section. This allows DNS to be extremely flexible, since any server can handle any request. If the server can't provide a specific answer to a client, it doesn't just dump out an error and continue. Instead, it offers a suggestion or pointer to another domain name server that it thinks can do a better job of handling the client's query. Since all of the information needed by the query itself and the response, whether complete or not, is contained in a single message, there's no need for the server to maintain state across requests.

Stateful Server Walk-through

We've looked at how it is possible to maintain state using a stateless protocol like HTTP using various client-side methods. Nevertheless, doing so required additional software beyond the HTTP server itself. Many server applications are capable of maintaining their own state information, including mail servers, file servers, and more. One example of a stateful protocol is the Post Office Protocol, or POP, also known as POP3. POP3 is a popular protocol for managing an electronic mailbox. Note that POP3 does not send or receive e-mail—those duties are delegated to mail transfer agents that use SMTP such as sendmail and qmail. For reference, the POP3 protocol is defined in RFC 1939. Let's walk through a typical POP3 session as a user checks his mailbox and manages the messages contained in it.

The POP3 protocol requires a TCP connection. So, the first step for a POP3 client is to make a connection to a POP3 server. As soon as the connection is established, the POP3 server sends a greeting to the client. At this point, a session is created for the client. This allocates resources on the server for that particular client. Once the greeting is sent, the client enters the *authorization* state on the server. In the authorization state, the client has to identify itself and authenticate itself to the server to proceed. Clients can use various authentication methods with the POP3 protocol. The simplest is a typical username and password negotiation. The client sends the username and password to the server, which in turn uses whatever method it is configured to use to determine whether this particular client should have access. In some cases, a POP3 server will keep its own database of usernames and passwords, and in other cases, the server will use the operating system's database of usernames and passwords to perform the authentication.

Assuming the server can authenticate the client, a file lock is placed on the user's mailbox. This prevents multiple connections to the same resource, which helps to preserve state. Once a lock is achieved on the mailbox, the server performs some processing, such as creating a list of the available messages. As soon as the server has authenticated the client and obtained a lock on the resources it needs, the session enters a new state.

The *transaction* state is where the bulk of communications happens for each session. It is in this state that the client instructs the server on how to handle each message using a variety of commands. The list of valid instructions in the transaction state is shown in Table 4-2.

Table 4-2. Valid Commands in the POP3 Transaction State

COMMAND	SERVER RESPONSE
STAT	A simple acknowledgement that the client's instruction was received.
LIST	A list of the message numbers available.
RETR	Given the number of a message, the server responds with the contents of that message.
DELE	Given the number of the message as an argument, the server marks the message for deletion.

As you can see, the number of commands that a client can issue in the transaction state is limited. Any other commands entered would generate an error message. Of special interest is the DELE command. When given, this command doesn't actually delete message in question, but instead simply marks the message for deletion. Messages marked for deletion aren't deleted until the next state, the *update* state.

The update state isn't allowed until the client sends the quit command (QUIT) to the server. At this point in the session, the server actually deletes any messages marked for deletion, and on completing this operation, it sends a status message to the client, releases any locks it may have on resources used during the session, and shuts down the TCP connection. There are a couple of exceptions to the update state. For example, if the quit command is issued while the client is still in the authorization state, the server will release any resources it may have locked and shut down the TCP connection *without* entering the intermediate transaction state; the session will go right from the authorization state to the update state.

Summary

In this chapter, we discussed the difference between stateful and stateless protocols and applications. Stateful servers store state information across client requests, while stateless servers do not. Examples of stateless protocols include HTTP and DNS. Examples of stateful protocols include POP3 and FTP. Key concepts covered in this chapter include the following:

- There is no automatic correlation between state and connection. A connectionless protocol doesn't automatically mean a stateless protocol.

- Stateless protocols like HTTP can require a connection.

- Maintaining state uses the concept of sessions, which are accessed using a session ID.

- There are various ways to maintain state, including storing state information on the client instead of storing it on the server.

- Developers can use additional application layers to add state management to stateless application protocols like HTTP.

Part Two

Design and Architecture

CHAPTER 5

Client-Server Architecture

A NETWORK SERVER APPLICATION THAT can handle only one client at a time isn't very useful. For example, consider an IRC chat application wherein only one client could connect to an IRC chat server at a time. How much fun would it be to chat with yourself? A server is typically required to handle multiple clients simultaneously.

Handling multiple clients at the same time requires solving several problems. The first issue is allowing multiple clients to connect and stay connected simultaneously. In this chapter, we cover three different general strategies for handling this: multiplexing, forking, and threads. The second issue is one of resources and how to efficiently utilize the memory and processor(s) available. The final issue is keeping the server responsive to each of the clients—in other words, not allowing a client to monopolize the server at the expense of the other connected clients. This is especially important when large amounts of data are to be transferred between the client and server.

This chapter will explain the various strategies available to handle multiple clients. In addition, we'll build servers of each type. We'll start off with a client test program.

Client Test Program

A server isn't much good without a client program to connect to it. In this chapter we'll look at and implement several types of servers. To see how they work we'll use a client test program. This will help us see how each server type handles multiple clients.

To test a server you'll need to open two xterm windows. In the first window, execute the server that you wish to test. In the second window, execute the client test program. You should see output in both the server and client windows.

Here's our test client program, client.c. We'll use it to test the various server examples throughout this chapter. First, we include the needed system header files:

```
/* client.c */
#include <stdio.h>
```

```
#include <sys/types.h>
#include <sys/socket.h>
#include <netinet/in.h>
#include <string.h>
```

We'll use the fork() system call to generate a number of child processes to simulate multiple clients connecting to the server at the same time. This is the forward declaration of the process function:

```
void child_func(int childnum);
```

This is our main() function. We check the command line to see how many child processes to create.

```
int main(int argc, char *argv[])
{
  int nchildren = 1;
  int pid;
  int x;

  if (argc > 1) {
    nchildren = atoi(argv[1]);
  }
```

Next, we loop and create the specified number of children. We will look at this later, but if fork() returns 0, then it has returned in the child process, so we call our child function.

```
  for (x = 0; x < nchildren; x++) {
    if ((pid = fork()) == 0) {
      child_func(x + 1);
      exit(0);
    }
  }
```

Once we've created all of the children, the parent process waits for them to finish before returning.

```
  wait(NULL);
  return 0;
}
```

Next, we create our child function. This is where we connect to the server.

```
void child_func(int childnum)
{
  int sock;
  struct sockaddr_in sAddr;
  char buffer[25];
```

We create our client socket and bind it to a local port.

```
  memset((void *) &sAddr, 0, sizeof(struct sockaddr_in));
  sAddr.sin_family = AF_INET;
  sAddr.sin_addr.s_addr = INADDR_ANY;
  sAddr.sin_port = 0;

  sock = socket(AF_INET, SOCK_STREAM, IPPROTO_TCP);
  bind(sock, (const struct sockaddr *) &sAddr, sizeof(sAddr));
```

Then we attempt to connect to whichever server is running on the local machine.

```
  sAddr.sin_addr.s_addr = inet_addr("127.0.0.1");
  sAddr.sin_port = htons(1972);

  if (connect(sock, (const struct sockaddr *) &sAddr, sizeof(sAddr)) != 0) {
    perror("client");
    return;
  }
```

Once connected, we send some characters to the server and read what the server sends back. We also insert some pauses, using sleep() to keep the clients from connecting and disconnecting so quickly that we don't have more than one connected to a server at the same time.

```
  snprintf(buffer, 128, "data from client #%i.", childnum);
  sleep(1);
  printf("child #%i sent %i chars\n", childnum, send(sock, buffer,
         strlen(buffer), 0));
  sleep(1);
  printf("child #%i received %i chars\n", childnum,
         recv(sock, buffer, 25, 0));
```

Finally, we close the connection and return.

```
  sleep(1);
  close(sock);
}
```

The test client can be compiled with the following command:

```
$>gcc -o client client.c
```

This runs the client with five child processes, each connecting to the server.

```
$>./client 5
```

Multiplexing

The first strategy for handling multiple connections that we'll discuss is *multiplexing*. Multiplexing is a way of handling multiple clients in a single server process. The application allows clients to connect to the server and adds them to a *watch list*. This watch list is just an array of socket descriptors. Then the operating system tells the application which clients (if any) need to be serviced or if a new client has established a connection.

As an example, think of a restaurant with only one waiter. The waiter is responsible for attending to all the tables at the same time. As customers come in and are seated, the waiter adds them to a mental list of tables to check on. Then, when a table needs attention, he attends to it. Of course, only one table may be serviced at a time, and the possibility exists of a single table using up all the waiter's time.

The select() Function

select() is a system function that allows us to specify a set of descriptors (sockets, in this case) that we are interested in. It is worth noting that select() works with any descriptor, including files, pipes, FIFOs, etc. The system puts our program to sleep, polls the sockets for activity, and wakes the program when an event occurs at one of the sockets. This keeps us from writing a busy loop and wasting clock cycles. The select() function prototype looks like this:

```
#include <sys/select.h>
int select(int n, fd_set *readfds, fd_set *writefds,
        fd_set *exceptfds, struct timeval *timeout);
```

The first parameter specifies the highest numbered descriptor (plus 1) to watch in the three sets. It is important to remember that you must add 1 to the highest numbered descriptor in the sets. The reason is that the watch lists are linear arrays of bit values, with 1 bit for every available descriptor in the system. What we are really passing to the function is the number of descriptors in the array that it needs to copy. Since descriptors start at 0, the number we pass is the largest descriptor number plus 1.

Next, we provide three descriptor sets. The first set contains descriptors to be watched for read events, the second for write events, and the third for exceptions or error events. Finally, we provide a timeval that specifies a timeout. If no event occurs in any of the sets before the timeout, then select() returns a 0. We can also specify a null pointer for the timeout parameter. In this case, the call will not return until an event happens on one of the watched descriptors. Otherwise, it returns the number of descriptors in the three sets.

It is important to note that select() does modify the descriptor sets that are passed to it. Upon return, the sets will contain only those descriptors that had some activity. To call select multiple times, we must retain a copy of the original sets. Other than a socket error, if any error occurs, then –1 is returned.

Four macros are provided to help deal with the descriptor sets. They are FD_CLR, FD_ISSET, FD_SET, and FD_ZERO. Each takes a pointer to a variable type fd_set. Except for FD_ZERO, each takes a descriptor as well. It is important to note that the behavior of these macros is undefined if you pass in a descriptor that is less than zero or greater than FD_SETSIZE. The macros are prototyped as follows:

- void FD_SET(int fd, fd_set *set): FD_SET flags a descriptor to be watched.

- void FD_CLR(int fd, fd_set *set): FD_CLR resets the flag set to a descriptor.

- int FD_ISSET(int fd, fd_set *set): After select() returns, FD_ISSET determines whether a descriptor is flagged or not.

- void FD_ZERO(fd_set *set): FD_ZERO clears the set so that no descriptors are watched.

A flagged descriptor indicates activity at the socket.
Here is a code fragment example of using select():

```
int sd; /* our socket descriptor */
fd_set sockreadset;

FD_ZERO(&sockreadset);
FD_SET(sd, &sockreadset);
select(FD_SETSIZE, sockreadset, NULL, NULL, NULL);
if (FD_ISSET(sockreadset))
    printf("Socket ready for read.\n");
```

In this example, the program will wait indefinitely for a read event to occur on the descriptor whose value is specified in sd.

A Multiplexing Server

In our example, the server uses select() to listen for new connections, check for client disconnects, and read events on existing connections. If a read event occurs on the server's listening socket, then a new connection is initiated and the server calls accept() to get the new socket descriptor. The new descriptor is then added to the server's watch set.

On the other hand, if a read event occurs on another socket, then the server calls recv to retrieve any data sent by the client. If no data is received, then the client has disconnected, and the server removes the respective descriptor from the watch set. Otherwise, the data is read and echoed back to the client. Figure 5-1 shows the basic architecture of a multiplexing server.

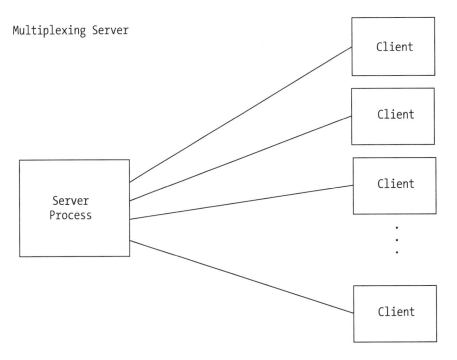

Figure 5-1. Basic architecture of a multiplexing server

Here is the program (server1.c) to implement the preceding example:

```
/* server1.c */
#include <stdio.h>
#include <sys/ioctl.h>
#include <sys/types.h>
#include <sys/socket.h>
#include <netinet/in.h>

int main(int argc, char *argv[])
```

Next, we set up the variables that we'll need. As select() modifies the set passed to it, we use two variables: one to maintain our state and another to interact with the select() function. We need to keep the master set separately:

```
{
    struct sockaddr_in sAddr;
    fd_set readset, testset;
    int listensock;
    int newsock;
    char buffer[25];
    int result;
    int nread;
    int x;
    int val;
```

Then we create the listening socket. This is the socket that will listen for incoming connections from the clients.

```
    listensock = socket(AF_INET, SOCK_STREAM, IPPROTO_TCP);
```

Afterward, we set the socket option SO_REUSEADDR. While debugging, you'll be starting and stopping your server often. Linux tends to keep the address and port that was used by your program reserved. This option allows you to avoid the dreaded "address in use" error.

```
    val = 1;
    result = setsockopt(listensock, SOL_SOCKET, SO_REUSEADDR, &val,
sizeof(val));
    if (result < 0) {
            perror("server1");
            return 0;
    }
```

Here, we bind the socket to the listening port. We use the special address INADDR_ANY to specify that we'll listen on all IP addresses associated with the server:

```
sAddr.sin_family = AF_INET;
sAddr.sin_port = htons(1972);
sAddr.sin_addr.s_addr = INADDR_ANY;

result = bind(listensock, (struct sockaddr *) &sAddr, sizeof(sAddr));
if (result < 0) {
  perror("server1");
  return 0;
}
```

We put the socket into "listen" mode so that we can accept incoming connections:

```
result = listen(listensock, 5);
if (result < 0) {
  perror("server1");
  return 0;
}
```

We initialize our descriptor set using FD_ZERO. Then we add the listening socket to the set so that the system will notify us when a client wishes to connect. Connection requests are treated as read events on the listening socket:

```
FD_ZERO(&readset);
FD_SET(listensock, &readset);
```

Notice that we assign our descriptor set to an alternate variable to be passed to the select() function. As noted previously, this is because select() will alter the set we pass, so that upon return, only those sockets with activity are flagged in the set. Our call to select() signifies that we are interested only in read events. In a real-world application, we would need to be concerned with errors and possibly write events. We loop through the entire set of descriptors. FD_SETSIZE is a constant set in the kernel and is usually 1024. A more efficient server implementation would keep track of the highest numbered descriptor and not loop through the entire set. FD_ISSET is used to determine if the descriptor is flagged as having activity. It returns a nonzero value if the supplied descriptor is set as having had activity; otherwise, it returns 0.

```
  while (1) {
    testset = readset;
    result = select(FD_SETSIZE, &testset, NULL, NULL, NULL);
    if (result < 1) {
      perror("server1");
      return 0;
    }

    for (x = 0; x < FD_SETSIZE; x++) {
      if (FD_ISSET(x, &testset)) {
```

If the activity is on the listening socket, then we accept the new connection and add its socket to our watch set. Otherwise, we read characters from the client. If the number of characters read is less than or equal to zero, then the client is assumed to have closed the connection. We close the connection on our side and remove the descriptor from our watch list. Otherwise, we echo the characters to the screen and back to the client.

```
        if (x == listensock) {
          newsock = accept(listensock, NULL,NULL);
          FD_SET(newsock, &readset);
        } else {
          nread = recv(x, buffer, 25, 0);
          if (nread <= 0) {
            close(x);
            FD_CLR(x, &readset);
            printf("client on descriptor #%i disconnected\n", x);
          } else {
            buffer[nread] = '\0';
            printf("%s\n", buffer);
            send(x, buffer, nread, 0);
          }
        }
      }
    }
  }
}
```

The server can be compiled with a command similar to the example client. Figure 5-2 shows a sample of the output obtained on executing the program.

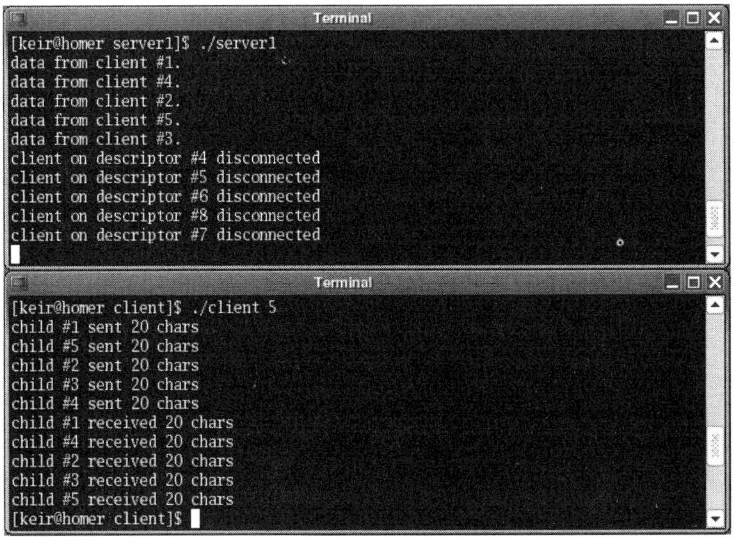

Figure 5-2. Output from a multiplexing server

Notice that, for a brief time, all five clients are connected at the same time.

Forking

In the UNIX environment, the traditional way to handle multiple clients is to use the fork() system call. When an application calls fork(), an exact duplicate of the calling program is made, right down to the program counter (PC), and a new child process is started with that copy. Everything (except the parent's *process ID*, or PID) is copied. This includes the parent's heap, stack, data space, and all open descriptors. Then, the system call returns twice: once in the calling program and the next time in the child process. The return value in the calling program is the PID of the new child process, while in the child process it is 0.

This can be a little confusing at first. How can a function that is called once return twice, you ask? If you think carefully about what the fork() call does, though, it is very logical. Calling fork() makes an exact copy of the program. This means that when the copy begins execution, it starts at the exact place the calling program was, which is the fork() call.

Let's see, in a little more detail, the consequences of copying descriptors. As mentioned previously, when the child process is created, everything is copied to the child, including all open descriptors. The Linux kernel keeps a reference count for each descriptor. So, when a child is created, the reference count is incremented for each copy. As a result, the client must close the descriptor of the listening socket used by the parent process, and the parent must close the descriptor of the client socket used by the child process. This will become evident on executing the program `server2.c`. If `close()` is not called on these sockets, the reference count in the kernel will be wrong, resulting in open or stale connections potentially abusing or exhausting system resources as time goes on.

Using the `fork()` system call to handle multiple clients has several advantages. First, it's simple. Creating a new process to handle each client is easy to implement. Second, using a process per client keeps any one client from monopolizing the server, because the Linux kernel will preemptively swap the processes in and out. Third, other child processes won't be affected if one of the child processes crashes, because the kernel prevents one process from damaging memory in another process.

The `fork()` system call isn't without its disadvantages, however. The most notable problem with the multiprocess approach is the lack of shared memory. Over the years, shared memory solutions (like `shmget()`) have been made available for multiprocess applications, but it isn't as elegant as with a threaded approach. `shmget()` is a system call that allows the allocation of a shared memory segment that can be accessed by multiple processes. The way it works is that the parent process creates a shared memory segment upon startup. Then, as each child is created, it inherits the attachment to the shared memory. Even with the shared memory, access to it must be synchronized with semaphores. Finally, with large programs, significant resources can be used because everything must be copied for each child, resulting in slow performance and potential exhaustion of resources.

 CAUTION *When using the `fork()` system call, you must be very careful to not create zombies. Zombies are child processes that occur when the parent process exits without calling `wait()` or `waitpid()` on the child process. The kernel keeps the exit information for these child processes until the parent process calls `wait()` or `waitpid()` to retrieve it. If the parent exits without retrieving the exit information, the child processes remain in a zombie state. Eventually the kernel will clean them up, but it is best to avoid them in the first place to free up system resources. The simplest way to handle this issue is by trapping the `SIGCHLD` signal and calling `waitpid()`. This is demonstrated in the forking server in the next section.*

One Process Per Client

The simplest architecture for a multiprocess server is to use one process per client. The server simply waits for a client to connect and then creates a process to handle it. From an application design standpoint, this is much less cumbersome than the multiplexing approach we examined earlier. Each client has a dedicated process, and the client logic flows linearly without worrying about stopping to service other connected clients, as compared to multiplexing, where a single process must deal with all clients simultaneously.

A Forking Server

In the following program (server2.c), the initial process waits for a client to connect. It then calls fork() to create a new child process to handle the client. Next, the child process reads the data from the client and echoes it back. Finally, the connection is closed, and the child exits. Meanwhile, the parent process loops back to listen for another connection. Figure 5-3 shows the basic architecture for a multiprocess server.

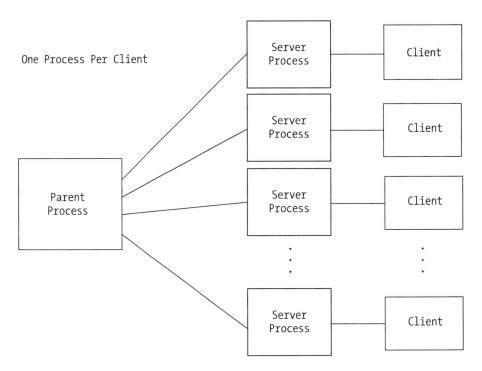

Figure 5-3. Basic architecture for a multiprocess server

The initial section of the code is similar to the earlier program, server1.c:

```
/* server2.c */
#include <stdio.h>
#include <sys/ioctl.h>
#include <sys/types.h>
```

```
#include <sys/socket.h>
#include <netinet/in.h>
```

To trap the child exits and prevent zombies, we also need the following two header files:

```
#include <sys/wait.h>
#include <signal.h>
```

Here's our signal handler. It simply calls `waitpid()` for any exited children. The reason we call it in a loop is that there may not be a one-to-one correlation between exited children and calls to our signal handler. POSIX does not allow for the queuing of signal calls, so our handler may be called once when several children have exited and we need to call `waitpid()` for each one.

```
void sigchld_handler(int signo)
{
  while (waitpid(-1, NULL, WNOHANG) > 0);
}
```

Next, we declare the variables that we will need.

```
int main(int argc, char *argv[])
{
  struct sockaddr_in sAddr;
  int listensock;
  int newsock;
  char buffer[25];
  int result;
  int nread;
  int pid;
  int val;
```

Then we create the socket that will accept the incoming connections.

```
  listensock = socket(AF_INET, SOCK_STREAM, IPPROTO_TCP);
```

Here we set our SO_REUSEADDR option.

```
  val = 1;
  result = setsockopt(listensock, SOL_SOCKET, SO_REUSEADDR, &val, sizeof(val));
  if (result < 0) {
          perror("server2");
          return 0;
  }
```

We then bind it to a local port and all addresses associated with the machine.

```
sAddr.sin_family = AF_INET;
sAddr.sin_port = htons(1972);
sAddr.sin_addr.s_addr = INADDR_ANY;
result = bind(listensock, (struct sockaddr *) &sAddr, sizeof(sAddr));
if (result < 0) {
  perror("server2");
  return 0;
}
```

Afterward, we put the socket into listening mode to listen for incoming connections.

```
result = listen(listensock, 5);
if (result < 0) {
  perror("server2");
  return 0;
}
```

Before we start looping, we install our signal handler.

```
signal(SIGCHLD, sigchld_handler);
```

We then call accept() and allow it to block waiting for connection requests from clients. After accept returns, we call fork() to create a new process. If it returns 0, then we are in the child process; otherwise, the PID of the new child is returned.

```
while (1) {
  newsock = accept(listensock, NULL, NULL);
  if ((pid = fork()) = = 0) {
```

Once in the child process, we close the listening socket. Remember that all descriptors are copied from the parent process to the child. The child process does not need the listening socket any longer, so we close the child's reference on that socket. However, the socket will remain open in the parent process. Next, we read characters from the client and echo them to the screen. Finally, we send the characters back to the client, close the socket, and exit the child process:

```
printf("child process %i created.\n", getpid());
close(listensock);
```

```
    nread = recv(newsock, buffer, 25, 0);
    buffer[nread] = '\0';
    printf("%s\n", buffer);
    send(newsock, buffer, nread, 0);
    close(newsock);
    printf("child process %i finished.\n", getpid());
    exit(0);
}
```

This line is only reached in the parent process. Since the child process has a copy of the client socket, the parent process closes its reference here to decrease the kernel reference count. The socket will remain open in the child process:

```
    close(newsock);
  }
}
```

The server can be compiled with a command similar to the example client. Figure 5-4 shows sample output obtained on executing the preceding program. The client was run with five child processes.

Figure 5-4. Output from a multiprocess server

Preforking: Process Pools

While the preceding strategy is simple to implement, there is a performance penalty to be paid. Creating a copy of a running process is expensive (in terms of time as well as resources), especially for large applications. As clients start connecting in large numbers, there can be a noticeable delay in launching the child process.

One strategy to mitigate the startup costs for a process is to fork a number of processes into a "process pool" when the application starts. This is called *preforking*, and it restricts all of the costs associated with creating a child process to the initialization section of the application. When a client connects, the process to handle it has already been created. Using this method, accept() is not called in the parent process, but in each child process. Unlike the previous example, the listening socket descriptor will not be closed in the child process. In fact, all of the children will be calling accept() on the same listening socket. When a client connects, the kernel chooses one of the children to handle the connection. Since the child is already running, there is no process creation delay.

Example: Apache Web Server

The original Apache Web Server (prior to version 2), http://httpd.apache.org, uses process pools. However, it takes them one step further by making the process pool size dynamic. In the Apache configuration file, you are able to specify the number of initial children, the maximum number of children, the minimum number of idle children, and the maximum number of idle children.

The initial and maximum number of children is pretty straightforward. Specifying the minimum and maximum number of idle children allows the server to handle sudden spikes in usage. The parent process continually checks on the child processes to see how many are idle. It then terminates extra children or creates new children depending on the settings. Using configuration settings, the server can be finely tuned for maximum performance.

Apache version 2 takes this even a step further by introducing *thread pools*. Thread pools are similar to process pools in that you generate the handlers to deal with connecting clients during the initialization of the application, but you are creating threads instead of processes. We'll talk about thread pools in the section "Prethreading: Thread Pools."

A Preforking Server

In the following program (server3.c), the parent server process uses a loop to create the specified number of child processes. On execution, we can pass in the number of children to fork, on the command line. The parent server process then calls wait() to keep it from returning before any of its children. If we don't insert this call, the parent process will end immediately. Each child then calls accept on the same listening socket and waits for a client connection. When a connection is made, the operating system chooses one of the children to signal using a "first in, first out" methodology. That child receives the data from the client and echoes it back. Finally, the connection is closed, and the child calls accept() again to wait for another client. Figure 5-5 shows the basic architecture for process pools.

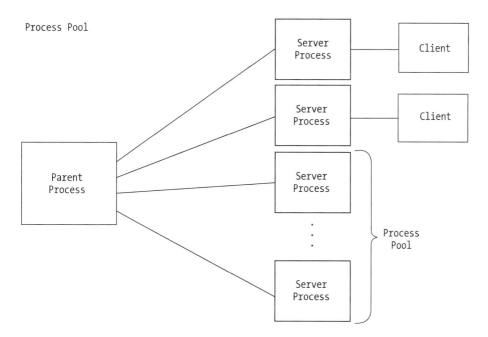

Figure 5-5. Basic architecture for process pools

The initial section is again similar to the earlier programs, except that we check the command line to see how large a process pool to create:

```
/* server3.c */
#include <stdio.h>
#include <sys/ioctl.h>
#include <sys/types.h>
#include <sys/socket.h>
#include <netinet/in.h>

int main(int argc, char *argv[])
{
```

First, we declare the variables that we will need.

```
struct sockaddr_in sAddr;
int listensock;
int newsock;
char buffer[25];
int result;
int nread;
int pid;
int nchildren = 1;
int x;
int val;
```

Then, we check the command line to see how many processes will be in our process pool. If nothing is specified, then we create only one listening process.

```
if (argc > 1) {
  nchildren = atoi(argv[1]);
}
```

We create the socket that will listen for incoming connections.

```
listensock = socket(AF_INET, SOCK_STREAM, IPPROTO_TCP);
```

Again, we set the SO_REUSEADDR option.

```
val = 1;
result = setsockopt(listensock, SOL_SOCKET, SO_REUSEADDR, &val, sizeof(val));
if (result < 0) {
        perror("server3");
        return 0;
}
```

Next, we bind it to a local port and all addresses associated with the machine.

```
sAddr.sin_family = AF_INET;
sAddr.sin_port = htons(1972);
sAddr.sin_addr.s_addr = INADDR_ANY;

result = bind(listensock, (struct sockaddr *) &sAddr, sizeof(sAddr));
if (result < 0) {
  perror("server3");
  return 0;
}
```

Now we put it into listening mode.

```
result = listen(listensock, 5);
if (result < 0) {
  perror("server3");
  return 0;
}
```

We create the specified number of child processes for the process pool using the fork() system call:

```
for (x = 0; x < nchildren; x++) {
  if ((pid = fork()) == 0) {
```

Each child process calls accept on the same listening socket. When a client connects, the system will choose the next child in line to notify:

```
while (1) {
  newsock =  accept(listensock, NULL,NULL);
```

Once a client connects, we read characters it sends, echo them to the screen and client, and close the connection:

```
printf("client connected to child process %i.\n", getpid());
nread = recv(newsock, buffer, 25, 0);
buffer[nread] = '\0';
printf("%s\n", buffer);
send(newsock, buffer, nread, 0);
close(newsock);
printf( "client disconnected from child process %i.\n", getpid());
      }
    }
  }
```

This tells the parent process to wait until all of the children have been completed, before continuing. Of course, none of the children in this example will ever be completed:

```
  wait(NULL);
}
```

Figure 5-6 shows a sample of the output obtained on executing the program. The client was run with five child processes.

```
Terminal                                                          _ □ X
[keir@homer server3]$ ./server3 3
client connected to child process 11986.
client connected to child process 11987.
client connected to child process 11988.
data from client #1.
client disconnected from child process 11986.
client connected to child process 11986.
data from client #4.
client disconnected from child process 11986.
client connected to child process 11986.
data from client #5.
client disconnected from child process 11986.
data from client #2.
client disconnected from child process 11987.
data from client #3.
client disconnected from child process 11988.

Terminal                                                          _ □ X
[keir@homer client]$ ./client 5
child #1 sent 20 chars
child #2 sent 20 chars
child #3 sent 20 chars
child #4 sent 20 chars
child #5 sent 20 chars
child #1 received 20 chars
child #2 received 20 chars
child #3 received 20 chars
child #4 received 20 chars
child #5 received 20 chars
[keir@homer client]$
```

Figure 5-6. Output from a preforking server

Notice that the processes are used in the order in which they called accept().
Since we have more clients than processes in the process pool, earlier processes
are reused for new clients once they become free.

Multithreading

More recently, using threads has become the preferred method for handling
multiple clients. *Threads* are lightweight processes that share the main memory
space of the parent process. Because of this, they use fewer resources than a
multiprocess application, and they enjoy a faster context-switch time. However, multithreaded applications are not as stable as multiprocess applications.
Because of the shared memory if, say, a buffer overrun occurs in one thread, it
can impact other threads. In this way, one bad thread can bring down the entire
server program. This isn't the case with multiprocess applications, where the
memory in each process is protected from alteration from another process by
the operating system. This keeps an errant process from corrupting the memory
of another process.

Before moving on, let's talk a little more about shared memory in multi-threaded server applications. If not handled correctly, the shared memory can be a double-edged sword. Remember that global variables will be shared by all threads. This means that to keep client-specific information, you must take advantage of the thread-local storage mechanisms provided by your thread library. These allow you to create "thread-global" values that aren't shared between threads.

If you do have global variables that need to be shared between threads, it is very important to use the synchronization objects like mutexes to control access to them. Without synchronization objects, you can run into very strange behaviors and even unexplained program crashes. Most often this occurs when one thread is writing to a variable when another is reading or writing to the same variable. This situation can cause memory corruption, and it may not show itself immediately but will eventually cause problems. Multithreaded applications are hard enough to debug, so synchronize access to all global variables and structures.

The version of POSIX threads distributed with most flavors of Linux was developed by Xavier Leroy. His website, `http://pauillac.inria.fr/~xleroy/linuxthreads`, has more information. In addition, there are many other resources on the Internet for references on pthread programming. You can find a new thread library based on GNU's pth library at `http://oss.software.ibm.com/developerworks/opensource/pthreads`.

As with the multiprocess strategy, using one thread per client is the simplest multithreaded server architecture. Again, the client logic in each thread does not have to stop to service other connected clients, but is free to focus on one client. One caveat, though, is that the maximum number of threads allowed on a system is far less than the maximum number of processes. With a server that needs to maintain a large number of persistent connections, you may want to consider using one of the other architectures presented in this chapter.

A Multithreaded Server

Note the multithreaded server's similarity to the multiprocess model. In the following program (`server4.c`), the parent server process waits for client connections. When a connection occurs, the server creates a new thread and passes the new socket descriptor to it. The new thread then reads data from the client and echoes it back. Finally, the connection is closed, and the thread exits. Meanwhile, the parent process loops and waits for another connection. Figure 5-7 shows the basic architecture for a multithreaded server.

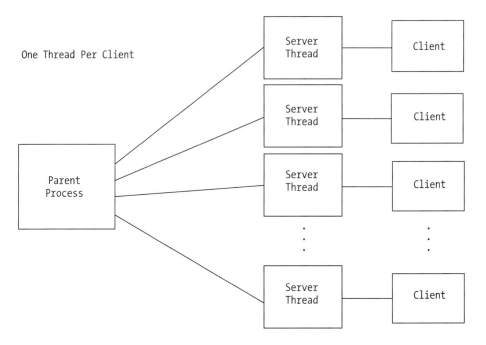

Figure 5-7. Basic architecture for a multithreaded server

Again, the initial section of the code is similar to that in the previous programs:

```
/* server4.c */
#include <stdio.h>
#include <sys/ioctl.h>
#include <sys/types.h>
#include <sys/socket.h>
#include <netinet/in.h>
#include <pthread.h>

void* thread_proc(void *arg);

int main(int argc, char *argv[])
{
```

First, we declare the variables that we will need.

```
struct sockaddr_in sAddr;
int listensock;
int newsock;
int result;
pthread_t thread_id;
int val;
```

Next, we create the socket that will listen for incoming connections.

```
listensock = socket(AF_INET, SOCK_STREAM, IPPROTO_TCP);
```

Now we set the SO_REUSEADDR socket option.

```
val = 1;
result = setsockopt(listensock, SOL_SOCKET, SO_REUSEADDR, &val, sizeof(val));
if (result < 0) {
        perror("server4");
        return 0;
}
```

Then, we bind it to a local port and all addresses associated with the machine.

```
sAddr.sin_family = AF_INET;
sAddr.sin_port = htons(1972);
sAddr.sin_addr.s_addr = INADDR_ANY;

result = bind(listensock, (struct sockaddr *) &sAddr, sizeof(sAddr));
if (result < 0) {
  perror("server4");
  return 0;
}
```

We then put the socket into listening mode.

```
result = listen(listensock, 5);
if (result < 0) {
  perror("server4");
  return 0;
}
```

As in `server2.c`, we call `accept()` and let it block until a client tries to connect:

```
while (1) {
  newsock =  accept(listensock, NULL,NULL);
```

Once a client connects, a new thread is started. The descriptor for the new client socket is passed to the thread function. Since the descriptor is passed to the function instead of being copied, there will be no need for the parent thread to close the descriptor:

```
result = pthread_create(&thread_id, NULL, thread_proc, (void *) newsock);
if (result != 0) {
  printf("Could not create thread.\n");
}
```

Since the parent thread will be in a continuous loop, there will be no need to ever join one of the child threads. Therefore, we call `pthread_detach()` to keep zombies from occurring. A zombie is a process (or thread, in this case) that has returned and is waiting for its parent to check its return value. The system will keep the zombies around until the return value is checked, so they just take up resources. In our example, we aren't interested in the thread's return value, so we tell the system by calling `pthread_detach()`. Then, we call `sched_yield()` to give the new thread a chance to start execution by giving up the remainder of the parent's allotted time-slice.

```
      pthread_detach(thread_id);
      sched_yield();
    }
  }

void* thread_proc(void *arg)
{
  int sock;
  char buffer[25];
  int nread;
```

In our thread function, we cast the passed argument back to a socket descriptor. Notice that we don't close the listening socket as we did in `server2.c`. In a threaded server, the descriptors aren't copied to the child process, so we don't have an extra listening socket descriptor in the child. Next is the familiar routine: read characters, echo them to the screen and client, and close the connection.

```
        printf("child thread %i with pid %i created.\n", pthread_self(),
              getpid());
        sock = (int) arg;
        nread = recv(sock, buffer, 25, 0);
        buffer[nread] = '\0';
        printf("%s\n", buffer);
        send(sock, buffer, nread, 0);
        close(sock);
        printf("child thread %i with pid %i finished.\n", pthread_self(),
              getpid());
    }
```

The server can be compiled with the following command. Notice that we are linking with the pthread library. This is the library that gives us the threading capabilities.

```
gcc -o server4 -lpthread  server4.c
```

Figure 5-8 shows a sample of the output obtained on executing the program. The client was run with five child processes.

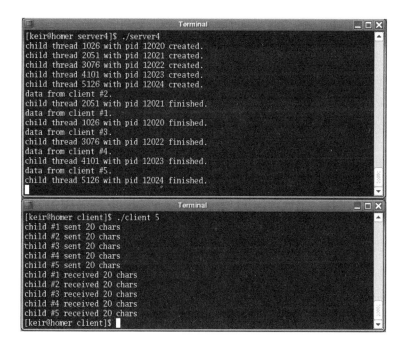

Figure 5-8. Output from a multithreaded server

Notice that, for a short time, all of the clients are connected at the same time.

Thread pools operate in a very similar manner to process pools. Our strategy is to create a certain number of threads when the application initializes. We then have a pool of threads to handle incoming client connections, and we avoid the costs associated with waiting to create a thread when the request is made. In addition, with shared memory, it is much easier to implement dynamic thread pools in which we can resize our thread pool at runtime depending on the load requirements.

On the downside, if one thread crashes, it can bring down the entire server application. This is due to the fact that all of the threads, including the main application process, use the same memory space and resources (for example, file descriptors). So, for example, if one of the threads encounters a buffer overrun problem, it can corrupt memory being used by another thread. This is not the case with multiple processes, because the operating system prevents one process from writing over the memory in another process. Great care must be taken when designing a multithreaded server to prevent an errant thread from affecting the others.

Figure 5-9 shows the basic architecture for a prethreaded server application.

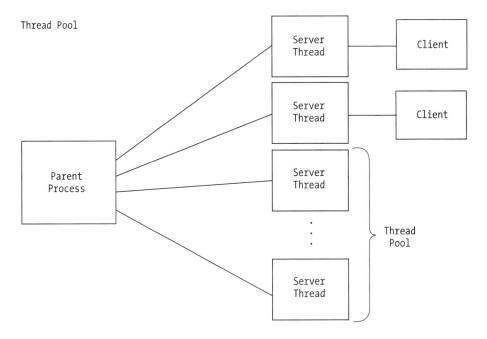

Figure 5-9. Basic architecture for a prethreaded server application

In the following program (server5.c), the number of threads in the pool is passed in on the command line. The parent process then uses a loop to spawn the requested number of threads, passing the descriptor of the listening socket. It then calls pthread_join() to keep it from returning before any of its threads. If we didn't insert this call, the parent process would end immediately and cause all its threads to return. Each thread then calls accept on the same listening socket and waits for a client connection. When a connection is made, the operating system chooses one of the threads to signal using a "first in, first out" methodology. This thread receives the data from the client and echoes it back. Finally, the connection is closed, and the thread calls accept() again to wait for another client.

These lines are very similar to the section in the program server3.c:

```
/* server5.c */
#include <stdio.h>
#include <sys/ioctl.h>
#include <sys/types.h>
#include <sys/socket.h>
#include <netinet/in.h>
#include <pthread.h>

void* thread_proc(void *arg);

int main(int argc, char *argv[])
{
```

First, we declare the variables that we will need.

```
struct sockaddr_in sAddr;
int listensock;
int result;
int nchildren = 1;
pthread_t thread_id;
int x;
int val;
```

We check the command line to see how many threads should be in our thread pool. If none is specified, then we will create a single thread.

```
if (argc > 1) {
   nchildren = atoi(argv[1]);
}
```

Next, we create the socket that will listen for incoming connections.

```
listensock = socket(AF_INET, SOCK_STREAM, IPPROTO_TCP);
```

Then, we set the SO_REUSEADDR option.

```
val = 1;
result = setsockopt(listensock, SOL_SOCKET, SO_REUSEADDR, &val, sizeof(val));
if (result < 0) {
        perror("server5");
        return 0;
}
```

We bind it to a local port and to all addresses associated with the machine.

```
sAddr.sin_family = AF_INET;
sAddr.sin_port = htons(1972);
sAddr.sin_addr.s_addr = INADDR_ANY;

result = bind(listensock, (struct sockaddr *) &sAddr, sizeof(sAddr));
if (result < 0) {
  perror("server5");
  return 0;
}
```

We now put it into listening mode.

```
result = listen(listensock, 5);
if (result < 0) {
  perror("server5");
  return 0;
}
```

Afterward, we create our pool of threads. Notice that we pass the descriptor for the listening socket instead of the client:

```
for (x = 0; x < nchildren; x++) {
  result = pthread_create(&thread_id, NULL, thread_proc,
                          (void *) listensock);
  if (result != 0) {
    printf("Could not create thread.\n");
  }
  sched_yield();
}
```

Here, we call `pthread_join()`. This has the same effect that calling `wait()` did in `server3.c`. It keeps the parent thread from continuing until the child threads are finished:

```
    pthread_join (thread_id, NULL);
}

void* thread_proc(void *arg)
{
  int listensock,  sock;
  char buffer[25];
  int nread;

  listensock = (int) arg;

  while (1) {
```

Each thread calls `accept()` on the same listening socket descriptor. Just as in `server3.c`, when a client connects, the kernel will choose a thread in which `accept()` returns:

```
    sock =  accept(listensock, NULL, NULL);
```

Once `accept()` returns, we read the data from the client and echo it back. Then we close the connection.

```
      printf("client connected to child thread %i with pid %i.\n",
              pthread_self(), getpid());
      nread = recv(sock, buffer, 25, 0);
      buffer[nread] = '\0';
      printf("%s\n", buffer);
      send(sock, buffer, nread, 0);
      close(sock);
      printf("client disconnected from child thread %i with pid %i.\n",
              pthread_self(), getpid());
  }
}
```

The server can be compiled with the following command:

```
gcc -o server5 -lpthread server5.c
```

This will run the server with five threads in the thread pool:

```
./server5 5
```

Figure 5-10 shows a sample of the output obtained on executing the program. The client was run with five child processes.

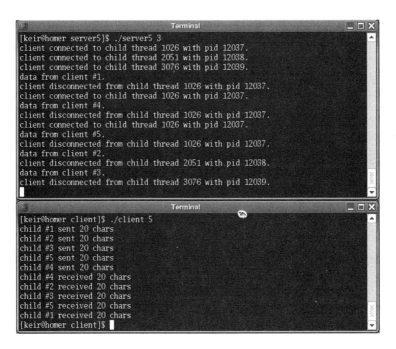

Figure 5-10. Output from a prethreaded server

Notice that the threads are used in the order in which they called accept(). Since we have more clients than threads in the thread pool, earlier threads are reused for new clients once they become free.

Combining Preforking and Prethreading

Starting with version 2 of the Apache Web Server, the Apache Project (http://httpd.apache.org) implemented a hybrid of the preforking and prethreading strategies. What the group hoped to achieve was the speed of prethreading combined with the stability of preforking.

As mentioned earlier in the chapter, a multiprocess server doesn't crash when one of the child processes crashes, but it suffers from slower context switching. Multithreaded servers, on the other hand, do crash when one of the child threads crashes, but have faster context switching. The developers at Apache have combined the two approaches to increase the benefits while minimizing the drawbacks. Figure 5-11 shows this hybrid architecture.

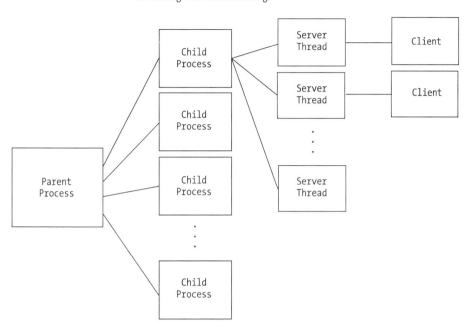

Preforking and Prethreading

Figure 5-11. Combining preforking with prethreading

The way it works is by preforking a number of server processes. However, these processes do not handle client connections. Instead, each child process spawns a finite number of threads. The threads handle client connections. Thus, when dealing with multiple clients, the server enjoys fast context-switching. As for crashes, if a thread crashes, it takes out only other threads from the same child process instead of the whole web server. Apache also provides a setting that sets a number of requests that a process handles before it is terminated and a new process (with child threads) is created. This ensures that resource leaks in any one process will be cleaned up periodically.

TIP *Don't forget about multiplexing. Multiplexing can be added to a multiprocess or multithreaded server to increase scalability. Using this strategy, you can handle very large numbers of simultaneous users because each process or thread can handle more than one client. You can even combine all three and have a multiprocess, multithreaded server with multiplexing.*

Which Method Should You Choose?

Your choice of method should be made based on the requirements of the server you want to develop and the available resources in the environment in which the server will run. Multiplexing is ideal for a low-volume server to which clients will not stay connected for a long period of time. The danger with a multiplexing server is that any one client might monopolize the server's time and cause it to stop responding to the other connected clients. In addition, a multiplexing server cannot take advantage of symmetric multiprocessing (SMP) capabilities. The reason is that a multiplexing server consists of a single process and, since a process cannot be spread across multiple CPUs, the server will only ever use one CPU.

For ease of implementation, you can't beat one process or thread per client. Processes win in stability, while threads win in context-switch time, resource use, and shared memory. Here, you must determine whether you need to coordinate the actions of clients. In a web server, for example, the clients are autonomous. So, the lack of shared memory isn't really a concern. On the other hand, if you're designing a multiuser enterprise application, then coordinating clients can be very important, and shared memory is essential. Of course, while using process pools can help with the context switching, when a client connects, it will still suffer from the lack of simple shared memory.

Table 5-1 summarizes the pros and cons of each method.

Dealing with Large Amounts of Data

In practice, the data transmitted between the client and the server is much larger than that dealt with in the examples earlier in this chapter. Such large amounts of data generate a few issues. First, large amounts of data will be broken up in the underlying transport layer. IP has a maximum packet size of 65,536 bytes, but even smaller amounts of data may be broken up depending on buffer availability. This means that when you call `recv()`, for example, it may not return all of the data the first time, and subsequent calls may be required. Second, while you are sending or receiving large amounts of data, you require your user interface to be responsive. In this section, we will address these issues.

Nonblocking Sockets

The first step to carry out large-sized data transfers is to create nonblocking sockets. By default, whenever we create a socket, it will be a blocking socket. This means that if we call `recv()` and no data is available, our program will be put to sleep until some data arrives. Calling `send()` will put our program to sleep if there is not enough outgoing buffer space available to hold all of the data we want to send. Both conditions will cause our application to stop responding to a user.

Table 5-1. Method Pros and Cons

METHOD	CODE COMPLEXITY	SHARED MEMORY	NUMBER OF CONNECTIONS	FREQUENCY OF NEW CONNECTIONS	LENGTH OF CONNECTIONS	STABILITY	CONTEXT SWITCHING	RESOURCE USE	SMP AWARE
Multiplexing	Can be very complex and difficult to follow	Yes	Small	Can handle new connections quickly.	Good for long or short connections.	One client can crash the server.	N/A	Low	No
Forking	Simple	Only through shmget()	Large	Time is required for a new process to start.	Better for longer connections. Reduces start penalty.	One client cannot crash the server.	Not as fast as threads	High	Yes
Threading	Simple	Yes	Large, but not as large as forking	Time is required for a new thread to start.	Better for longer connections. Reduces thread start penalty.	One client can crash the server.	Fast	Medium	Yes
Preforking	Can be complex if using a dynamic pool and shared memory	Only through shmget()	Depends on the size of the process pool	Can handle new connections quickly if the process pool is large enough.	Good for long or short connections.	One client cannot crash the server.	Not as fast as threads	High	Yes
Prethreading	Only complex if using a dynamic pool	Yes	Depends on the size of the thread pool	Can handle new connections quickly if the thread pool is large enough.	Good for long or short connections.	One client can crash the server.	Fast	Medium	Yes
Preforking plus prethreading	Complex	Yes, but only within each process	Depends on pool sizes	Can handle new connections quickly if pools are large enough.	Good for long or short connections.	One client will crash only its parent process, not the whole server.	Fast	Similar to threading, but depends on how much preforking is done	Yes

Creating a nonblocking socket involves two steps. First, we create the socket as we would usually, using the socket function. Then, we use the following call to `ioctl()`:

```
unsigned long nonblock = 1;
ioctl(sock, FIONBIO, &nonblock);
```

With a nonblocking socket, when we call `recv()` and no data is available, it will return immediately with `EWOULDBLOCK`. If data is available, it will read what it can and then return, telling us how much data was read. Likewise with `send()`, if there is no room in the outgoing buffer, then it will return immediately with `EWOULDBLOCK`. Otherwise, it will send as much of our outgoing data as it can before returning the number of bytes sent. Keep in mind that this may be less than the total number of bytes we told it to send, so we may need to call send again.

The `select()` call from the section on multiplexing is the second step to carry out large-sized data transfers. As mentioned earlier, we use `select()` to tell us when a socket is ready for reading or writing. In addition, we can specify a timeout, so that in case a socket is not ready for reading or writing within a specified time period, `select()` will return control to our program. This allows us to be responsive to a user's commands while still polling the socket for activity.

Putting It All Together

Combining nonblocking sockets with `select()` will allow us to send and receive large amounts of data while keeping our application responsive to the user, but we still need to deal with the data itself. Sending large amounts of data is relatively easy because we know how much we need to send. Receiving data, on the other hand, can be a little harder unless we know how much data to expect. Because of this, we will need to build into our communications protocol either a method to tell the receiving program how much data to expect or a fixed data segment size.

Communicating the expected size of the data to the receiver is fairly simple. In fact, this strategy is used by HTTP, for example. The sender calculates the size of the data to send and then transmits that size to the receiver. The receiver then knows exactly how much data to receive.

Another option is to use a fixed-sized segment. In this way, we will always send the same amount of data in each segment sent to the receiver. Because of this, the sender may need to break up data into multiple segments or fill undersized segments. Therefore, care must be taken in determining the segment size. If our segment size is too large, then it will be broken up in the transport and will be inefficient. If it is too small, then we will incur a lot of underlying packet overhead by sending undersized packets. The extra work on the sending side pays off on the receiving side, however, because the receiving is greatly simplified.

Since the receiver is always receiving the same amount of data in each segment, buffer overruns are easily preventable. Using fixed sizes can be a little more complex on the sending side, but simpler on the receiving side.

Finally, here is some code that demonstrates sending data using nonblocking sockets and select(). The strategy for receiving data is very similar.

```
int mysend(int sock, const char *buffer, long buffsize)
{
```

 NOTE *This code does not deal with the Big Endian/Little Endian issue. It sends a buffer of bytes in the order provided. If you will be dealing with clients and servers that use differing byte orders, then you will need to take care in how the data is formatted before sending with this function.*

First, we declare some variables that we'll need.

```
fd_set fset;
struct timeval tv;
int sockStatus;
int bytesSent;
char *pos;
char *end;
unsigned long blockMode;
```

Then, we set the socket to nonblocking. This is necessary for our send but can be removed if we are already using nonblocking sockets.

```
/* set socket to non-blocking */
blockMode = 1;
ioctl(sock, FIONBIO, &blockMode);
```

Now we set up a variable to keep our place in the outgoing buffer and a variable to point to the end of the buffer.

```
pos = (char *) buffer;
end = (char *) buffer + buffsize;
```

Next, we loop until we get to the end of the outgoing buffer.

```
while (pos < end) {
```

We send some data. If send() returns a negative number, then an error has occurred. Note that 0 is a valid number. Also, we want to ignore an error of EAGAIN, which signifies that the outgoing buffer is full. Our call to select() will tell us when there is room again in the buffer.

```
bytesSent = send(sock, pos, end - pos, 0);
if (bytesSent < 0) {
    if (bytesSent == EAGAIN) {
        bytesSent = 0;
    } else {
        return 0;
    }
}
```

We update our position in the outgoing buffer.

```
pos += bytesSent;
```

If we are already to the end of the buffer, then we want to break out of the while loop. There is no need to wait in the select() because we are already done.

```
if (pos >= end) {
    break;
}
```

Next, we get our watch list ready for select(). We also specify a timeout of 5 seconds. In this example, we treat a timeout as a failure, but you could do some processing and continue to try and send. It is important to use select() here because if the outgoing buffer is full, then we end up with a tight busy-wait loop that can consume far too many CPU cycles. Instead, we allow our process to sleep until buffer space is available or too much time has lapsed without space becoming available.

```
FD_ZERO(&fset);
FD_SET(sock, &fset);
tv.tv_sec = 5;
tv.tv_usec = 0;
sockStatus = select(sock + 1, NULL, &fset,  &fset, &tv);
if (sockStatus <= 0) {
    return 0;
}
}

return 1;
}
```

Summary

In this chapter, we looked at the different ways to handle multiple, simultaneous clients. First, we examined how to handle multiple clients in a single server process by using multiplexing. Then, we moved on to multiprocessing servers and the single process per client versus a process pool. Next, we introduced multithreaded servers. Much like multiprocess servers, multithreaded servers can be either a one-thread-per-client or a thread-pooled architecture. Afterward, we looked at an interesting approach used by the Apache Web Server version 2, in which multiprocessing is combined with multiple threads. We closed the chapter by covering how to handle sending and receiving large amounts of data by using nonblocking sockets and the `select()` system call.

In the next chapter, we'll examine what's involved in implementing a custom protocol.

Implementing Custom Protocols

WHEN DEVELOPING A CLIENT-SERVER application, you have to make protocol choices at two levels. First, you must choose a transport protocol. The most common types are TCP and UDP. We will look at that decision in Chapter 7. The second choice is at the application level. Some common application protocols include HTTP, FTP, and SMTP.

In this chapter we'll cover application protocols and how to design our own to be used in the chat application we develop in Chapter 9. Finally, we'll examine how to register our custom protocol with the system.

What Is a Protocol?

A *protocol* is a set of rules that the client and server each follow for communication to take place. We use protocols in real life all the time. For instance, consider going to a fast-food restaurant for lunch. The protocol we follow looks something like Figure 6-1.

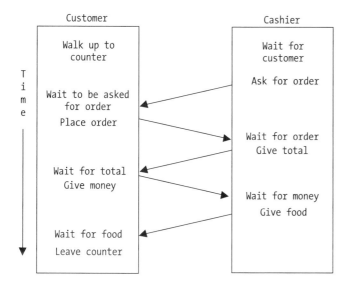

Figure 6-1. Fast-food restaurant protocol

First, we approach the counter and wait to be asked for our order. After we are asked, we place our order and wait to be given a total to pay. Once the total is provided, we pay and wait for our food to be delivered. After receiving the food, we leave the counter.

Now, compare this to Figure 6-2, which shows the HTTP protocol steps. In this case, the client is requesting a file instead of a hamburger, but the idea is the same. Most protocols consist of a "conversation" between the client and the server, with the client making requests that the server fulfills.

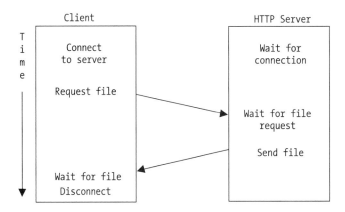

Figure 6-2. HTTP protocol

Designing a Custom Protocol

Designing a custom protocol for your client and server to communicate involves figuring out what services that the client will need to request and how the server will respond. The following sections outline some considerations when designing a custom application protocol.

What Will the Message Format Be?

Traditionally, client-server protocols have been text-based and, therefore, the format was based on delimiters. For example, in SMTP, each command is terminated by a carriage return/linefeed pair. In addition, each command line consists of a command followed by a space and then any parameters.

Text-based protocol messages also depend on context sensitivity. By that, we mean that the ordering of the parameters in a message is important, especially when using delimiters. When parsing a command, the application will first look at which command it is. Then, once the command is determined, the application knows how many parameters to expect. So, for example, if a command should have two parameters, then the delimiter can occur in the second parameter without being interpreted as a delimiter. This is very convenient when the delimiter is a space.

If you decide upon a binary protocol, then the format will be even more important. For example, you will need to address the Big Endian/Little Endian problem in addition to differing data type sizes on different client-server hardware architectures.

Our message format will be similar to the one used by the IRC protocol. This protocol is described in RFC 1459—you can find it by performing a quick Google search for "IRC+RFC". The basic format for a message is a command followed by one or more parameters. Each of the parameters is separated by a space, and the entire command is terminated by a carriage return/linefeed pair.

We will also make use of context sensitivity. Messages sent via chat frequently contain spaces. On those commands that messages are sent, we will make the message be the last parameter. In this way, we won't have to worry about the spaces because the parser will know that it's already on the final parameter and won't be looking for more delimiters.

The client commands consist only of alpha characters. The server has two types of messages that will be sent to clients: replies to client commands and independent messages. A reply to a client command will be a numeric code followed by a space and then a user-friendly description. These are used only to signify the success or failure of the client command. Independent messages from the server will follow the same format rules as client commands. With the server following these rules, the client will immediately know whether a particular message is a reply to a command or an independent message. It simply checks to see if the command starts with a numeric identifier or an alpha sequence.

Will the Server Be Passive or Active?

If the server is passive, then it will only ever act when prompted by the client. Communication is initiated only by the client through the submission of a command. Once the server has executed the command and provided a response, it simply waits for the client to submit another request. This is how traditional client-server protocols were designed. For example, SMTP, POP, and HTTP all work this way.

If it is active, then it may need to communicate information to the client without the client asking for anything. In this case, the server is not only waiting for the client to submit a request, but also may send a message to the client on its own. Therefore, the client must always be open to receiving messages from the server, even when it hasn't submitted a command. A chat server is a good example of an active server. Once a client is connected, the server may relay messages to it from other users without the client requesting anything.

Our server will be active. When chatting with other users, the server can have a message to deliver to the client at any time. Because of this, we need to not only be able to send requests to the server, but also be prepared to receive both responses to our requests and independent messages. In this case, the messages from the server will need to be marked in such a way that we know whether they are responses to a request or messages from another user.

Will the Server Handle Multiple Requests?

Most traditional protocols (SMTP, HTTP, POP, etc.) are set up to only handle one request from a client at a time. This means that once a client submits a command, it must wait for the server to respond before submitting another. Note that this is a different issue than whether the server can handle requests from multiple clients. We looked at solutions to that in Chapter 5.

If the client can send a request before the server has completed a previous request, then a mechanism for identifying the requests is needed. Usually each message is stamped with a unique identifying number so that when the server provides a response, the client will need to know which request has been fulfilled.

An interesting implementation of extending a traditional protocol to handle multiple requests is described in RFC 1854: SMTP Service Extension for Command Pipelining. (You can find it on the Web by doing a Google search for "RFC+1854".) In this case, while the server can handle multiple requests from a client, it responds to the requests in order. This eliminates the need for any identifying numbers for the commands/responses, but it does require the client to match up the responses with the corresponding command.

For our chat server, the client will need to make only one request at a time. This application does not have to do the extensive calculations or data gathering that would necessitate allowing the client to queue requests. Each request made by the client will have an immediate success/failure reply from the server.

Will the Protocol Be Sessioned or Sessionless?

This concept was covered in Chapter 4, but it's important in the design of a custom protocol. Recall that with a sessionless protocol, state is not maintained between client requests as it is with a sessioned protocol.

We will use a sessioned protocol for our chat server. Once we go through the login procedure with the client, the server will retain the client's nickname and associate it with the connection. A good reason for this has to do with the nick-names. When a client logs in, it will request to be known by a certain nickname in the virtual room. This nickname needs to be unique to the room and, as such, will be checked against the nicknames already in use. Once a nickname is accepted, the user is logged in and the nickname is tied to the connection (session).

If we used a sessionless protocol, then the nickname would need to be transmitted with each message sent. In this case, it would be impossible to pre-vent two clients from using the same nickname in the same virtual room. This would make conversations very confusing indeed!

Will the Protocol Use Plain Text or Binary?

We will cover this topic in more detail in Chapter 7. Each has its advantages and disadvantages. For example, while text is human-readable, which is easier to debug for example, it usually consumes more bandwidth than a comparable binary format.

For our protocol, plain text will be the best choice. We won't send any com-plicated objects or files—just text messages. Also, it will make the application much easier to debug, as you'll see in Chapter 8. Because we've chosen plain text, however, we'll need to decide upon a very specific layout to each text mes-sage so that it can be easily parsed.

How Will Authentication Be Handled?

Security has become an increasingly important issue for network applications. One aspect of security is authenticating a user. This involves not only verifying that the user is authorized to connect to the server, but also ensuring that the user is who she says she is. We discuss this topic in greater detail in Part Three of this book.

For our purposes, we'll allow anyone to connect to the chat server as long as that person provides a unique nickname. Therefore, our authentication will be very simple and consist of the client submitting a nickname for approval.

What About Privacy?

Another issue to address is privacy. When a client and server are communicating, it is easy for someone to eavesdrop on the conversation. When implementing a protocol, you must decide whether or not encryption is applicable. We discuss this topic in greater detail in Part Three of this book.

In our simple example, we won't provide any kind of encryption for the client-server communication. All commands and responses will be sent in plain text.

Our Chat Protocol

In this section, we will design a protocol to be used in the chat application we develop in Chapter 9. The client will need to be able to log into a server with a nickname and send text messages to other clients connected to the server. There will be two types of messages: public and private. When a client sends a public message, it will be relayed to each of the other clients that is connected to the "virtual room." A private message will be sent only to the user specified. Finally, a user may quit and leave the room.

In addition, we will adopt IRC's notion of a *room operator*. The first person to log into the server will be designated as an operator. An operator has three extra commands available. First, an operator can make another user an operator. Second, an operator can kick a user out of the room. And third, an operator can set the topic for the room.

Client Commands

In this section, we will cover each of the client commands as well as the possible server responses. Table 6-1 summarizes these commands.

Table 6-1. Client Commands

COMMAND	DESCRIPTION
JOIN	Used when the client connects to join the room and set its nickname.
MSG	Posts a message to the entire room.
PMSG	Sends a private message to a single user.
OP	Gives room operator privileges to another user. This can be used only by a room operator.
KICK	Kicks a user out of the room and disconnects him. This can be used only by a room operator.
TOPIC	Sets the topic for the room. This can be used only by a room operator.
QUIT	Used when the client wishes to disconnect.

The following sections describe each command in more detail. Note that a client may have only one outstanding command at a time, so neither the command nor the responses have any kind of identifying number.

JOIN

The first command that a client issues after connection is the JOIN command. Its syntax is as follows:

```
JOIN <NICKNAME>
```

The client sends the JOIN command and the nickname that the user would like to use. Because our commands are space delimited, a nickname cannot contain a space. In addition, the nickname must not be currently used by any other client. The server will respond with one of the following:

```
100 OK
200 NICKNAME IN USE
201 INVALID NICKNAME
999 UNKNOWN ERROR
```

In our protocol, the server response 100 will always mean that the command was executed successfully. Any other response is an error code. Each error code is followed by a short description of the error. We'll reserve code 999 for an error for which we didn't plan.

MSG

This is the command for a public message, and it has the following syntax:

```
MSG <ROOM MESSAGE>
```

Notice that the only parameter is the message itself. A message submitted with this command will be relayed to every other client connected to the server. Remember, too, that we use a carriage return/linefeed to signify the end of a command. Because of this, we need to be careful to not allow them within the ROOM MESSAGE. We can, however, have spaces in the message. Since the MSG command takes only a single parameter, everything up to the carriage return/linefeed will be considered the message.

The server can respond with one of the following:

```
100 OK
999 UNKNOWN ERROR
```

Since this command is very general in nature, it will most likely always be successful. However, to allow for future uses, it is always good to leave open the possibility for failure.

PMSG

This is the command for a private message. It has the following syntax:

```
PMSG <NICKNAME> <MESSAGE>
```

Since this is a private message intended for a single user, we specify not only the message, but also the nickname of the recipient. Remember that the NICKNAME cannot contain spaces, but the MESSAGE may. Since the message is the last parameter and we know that the PMSG command only takes two parameters, we will consider everything after the NICKNAME up to the carriage return to be the MESSAGE.

The server can respond with one of the following:

```
100 OK
202 UNKNOWN NICKNAME
999 UNKNOWN ERROR
```

The return codes here are the same as for MSG, but with one addition. If the message is sent to a nickname that is not in the room, then error 202 is returned.

OP

This is the command for giving another user operator privileges. It can be executed only by someone who already has operator status. It has the following syntax:

```
OP <NICKNAME>
```

The only parameter for this command is a NICKNAME. The server can respond with the following:

```
100 OK
202 UNKNOWN NICKNAME
203 DENIED
999 UNKNOWN
```

Besides the responses that you've already seen, a denied response is possible. Remember that only a client with operator status can make another user an operator. If a client that is not an operator executes the `OP` command, error 203 will be returned.

KICK

Operators also have the ability to kick another client out of the room. The `KICK` command has the following syntax:

```
KICK <NICKNAME>
```

The only parameter for this command is a `NICKNAME`. The server can respond with the following:

```
100 OK
202 UNKNOWN NICKNAME
203 DENIED
999 UNKNOWN
```

The responses for this command are the same as for `OP`. The command will succeed if the client executing it is an operator and the `NICKNAME` is known.

TOPIC

Another operator-only command allows the client to change the topic in the room. The topic is for informational purposes only and simply tells the users logging on what the users in the room are talking about. For instance, the topic might be "Network Programming on Linux" and the users would be helping each other with their Linux network programming.

When a topic is set, it is relayed to all clients connected to the server. In addition, after a client successfully logs in, the current room topic is sent. The syntax for the `TOPIC` command is

```
TOPIC <TOPIC NAME>
```

The only parameter for this command is a TOPIC NAME. Note that because the TOPIC command takes only one parameter, the TOPIC NAME may contain spaces. The server can respond with the following:

```
100 OK
203 DENIED
999 UNKNOWN
```

The responses for this command are similar to the other operator-only commands.

QUIT

Finally, we have a message that the client uses to disconnect from the server. When the server receives this command, it will relay it to all of the remaining connected clients. Its syntax is as follows:

```
QUIT
```

No parameters are required, and the server has only two responses available:

```
100 OK
999 UNKNOWN
```

Server Messages

Since we're going to have an active server, it can send out messages to the clients at any time. Table 6-2 summarizes these messages.

Table 6-2. Server Messages

MESSAGE	DESCRIPTION
JOIN	Tells the client that a user has joined the room
MSG	Relays a message that was posted to the room
PMSG	Relays a private message to the client to which it was sent
OP	Tells the client that a user has been given operator status
KICK	Tells the client that a user has been kicked out of the room
TOPIC	Tells the client that the topic for the room has been set/changed
QUIT	Tells the client that another user has left the room

Notice that the commands in Table 6-1 are the same as the commands that the client can send. Each one relays a successful client command to each of the other connected clients. The following sections cover each message and its syntax.

JOIN

The JOIN message is sent to all connected clients to tell them that a new user has joined the room. In addition, it is used when a client first connects to send the list of clients already connected. A JOIN message will be sent for each client that is in the room at the time a client connects. Its syntax is as follows:

```
JOIN <NICKNAME>
```

The only parameter is the NICKNAME of the new user. Upon receiving this message, the client can update its list of who is in the room. Usually, a chat program will provide this list graphically to the user at all times.

MSG

The MSG message is sent to all connected clients when a client posts a message to the room. It has the following syntax:

```
MSG <NICKNAME> <ROOM MESSAGE>
```

Note that the server version of the MSG message has two parameters. In addition to the message that was posted, the NICKNAME of the user that posted the message is sent. The client can then use this information to communicate to the user who is saying what.

PMSG

The PMSG is sent to a single client when a private message has been posted. It has the following syntax:

```
PMSG <NICKNAME> <MESSAGE>
```

Like MSG, PMSG has two parameters. The first parameter is the NICKNAME of the client that sent the private message and the second is the message itself.

OP

The OP message is sent to all connected clients to inform them that a user has been given room operator privileges. Most chat clients choose to use this information to highlight that nickname in the room user list. The OP message is also used in conjunction with the JOIN message when a client first connects to tell the joining client which members of the room are operators. It has the following syntax:

```
OP <NICKNAME>
```

This message has a single parameter that indicates which user was given the room operator status.

KICK

When a room operator kicks out another user, the server will send a KICK message to all of the connected clients. This lets them know two things: first, that they can remove that user from their list of users in the room, and second, that the user was kicked out rather than leaving on his or her own. It has the following syntax:

```
KICK <KICKED NICKNAME> <OP NICKNAME>
```

The KICK message has two parameters, both of them nicknames. The first parameter is the NICKNAME of the user that was kicked out of the room. The second parameter identifies the room operator who did the kicking.

TOPIC

Room operators are the only users who are able to set the topic for the room. When the topic is set, all connected clients get a TOPIC message to let them know what the topic is. The client application will usually display this to the user somewhere on the screen. The TOPIC message has the following syntax:

```
TOPIC <OP NICKNAME> <TOPIC>
```

The TOPIC message has two parameters. Not only is the new TOPIC specified, but also the nickname of the operator that set the topic is specified.

QUIT

When a user leaves the room, either by issuing a QUIT command or by becoming disconnected in some way, the server will send a QUIT message to all remaining connected clients. This allows them to update their list of those room members. It has the following syntax:

```
QUIT <NICKNAME>
```

The QUIT message has a single parameter that specifies which user left the room.

Our Chat Protocol in Action

Now we will put it all together and see what a typical client-server session would look like. Here is an example session. The client commands are in **bold**. The line numbers are for the discussion that follows and are not part of the protocol.

```
 1:  JOIN madchatter
 2:  100 OK
 3:  TOPIC topdog Linux Network Programming
 4:  JOIN topdog
 5:  OP topdog
 6:  JOIN lovetochat
 7:  JOIN linuxlover
 8:  JOIN borntocode
 9:  MSG hi all!
10:  100 OK
11:  MSG topdog welcome madchatter.
12:  OP madchatter
13:  MSG linuxlover hi mad!
14:  MSG lovetochat hi!
15:  MSG borntocode sup chatter.
16:  PMSG lovetochat linuxlover is getting a bit too obnoxious and topdog won't
     do anything.
17:  PMSG lovetochat no prob.  i'll take care of it.
18:  100 OK
19:  KICK linuxlover
20:  100 OK
21:  PMSG lovetochat he's gone.
22:  100 OK
23:  PMSG lovetochat thanks!
...
```

After connecting, we issue the JOIN command as seen in line 1. The server then checks to make sure that our nickname is valid and not used. We get the success response in line 2. Next, we start to receive messages from the server telling us the room topic in line 3 and the current members of the room in lines 4, 6, 7, and 8. Note that in line 5, we are told that topdog is a room operator.

In line 9, our client issues a command to post a message to the room, and we get the success response in line 10. We get messages that relay two commands issued by topdog. First, we get a message that topdog posted to the entire room, and second, we are informed that we have been given room operator privileges. These are shown on lines 11 and 12.

In lines 13 and 14, we get three more messages from the server. Each is a message posted to the entire room.

In line 16, we get a private message from lovetochat. In line 17, our client issues the PMSG command to respond. We get the success reply from the server on line 18.

On line 19, we issue the KICK command and kick linuxlover out of the room. Notice that while we get a success response on line 20, we get no further message from the server about the KICK. The server will send out the KICK messages to all of the other connected clients, but not to the client that did the kicking.

Finally, in lines 21, 22, and 23, we have a couple of private messages.

Protocol Registration

Once we've created a custom application protocol, we'll want to register it with the system so that others know about it. Registering it with the system publishes the fact that this protocol exists and informs others which communications port that it uses. One big advantage here is that if the port number of the protocol needs to change, then it has to be updated in only one place, and the applications don't need to be recompiled. In Linux, this information is stored in the file /etc/services. Once the protocol is registered with the system, we can use the functions getservent(), getservbyname(), and getservbyport() to read the entries of this file from our application.

The /etc/services File

The services file is a text file of the form

```
service-name port/protocol [aliases ...] #comment
```

For example, to see the entries for the SMTP protocol, open a terminal and type the following:

```
cat /etc/services | grep smtp
```

You may see something similar to the following displayed:

```
smtp    25/tcp   mail
smtp    25/udp   mail
smtps   465/tcp          #SMTP over SSL (TLS)
```

Notice that we get two entries for SMTP on port 25: one for TCP and one for UDP. Even though SMTP uses only TCP for transport, it is common practice to register both TCP and UDP when adding an entry for an application protocol. In addition, notice that the SMTP entries each have an alias named MAIL. As you'll see in next section, the port numbers can be looked up using a name, and you can supply either the name of the protocol or one of its aliases. Finally, you'll see that we have an entry for secure SMTP using the TLS protocol.

If we wanted to register the chat protocol we developed in this chapter with the system, we can do that in the services file. First, we need to give our protocol a name. Let's use "apress-chat". Next, we need to decide on a port. Let's use 5296. With that information, we can add the following entries to the /etc/services file:

```
apress-chat    5296/tcp
apress-chat    5296/udp
```

The port numbers and transport protocol information for our chat protocol are now registered with the system and can be retrieved with the functions described in the next section.

Service Entry Functions

The system provides a set of functions for reading the entries of the services file in a uniform manner. The getservent(), getservbyname(), and getservbyport() functions each return a pointer to a servent structure. The structure is defined as follows:

```
struct servent {
        char•s_name              /* official service name */
        char•*s_aliases  /* alias list */
        int     s_port           /* port number */
        char    s_proto          /* protocol to use */
};
```

To use these functions, you'll need to include the <netdb.h> header file.

setservent()

The setservent() function opens the services file and rewinds the file pointer to the beginning. This allows you to call getservent() repeatedly to iterate over the service entries. The setservent() function has the following signature:

```
void setservent(int stayopen);
```

If stayopen is true, then the file will not be closed between calls to the getserv* functions.

getservent()

The getservent() function returns a structure that contains the service information for the next entry in the services file. It returns NULL if the end of the file has been reached. The getservent() function has the following signature:

```
struct servent *getservent(void);
```

endservent()

Once you have the services file open using setservent(), you close it by calling endservent(). Its signature looks like this:

```
void endservent(void);
```

getservbyname()

The getservbyname() function searches the services file for an entry that matches the provided name and protocol (i.e., TCP/UDP). You can search all protocols by specifying a NULL for proto. The function signature looks like this:

```
struct servent *getservbyname(const char *name, const char *proto);
```

For example, to search for the SMTP entry, you would call it as follows:

```
struct servent *s = getservbyname("smtp", NULL);
```

getservbyport()

Finally, you can search the `services` file entries by port number and protocol. Again, you can provide NULL for the protocol if you don't care whether it is TCP or UDP. The function is declared as follows:

```
struct servent *getservbyport(int port, const char *proto);
```

For example, to search for the entry that uses port 80 (HTTP), you would call it like this:

```
struct servent *s = getservbyport(80, NULL);
```

Summary

In this chapter, we examined what an application protocol is and covered some of the considerations you must take into account when designing one from scratch. Then we laid the foundation for the chat application we'll create in Chapter 9 by developing the protocol that it will use.

In the next chapter, we'll look at considerations for client-server communications and techniques for server development.

CHAPTER 7

Design Decisions

IN THIS CHAPTER, WE'LL LOOK at some of the considerations you must make when developing a client-server application. First, we'll examine the TCP and UDP transport protocols. In the last chapter, we covered developing a custom application protocol. In this chapter we'll weigh the costs and benefits of using an existing protocol versus developing one from scratch and whether or not we should use plain text or binary. We'll then look at client-server architecture and examine two- and three-tier architectures.

Finally, we'll focus on client-specific and server-specific considerations, in turn. Client-specific considerations include building a monolithic client versus a modular one. As for server-specific considerations, we'll consider daemonizing, privilege dropping, `chroot()` jails, and various logging options.

TCP vs. UDP

As you'll remember from Chapter 3, the TCP and UDP protocols are two ways to transmit data over the lower-level IP protocol. Here we'll compare and contrast these protocols so that you can choose which one will serve your particular application best.

Reliability

TCP is reliable, in that if a packet is lost it will be resent. If the packet ultimately can't be delivered, you'll be notified via an error condition.

UDP isn't reliable. If a packet is lost between the sender and receiver, the sender will not receive any kind of notification. This isn't always a problem. For example, if you're sending a heartbeat notification, it usually isn't a problem when one packet is lost. The application monitoring the heartbeat won't take action unless several packets are lost.

If your application requires instant notification when a packet is lost, then choose TCP. Otherwise, you might consider UDP.

Packet Ordering

TCP provides automatic ordering of packets to ensure that the receiving application is handed data in the order in which it was sent.

UDP doesn't provide automatic ordering. The packets arrive in whatever order they happen to be delivered by the intermediate network. This doesn't have to be a problem. You can add sequence numbers to your packets, or the order may not even be an issue. For example, a time-of-day server sends packets that are self-contained; packet ordering isn't an issue in this case.

If your application sends small, self-contained packets, then UDP may be a good choice. If your application sends larger pieces of information, then it's very convenient to use TCP instead of developing your own ordering scheme.

Flow Control

TCP provides automatic flow control to keep from flooding the receiver with packets; UDP does not. If you will be sending large amounts of data using UDP, then you will need to build some kind of flow-control mechanism into your application.

Full Duplex

TCP is *full duplex*. This means that an application can send and receive data on the same connected TCP port. In TCP, the protocol must keep multiple buffers and keep track of what is coming and going.

UDP is inherently full duplex. Since no connection is ever made on a UDP port, you can both send and receive on that port because each packet is independent.

Overhead

TCP has more protocol overhead than UDP. To provide the previously described services, the TCP protocol must perform connect/disconnect handshaking, maintain buffers, track packet delivery, and more.

UDP does not need to do any of this. It simply sends the packet on its way or receives a packet that has arrived.

TCP vs. UDP Conclusion

TCP and UDP each have their place. In fact, some applications use a combination of the two. For example, a lot of online multiplayer games use TCP for data transfer and UDP for things like a client heartbeat or to send opponent position updates.

TCP is generally a good choice, though, even with its associated overhead. Most of the overhead is in the connection. Therefore, if your application stays connected for any length of time, then the cost is mitigated. In addition, if you're sending any quantity of data, then it's cheaper to use TCP's built-in reliability, ordering, and flow control instead of building your own.

UDP is a good choice if you're sending small amounts of self-contained data, especially if you're sending it to many different places. Since no connection is made, it's very inexpensive, unlike TCP, which has to go through an entire three-way handshake for each connection.

Application Protocol Choices

When you choose the application protocol, you have two important choices to make. First, you'll need to decide whether to create the protocol from scratch or use an existing protocol. Second, if you create a protocol from scratch, you'll need to determine whether it should be plain text or binary.

Established vs. Custom

Choosing an established protocol can greatly simplify your development process. The protocol will have already been developed and tested. It will give you a framework in which you can work, and you can draw upon the experiences of others who have used it for applications.

When choosing an existing protocol, however, you must pay attention to how the protocol works and whether or not it will fit with your application. For example, some have chosen to use the HTTP protocol. The two most prominent examples are the Simple Object Access Protocol (SOAP) and the Internet Printing Protocol (IPP). SOAP is from the World Wide Web Consortium (W3C) and is described at http://www.w3.org/2000/xp/Group. IPP is described in RFCs 2565, 2567, 2568, and 2569. In both instances, the protocols are for applications where a client is requesting services from the server. For this, HTTP works well. For a chat program, though, HTTP does not work very well. A chat program requires that either the client or the server be able to send commands at any time.

Creating a protocol ensures that it does exactly what you need and want, but it requires more development time and testing. Of course, you'll be the only one to ever use your custom protocol, too, so you can't look at other implementations for guidance.

Binary vs. ASCII

The choice between binary and plain text involves determining which is better for your particular application. Each has its benefits and detriments.

Plain text is easier to debug because it is generally human readable. In fact, most Internet standard protocols are plain text. Plain text also deals with cross-platform issues. Most platforms read and interpret byte-length text in the same way. Platforms do not generally handle binary data in the same manner. No doubt you've heard of the Big Endian/Little Endian issue (this was covered in Chapter 2).

On the other hand, binary transmission can be much more efficient. Consider sending an image via SMTP, for example. SMTP mandates that the contents of the e-mail message be plain text. In order to work around this, binary objects such as images are encoded in Base64 or some other binary-to-text encoding scheme. Each increases the size of the resulting data by around one-third to one-half.

Client-Server Architecture

An important design decision involves the overall architecture of your client-server application. This determines where the application logic and application data will reside. In this section we'll look at the two most prevalent architectures: two-tier and three-tier.

Two-Tier Architecture

The two-tier architecture is traditionally how client-server applications were built. As you can see in Figure 7-1, this architecture consists of a client component and a single server component. With this style of application, the majority of application logic resides in the client, and the server is usually a simple provider of services and data.

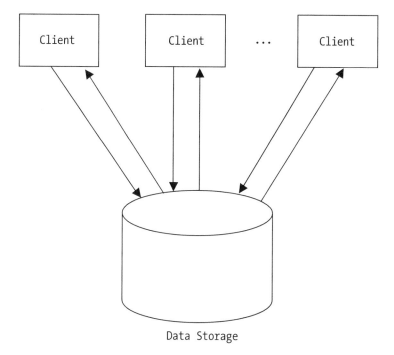

Figure 7-1. Two-tier architecture

While it's simple to implement, you can immediately see drawbacks to this design. First, scalability will be a concern. Since each client is independently accessing the data from the server, coordination can be slow. Second, anytime the application logic changes, a new client must be distributed. This can cause many problems for end users. Finally, the client is usually manipulating the application data directly. This can cause extensibility issues when, in the future, you would like to write a different client that works with the same server.

Three-Tier Architecture

Today, most large-scale network applications are designed using the three-tier architecture. In Figure 7-2, you can see that, in addition to the client component and single server component in the two-tier architecture, there is another middle server component. In this case, the application logic resides in the middle layer and the application data in the data layer.

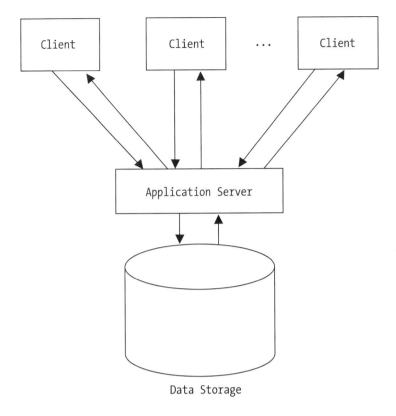

Figure 7-2. Three-tier architecture

While this architecture is somewhat more complex to implement, you obtain definite improvements over the two-tier design. First, you'll achieve a much higher level of scalability. The middle layer can coordinate data access and efficiently submit requests to the data layer. Second, you can alter application logic without necessarily requiring the distribution of a new client. Finally, other clients can easily be developed that use the services of the middle layer without worrying about the underlying application data being improperly accessed or manipulated. Three-tier architectures typically use two different types of clients: thick and thin.

Thick Clients

A *thick client* contains at least some of the application logic. This can range from data validation to more complex logic involving the overall process itself. In a two-tier architecture, all of the clients are thick clients. In a three-tier architecture, the clients are thick clients to a varying degree, and you can make a client as thick as desired.

Thin Clients

A *thin client* contains no application logic. Currently, the most popular form for a thin client is a web-based application. The user only needs a web browser to access the application. All application logic and data manipulation is performed by the server.

Client-Side Considerations

When developing your client-server application, keep in mind how (and by whom) the client will be developed. Traditional Internet servers tend to force the user to develop a monolithic client. Some newer servers, such as database servers, provide a client API to ease the development of a client.

Monolithic Client

A *monolithic* client, as shown in Figure 7-3, handles the network communications, application protocol management, and user interaction, all in the main application. Most Internet standard protocol clients are built in this way. Remember that protocols like HTTP, SMTP, POP3, and FTP are text based. Therefore, the client need only send and receive text streams to communicate with the server. While this means that the application is very easy to debug, it can add to the overall complexity of the client application. For example, the client developer will need to understand the application protocol and be able to implement it.

```
User Interaction
Application Logic
Protocol Implementation
Socket Programming
```

Figure 7-3. Monolithic client architecture

Many libraries have been developed to cope with this issue. For example, the libspopc (http://brouits.free.fr/libspopc) library provides encapsulation of the POP3 protocol. It provides a high-level API for accessing a POP3 server without the client creating sockets or knowing the POP3 protocol.

Modular Client

A *modular* client, as shown in Figure 7-4, uses an external library provided by the server developer. This library encapsulates the network communications and application protocols. The client, therefore, must only worry about the user interaction. This makes it very easy for someone to develop a client. In addition, you can change the application protocol without changing any of the client code.

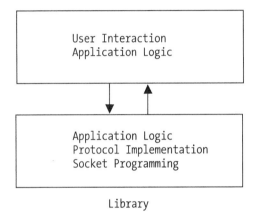

Library

Figure 7-4. Modular client architecture

An example of this type is the database client. Most database servers come with a set of client libraries. These libraries handle all of the underlying socket communications as well as the application-level communication.

Server-Side Considerations

In this section, we'll examine four very useful server-side considerations. First, we'll look at the common practice of daemonizing your server. Next, we'll look at system logging. Servers should always provide a log of their activities, and we'll describe how to use the system logger. We'll then cover security by looking at how to do "privilege dropping" and chroot() jails. Both techniques are useful for creating a safe server process.

Daemonizing

When you're writing a network server, quite often it's a good idea to make it a daemon. A *daemon* is a program that runs in the background and isn't attached to any terminal. Normally, when you execute a program, it's attached to the active terminal. Its standard input, output, and error streams are connected to the terminal, and if the terminal is closed then the program is terminated.

Now, you may be familiar with using the ampersand (&) to start an application in the background from a shell. This is not the same as a daemon. While this does work in certain cases, it is not usable from an rc script during system boot, which is when most daemons are started.

Daemons are designed to be run without direct user interaction and to execute as long as the system is running. Some well-known examples of daemons are cron (program scheduler), httpd (web server), and named (DNS server). To create your own daemon, you must follow a strict set of rules.

1. Call the fork() system call and allow the parent to exit. This initially detaches your program from the calling shell and returns control to it. In addition, this call ensures that while your process is a member of a process group, it is not the process group leader.

2. Call setsid(). The setsid() system call creates a new process group and a new session group. It then makes your process the only member and leader of both groups. This sets up the following situation: your process is a session group leader, a process group leader, and you have no controlling terminal.

3. Call fork() again and allow the parent to exit. Now the session group and process group leader has exited. Since our process is not a leader, it cannot possibly ever have a controlling terminal.

4. One of the issues with a long-running process is that it could accidentally keep a directory in use. Worse still, that directory could be on an NFS mount or some other remote resource. To prevent that from happening, the next step is to execute chdir("/"). This changes our working directory to the root directory. Now, this isn't an absolute. We could also change the directory to the location where the daemon's files reside. We simply need to make sure that we choose a safe location that won't interfere with the normal system operation.

5. Next, we call umask(0). This clears the file-mode creation mask since we can't be sure of what it is at this point. When we called fork(), we inherited whatever the current mask happened to be at the time. If we're creating files in our process, this allows us to specify exactly what mode will be used.

6. Finally, we need to close any open file descriptors. It is unknown at this point which descriptors we may have inherited through fork(). At the very least, we need to close descriptors 0, 1, and 2. These are stdin, stdout, and stderr. If you want to be thorough, you can call sysconf() with the _SC_OPEN_MAX parameter. This will return the total number of descriptors that a process can have. With this value, you can loop through and close each in turn.

Now that we've gone through the process of starting a daemon, we'll look at the actual code required. We'll create a daemonizing function that can be called from main() in any program to turn it into a daemon. Hang on to this example, because we'll build on it in the following sections.

First, we include the needed system header files.

```
#include <unistd.h>
#include <sys/types.h>
```

Now for the function:

```
int daemonize()
{
    pid_t pid;
    long n_desc;
    int i;
```

Here is our first fork() call. This initially detaches the process from the terminal. Note that the parent exits.

```
    if ((pid = fork()) != 0) {
        exit(0);
    }
```

Now we make the call to setsid().

```
setsid();
```

We are now the process group and session group leader. In addition, we have no controlling terminal. We call fork() again for good measure and have the parent exit. This ensures that we cannot regain a controlling terminal.

```
if ((pid = fork()) != 0) {
    exit(0);
}
```

Next, we change the current directory to the root directory and clear the file mode mask.

```
chdir("/");
umask(0);
```

Finally, we close all available file descriptors and return success.

```
n_desc = sysconf(_SC_OPEN_MAX);
for (i = 0; i < n_desc; i++) {
    close(i);
}

return 1;
}
```

Logging

An important feature of any server is the ability to log events. This is very helpful to the person who is responsible for administering the server program. The information contained in the log can inform the user of not only the server activity, but also problems that the server encounters.

One strategy is to open a file and write events to it. A lot of server applications allow you to specify the log location in a configuration file. The only requirement is that your application has the appropriate permissions to write to the specified file. Many server applications choose this route, and it is trivial, so we won't discuss it here.

Another option is to use the system logging facility. Linux keeps a central log file called messages that is usually located in /var/log. This file contains all messages relayed through the syslog facility. We will now look at how to use syslog and expand on our daemonizing example.

To use syslog, we first open a connection to the logger by calling openlog(). Its signature is as follows:

```
#include <syslog.h>
void openlog(const char *ident, int option, int facility);
```

The first parameter is an identifying string that is prepended to each log message. Usually, this is the name of the program that is doing the logging. The second parameter is one or more of the following options OR'd together:

- LOG_CONS: This instructs syslog to write the log message to the console if the logger is unavailable for some reason.

- LOG_NDELAY: This creates an immediate connection to the logger. Normally, the connection won't be made until the first log message is sent.

- LOG_PERROR: This causes the log message to be sent to stderr in addition to the system logger.

- LOG_PID: This also prepends the program's process identifier to the log message.

The final parameter identifies to the logger the type of program that it is logging. This is referenced in the syslog configuration and can be used to treat certain programs' messages differently. The value is one of the following:

- LOG_AUTHPRIV: A security/authorization message.

- LOG_CRON: A clock daemon, usually cron and at.

- LOG_DAEMON: A general system daemon.

- LOG_FTP: The FTP daemon.

- LOG_KERN: For kernel messages.

- LOG_LPR: The printer daemon.

- LOG_MAIL: The mailer daemon.

- LOG_NEWS: The news daemon.

- LOG_SYSLOG: Internal messages from the syslog daemon.

- LOG_USER: For general user-level messages. This is what you would use most often.

- LOG_UUCP: Messages from the UUCP daemon.

The call to openlog() isn't strictly required, but without it, you do not have the opportunity to specify the identity of your program or the options.

Next, we can send messages to the logger with syslog(). Its signature is as follows:

```
void syslog(int priority, const char *format, ...);
```

If you'll notice, it is very similar to printf(). In fact, after specifying the priority, the remaining parameters behave exactly like printf(). The possible priority values are as follows:

- LOG_EMERG: Indicates that the system is in an unusable state

- LOG_ALERT: Indicates that some kind of immediate action is required

- LOG_CRIT: A critical message

- LOG_ERR: An error message

- LOG_WARNING: Indicates a warning

- LOG_NOTICE: Specifies that something important but normal has occurred

- LOG_INFO: A simple informational message

- LOG_DEBUG: A debug message

Finally, when your program is finished using the system logger, it calls closelog(). This is its signature:

```
void closelog();
```

Now, let's expand our example from the daemonizing section to write a message to the system log. First, we need to add the header file for syslog to the #includes.

```
#include <syslog.h>
```

Next, we create a `main()` function that calls our `daemonize()` function.

```
int main(int argc, char **argv)
{
    daemonize();
```

Finally, we add the calls to the system logger to log a "Hello World!" message from our program.

```
    openlog("test_daemon", LOG_PID, LOG_USER);
    syslog(LOG_INFO, "%s", "Hello World!");
    closelog();

    return 1;
}
```

You can now compile and execute the test program. After it runs, you can execute the following to see the entry that was created. Note that you may need to be root.

```
cat /var/log/messages | grep test_daemon
```

You should see something similar to the following output:

```
Dec 14 11:14:00 homer test_daemon[19366]: Hello World!
```

Privilege Dropping

In Linux, every process is associated with a user and must operate under the access rights for that user. When you write a server application, it is a good idea to have it run under a nonprivileged user. That way, if the application is hacked, damage to the system is minimal. Imagine the damage that could be caused if the server were run as root and was hacked.

On the other hand, sometimes your application needs to be able to do something that only a superuser can do. For example, the `chroot()` jail we discuss next can be used only by a superuser. Another frequent need is to bind to a port that is less than 1024. For example, a web server would need to bind to port 80. This can be done only by root or by a superuser.

To achieve both of these goals, we employ a process called *privilege dropping*. When our server application is started, we execute it as root (or setuid root). Then we do whatever we need to do as root and give up the superuser privilege for the remainder of the application.

The command for changing the associated user ID is setuid(). Its signature is as follows:

```
#include <unistd.h>
int setuid(uid_t uid);
```

When a process with superuser privileges executes this command, it sets all three user IDs (*real, effective,* and *saved)* to the specified ID. Afterward, it is impossible for the process to regain superuser privileges.

Note that the setuid() command requires the uid of the user. When writing a server, you'll want the user to be able to specify which uid the server should run under. To provide maximum flexibility, you should allow the user to specify either the numeric user ID or the username. If the username is provided, then you can use the getpwid() command to retrieve the uid for the given username. Its signature is as follows:

```
#include <pwd.h>
#include <sys/types.h>
struct passwd *getpwnam(const char *name);
```

The setppuid() command returns a pointer to a passwd structure if the username is valid. Otherwise, it returns NULL. The passwd structure is defined as follows:

```
struct passwd {
      char      *pw_name;
      char      *pw_passwd;
      uid_t     pw_uid;
      gid_t     pw_gid;
      char      *pw_gecos;
      char      *pw_dir;
      char      *pw_shell;
};
```

It is also worth noting that Linux keeps track of a file system user ID as well. Sometimes it is useful to keep a higher privilege for the main process, but drop privileges for disk access. The setfsuid() command accomplishes this, but it is not required if the calling process is associated with superuser privileges. In that case, the fsuid is set automatically by setuid.

Now, let's look at this in action. We'll use our daemonize() function, but provide a new main(). First, we add the following to our list of #includes:

```
#include <pwd.h>
```

Here's our new `main()` function:

```
int main(int argc, char **argv)
{
```

We then declare a structure pointer to be used with the `getpwnam()` function. We also hard-code the username that we will be using for the privilege dropping. You will want to either create a user called "nopriv" or change the string to an existing nonprivileged user on your system. In practice, you will want to make this a user-specified parameter.

```
struct passwd *pws;
const char *user = "nopriv";
```

Now we attempt to retrieve the user ID associated with our nonprivileged user. If the `getpwnam()` function returns a `NULL`, then the username was not found.

```
pws = getpwnam(user);
if (pws == NULL) {
    printf ("Unknown user: %s\n", user);
    return 0;
}
```

Next, we call our `daemonize()` function and drop our privileges.

```
daemoniz();
setuid(pws->pw_uid);
```

Finally, we set up an endless loop so that we can observe the effects of `setuid()`.

```
while (1) {
    sleep(1);
}
return 1;
}
```

Compile the program as `daemon2` and execute it as the superuser. You can use the following command to see that the `setuid()` call worked:

```
ps -ajx | grep daemon2
```

You should see something similar to the following output:

```
     1 27996 27995 27995 ?           -1 S      502   0:00 ./daemon2
 27959 27998 27997 27350 pts/2 27997 S          0   0:00 grep daemon2
```

Notice that the grep command is associated with user ID 0, which is the superuser, but the daemon2 process is associated with user ID 502, which is the nopriv user on this particular system. You can stop the daemon2 process by sending it the term signal. In this case, it would be

```
kill -TERM 27996
```

Next, experiment with running this program as a user other than the superuser or "nopriv." Log in as a different user or use the su command to assume another user. Then execute the preceding program. Notice that when you look at the process with ps, the setuid call does not change the user ID. The call to setuid() will fail, and the process will continue to run under the user you are logged in as.

chroot() Jails

Another means for securing a server involves limiting its access to the file system. The Linux file system hierarchy starts with "/" or the root directory. The chroot() command allows you to redefine where the root directory is for a particular process. This is called a chroot() *jail*.

For example, let's say that we have created a user ID called myserv for our server to run under, and we've given it a home directory, /home/myserv. We can change the root directory for our server to /home/myserv. This means that the server can only access files that are under /home/myserv. If the server changes the directory to "/", it will still be in the /home/myserv directory, although if it queries for the current directory it will be returned as "/".

Only root or a superuser can execute the chroot() command. So, if you are employing privilege dropping, remember to chroot() before dropping your privileges. The signature for chroot() is as follows:

```
#include <unistd.h>
int chroot(const char *path);
```

One very important point to remember about the chroot() command is that it does not change the current directory. This means that if you call chroot(), the server still has access to the current directory, even if it is outside of the chroot()

jail! Therefore, it is advisable to call `chdir("/")` immediately after calling `chroot()`. This will ensure that the server is in the jail.

Summary

In this chapter, we covered some of the considerations that you need to make when designing a networked application. First, we looked at choosing between the TCP and UDP transport protocols. Next, we looked at application protocols. Here, the issues are whether to use an established protocol or roll your own, and whether to use binary or plain-text transmission. Then, we looked at overall client-server architecture before moving on to client-specific issues. Finally, we looked at server-specific issues that included daemonizing the server, the system logger, privilege dropping, and `chroot()` jails.

In the next chapter we'll look at the client-server development process and debugging.

CHAPTER 8

Debugging and Development Cycle

DEBUGGING CLIENT-SERVER NETWORK applications poses some unique challenges. You need to debug not only the programs themselves, but also the communication between them. In this chapter, we will first look at some tools to help with the debugging process. Next, we will address another unique issue with client-server programming: which do you develop first, the client or the server? Then we will examine the overall process of debugging a client-server network application. Finally, we will discuss defensive programming techniques.

Tools

Debugging applications is not an easy thing to do. Debugging applications talking to each other is even harder. In this section, we will cover some tools that can aid in debugging your network applications.

 NOTE *Some of the examples in this section refer to the chat application presented in Chapter 9. It may be useful to revisit this section after examining the chat application and trying some of these tools yourself.*

netstat

netstat is a tool used to list the socket activity on a particular machine. By default, it shows both client and server connected sockets along with other useful information. You can use the -l option to show unconnected sockets in the LISTEN state. If you invoke it as root or superuser you can also see the process that owns the socket by invoking the -p option. Here is a sample entry for a web server using `netstat -lp`:

```
Proto   Recv-Q  Send-Q  Local Address  Foreign Address  State   PID/Program Name
tcp     0       0       *:http         *:*              LISTEN  2933/httpd
```

`Proto` is the protocol of the socket. This can be `tcp`, `udp`, or `unix`. `Recv-Q` is the number of bytes in the receive queue. These are bytes that have been received from the network, but the application bound to the socket has not yet read them. `Send-Q` shows the number of bytes that have been sent but have not been acknowledged. `Local Address` displays the local address and port to which the socket is bound. If the address is an asterisk (*), then it is bound to all local interface addresses. If the port number has an entry in the `services` file, then the service name is displayed; otherwise, the port number will be shown. `Foreign Address` displays the same information as `Local Address`, but for the remote socket. `State` shows the state of the socket. In our example, it is in the `LISTEN` state because the web server is waiting for connections. Other common states include `ESTABLISHED`, `TIME_WAIT`, and `CLOSED`. The man page for `netstat` describes all of the possible states. Finally, `PID/Program Name` shows the process ID and program associated with the socket.

`netstat` is useful for debugging both clients and servers. For servers, you can verify that they are listening on the correct address/port combination. This is helpful in finding errors where you have forgotten to use `htons()` when assigning the port number. In addition, you can see how many clients are connected to your server and what state the sockets are in. For the client, it is sometimes useful to know the local port number that has been assigned to the socket it is using.

Ethereal

Ethereal (`http://www.ethereal.com`) is a GUI tool that allows you to capture and examine data packets on your network. In the past, tools like `tcpdump` were used for this purpose. While `tcpdump` still has a use on servers without X Windows, Ethereal is much more flexible and allows you to easily see the packets and their contents in a visual way. It has support for many protocols and will automatically decode these for you. In addition, it can read dump files from `tcpdump` as well as files from some commercial sniffing tools.

Ethereal is a valuable tool for debugging your client-server network application. If you are already using one of the supported protocols (like HTTP), then it can easily show you the conversation between the client and server. If you are using a custom protocol like the one we use in Chapter 9, Ethereal can still help, because our protocol is text based. Figure 8-1 shows the contents of a JOIN command that the chat client sent to the chat server.

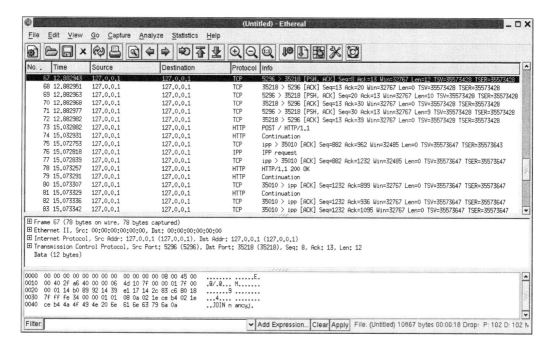

Figure 8-1. An Ethereal session

As you can see in the window just above the Filter box, the command JOIN n ancyj can be readily discerned from the remainder of the packet. Of course, if you are using a binary protocol it will be a little more difficult to pick out the contents of the packet.

There are some caveats to using Ethereal, though. First, you must be root or superuser to execute Ethereal. It must place the network device in promiscuous mode, and this is allowed only by root or superuser. Second, it will not help you if you are encrypting the communication between your client and server. All you will see is garbage. Finally, if you are trying to look at client-server communication on machines other than the one on which you are running Ethereal, make sure that you are using a hub and not a switch to connect these computers. Ethereal works by grabbing all network packets, even those not destined for your machine. A switch prevents this from happening.

netcat

netcat (or nc) is an extremely flexible tool not only for helping to debug your client or server, but also for development. netcat is capable of sending or receiving any kind of data over TCP or UDP. Built in the UNIX tool tradition, it is highly scriptable and can take input from the command line or stdin. Output is sent to stdout, with errors to stderr.

Here is an example session using netcat with stdin to connect to the chat server presented in Chapter 9. The server messages are in bold.

```
[chatsrv]$ nc 127.0.0.1 5296
JOIN nancyj
100 OK
JOIN linuxguy
OP linuxguy
JOIN nancyj
TOPIC Everything Linux!
MSG linuxguy hi!
100 OK
MSG nancyj linuxguy hi!
JOIN madchatter
```

As you can see, it is very easy to connect to a server and exercise it for debugging purposes. For debugging clients, nc can act as a server. In this mode, you can see what the client sends and manually send responses to the client.

gdb

While not strictly for network application development, gdb must be mentioned for completeness. It is invaluable for debugging applications under Linux. If its command-line nature is daunting, then try DDD (http://www.gnu.org/software/ddd). It is an excellent GUI front-end for gdb.

Figure 8-2 shows a DDD session with the chat server presented in Chapter 9. You can see that you can set breakpoints visually. Also, you have the ability to hover over a variable to see the current value.

Figure 8-2. A DDD session

Chicken or the Egg

A question that comes up quite often in network programming is this: "Which do you write first, the client or the server?" The answer really depends on the application being built, but usually it's "Both!" One of the significant factors is the choice of a plain-text or binary communication protocol. Let's look at each in turn.

If you choose a plain-text protocol, then you can develop either the client or the server and use netcat to simulate the missing piece. For example, the server for the chat application presented in Chapter 9 was completely developed and tested using netcat before a line of client code was written. Since netcat can also be used to simulate a server, the chat client could have been developed first. Why wasn't it? In the case of the chat application, all of the application logic is housed in the server. The client is simply a means to execute the commands and display the results. In fact, many different clients (GUI, text based, etc.) could be developed to use the same chat server. Using netcat, each of the commands could be easily tested independent of the client.

For a binary protocol, a tool like netcat isn't an option. In this situation, it's usually easiest to use a "bootstrap" strategy. This means that you write just enough of the server and the client to get them talking to each other using your basic protocol. Then, you add commands and features one by one into both the server and client. In this case, neither is written "first"—they are developed in parallel. Now, there is nothing that says this approach can't be used with an application using a plain-text protocol. In that case, you can use either approach.

Debugging

Effective debugging tends to be learned through experience. There are, however, some strategies that can be employed to help with the debugging process. In this section we will look at debug statements and source code analyzers.

Debug Statements

One of the simplest ways to see what is going on inside your program as it runs is to add debug output statements. You add lines of code like this:

```
#ifdef DEBUG
printf("Accepting client connection.\n");
#endif
```

to strategic areas of your program. Of course, you may want to put in more information than that—variable values, for example. Then you add a line like this:

```
#define DEBUG
```

to a common header file and comment it out when you don't want the debugging output. If you're using gcc, you can use the -D switch instead as follows:

```
gcc -D DEBUG -o myserver myserver.cpp
```

Not only can debug output statements help you document your program flow and variable values, but also they can be used to keep track of the "discussion" between a client and server. The output can expose errors in the conversation between client and server. It can also show whether any command parameters are incorrect or out of bounds. If you are using a text-based protocol, you can simply log the commands that are sent and received. If your protocol is binary, then you will want to write a small function to convert it into a human-readable form for logging.

Source Code Analyzers

Another strategy for debugging is to use a source code analyzer. Even though your program may compile without any warnings or errors, there can be subtle problems lurking. Analyzers use sets of rules that describe common programming pitfalls and potential mistakes. They then apply these rules to your source code and give you warnings about possible problems. You can then investigate further and determine whether or not a change is necessary.

The most famous source code analyzer is `lint`. `lint` has been available on UNIX systems for many years, but it was too difficult to use to garner widespread use. A free reimplementation of `lint` is called Splint (`http://www.splint.org`). The Splint project aims to be an easier-to-use, more thorough `lint`.

One drawback to Splint is that it works only with C code. There are several commercial `lint`-like products available that also work with C++ code. Two of the more popular are Gimpel's FlexeLint (`http://www.gimpel.com`) and Parasoft's CodeWizard (`http://www.parasoft.com`). In addition to the standard checks, CodeWizard even has rules corresponding to Scott Meyers's *Effective C++* books.

Defensive Programming

Creating a network application, especially one for the Internet, carries with it added responsibilities. You must take great care when coding the server and client to keep malicious users and programs from wreaking havoc with your application. In addition to crashing your application, security can also be compromised. Here we will focus on the stability aspects; the security issues are covered in Chapter 12. In this section we will look at four key areas that you should consider when writing your network application.

Respect Buffer Limits

One of the most common errors in network applications is the buffer overflow. A buffer overflow condition exists when data is written beyond the limit of the allocated memory.

Figure 8-3 shows the layout for a stack record. Note that the memory for the local variables will be written from bottom to top. An overflow usually occurs when data submitted from a client exceeds the amount expected by the server. The return address for the function can be overwritten, causing the application to behave in an undefined manner. Furthermore, part of the overflowing data can be interpreted as machine instructions that can be executed using the permissions of the process. This is called *stack smashing*.

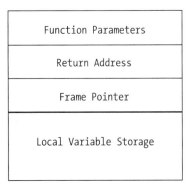

Figure 8-3. Layout of a stack record

After the return address is overwritten, your application's behavior is undefined. In the best case, it will crash, but in the worst case, it will continue to function erratically. A buffer overflow is a very hard bug to diagnose and fix. The best place to find and fix buffer issues is during development. Many tools are available for use during testing that can point out memory management issues. The two most popular are Electric Fence and Valgrind.

Electric Fence (`http://perens.com/FreeSoftware`) was developed by Bruce Perens and was one of the earliest solutions available. It works by redefining `malloc()` and `free()`. You simply compile a special version of your application that links against Electric Fence and start testing. It will halt your program whenever a memory error is encountered.

Valgrind (`http://valgrind.kde.org`) has become extremely popular of late. It takes a different approach from Electric Fence in that it isn't a library replacement for `malloc()` and `free()`; rather, it's a full execution environment that simulates an x86 CPU. As such, it doesn't require you to recompile your program with a special library. In addition to memory errors, Valgrind can help with optimization. It's actively developed and also has an excellent extension capability.

Even if you think you've found all of the buffer overflow problems during development, it's possible for one to slip through. Next, we'll look at two of the most popular solutions for runtime overflow protection. Both employ the technique of altering the stack record generated by the compiler to check for overflows.

StackGuard (`http://www.immunix.org/stackguard.html`) is a special version of the GCC compiler. It works by modifying the stack record that is generated for a function to contain not only the return address, but also a "canary" value. Then, when the function completes, a check is made for the canary value. If the value has been altered, StackGuard assumes that a buffer overflow has occurred and execution stops. While this can be harsh, it is better than allowing the overflow to occur.

Stack-Smashing Protector (`http://www.research.ibm.com/trl/projects/security/ssp`) uses the same basic approach as StackGuard, but adds reordering of local function pointers in the stack. This prevents the altering of local pointers to gain access to arbitrary memory locations.

 CAUTION   *Using one of these runtime solutions is not a replacement for good, solid defensive programming. While these solutions may keep your program from having a buffer overflow, your program will be shut down unceremoniously, resulting in frustrated users.*

You can find more information on the security aspects of buffer overflows, including safe library functions, in Chapter 12.

Expect the Unexpected

Another common failure in client-server applications is receiving unexpected information. This can be in the form of a malformed command or a command parameter that is outside of the expected boundaries. In either case, it is very important to validate the command as it is being read from the network. Once again, different strategies are employed depending on whether you are using a plain-text or binary protocol. We will look at each in turn.

For a plain-text protocol, you will typically employ some kind of grammar that specifies a valid command. So, the first step in validating the command is to verify that it is grammatically correct. This can be done either by creating a handmade parser or by using parser-generator tools such as `lex` and `yacc`. Then, each parameter should be checked to make sure that it falls within an accepted range. As soon as an irregularity is detected, an error message should be returned, the remainder of the command ignored, and perhaps even the connection terminated. Otherwise, you run the risk of the application failing in an unexpected manner.

When you use a binary protocol, even more care must be taken. This is because you are generally storing the incoming data directly into `structs` or class variables, and an inadvertent buffer overflow can occur. The grammar in a binary protocol is implicit, but values should be checked for validity as they are received. If a problem is detected, then an error message should be returned immediately and the remainder of the command discarded. Again, perhaps the connection should even be closed.

Limit Collateral Damage

Even if a catastrophic error occurs and your application crashes, you need to limit the collateral damage. This can be accomplished in two key ways: running as a nonprivileged user and using chroot() jails.

The first and most important way to limit collateral damage is to not run your application as root or superuser. Too often, an exploitable area is found in a server process that runs as root, and the exploiter is then able to gain root privileges. If you must have root privileges (for example, to bind to a port under 1024), then drop those privileges as soon as they are no longer needed. We covered privilege dropping and how to do it in Chapter 7.

For a server application, the best way to run it is with its own nonprivileged user. This shields the application from affecting anything else in the system. Once you have more than one server running under the same user, there is the possibility for them to hurt each other.

The other key way to prevent collateral damage is to use a chroot() jail. This was also covered in Chapter 7. A chroot() jail will ensure that a crashing process cannot harm files outside of its own area. Because the chroot() command requires root or superuser privileges, you must use it in conjunction with privilege dropping for maximum safety.

The security aspects of limiting a process's permissions are covered in Chapter 12.

Fail Gracefully, But Not Silently

When (not if) your application fails, great care must be taken to have it fail gracefully. And while your application should fail gracefully, it should not fail silently. Leaving around information to help determine the cause of failure is very important.

What does it mean for an application to fail gracefully? First and foremost, it means that Linux should not be the one shutting down your application and dumping core. Your application should catch the fatal error and shut itself down. This gives it a chance to notify those to which it is connected (clients or server) and release system resources, such as socket descriptors.

One way to ensure that your application fails gracefully is to check return values from system calls. This is very important. Always check return values, even for functions that you don't think will ever fail, because sometimes they will, and it will be very hard to track down the reason for the failure. In addition, your own functions should all return status codes, if possible. Checking the return codes will allow you to react to a failure and stop the program, if necessary, before the system does it for you.

NOTE *It is not always possible for a function to return a value. This is common in GUI applications when you are usually providing callback functions to a framework. In this case, it is sometimes helpful to store success/failure in global structures.*

If you are using C++, then another way to ensure that your application fails gracefully is to use try...catch blocks. Use them liberally in your main() function so that if any of your other functions fail outside of a try...catch block, then the outer catch will be called.

After your application fails, you will want to be able to determine the cause of the failure. This is where not failing silently comes into play. After the application successfully determines a failure, it should record as much information as possible about what was going on at the time. This should most definitely include the date and time of the failure, and it can include important variable values, such as the failed return value. For networking applications, it is also helpful to include the last communication buffer.

Summary

In this chapter, we explored various debugging tools and methods. In addition, we covered how to program defensively to help with stability and in troubleshooting problems.

In the next chapter, we will look at how to code a real-world chat application.

CHAPTER 9

Case Study: A Networked Application

IN THIS CHAPTER, we will bring together everything we've talked about in Parts One and Two and build a chat application. It will be written in C++ and consist of both a server and a GUI client. The server will be multithreaded as described in Chapter 5 and will use the chat protocol developed in Chapter 6.

The Server

The server has no user interface and would be a good candidate for a daemon, although we won't complicate it with our daemonize function from Chapter 7 here. The basic architecture of the server is that it will spawn a thread for each client that connects. It will have a global list of the connected clients, and each thread will relay server messages to that list. The list will be protected from simultaneous modification by means of a mutex. The main loop for each thread will first check to see if the client has sent a command. If it has, it is dealt with and a return code is sent. Then the thread checks to see if there are any pending messages to be sent to the client. This loop continues until the client disconnects or the user has been kicked out of the room.

First, we include the system headers and signify that we will be using the Standard Template Library (STL) namespace.

```
/* chatsrv.cpp */
#include <iostream>
#include <string>
#include <map>
#include <vector>
#include <stdio.h>
#include <sys/ioctl.h>
#include <sys/types.h>
#include <sys/socket.h>
#include <netinet/in.h>
#include <netinet/tcp.h>
#include <pthread.h>

using namespace std;
```

Next, we define a couple of constants. First, we signify that the server will listen on port 5296, and we set the maximum line length to be 1024 bytes.

```
/* #define's */
#define LISTEN_PORT    5296
#define MAX_LINE_BUFF  1024
```

Here we define two structures. The first will help us keep track of each connected client. We have two flags: one to signify whether the user is a room operator and the other to signify that the user was kicked out of the room. Finally, we have a vector of strings. This will contain a list of messages that are being relayed to the client.

```
/* Structures */
struct client_t {
    bool opstatus;
    bool kickflag;
    vector<string> outbound;
};
```

The second structure is for holding the client commands. We will parse the command into this structure for easier handling. The maximum number of operands for any command is two.

```
struct cmd_t {
    string command;
    string op1;
    string op2;
};
```

Now we declare some global variables. First, we have a mutex to synchronize access to the room topic. Then, we have the room topic variable. Next, we have a mutex to synchronize access to the client list. We are using an STL map keyed on username to hold our list of connected users. Each entry is a client_t structure.

```
/* Globals */
pthread_mutex_t room_topic_mutex;
string room_topic;
pthread_mutex_t client_list_mutex;
map<string, client_t> client_list;
```

Here are our forward declarations for the functions we will use:

```
/* Forward declarations */
void* thread_proc(void *arg);
int readLine(int sock, char *buffer, int buffsize);
cmd_t decodeCommand(const char *buffer);
int join_command(const cmd_t &cmd, string &msg);
int msg_command(const cmd_t &cmd, const string &nickname, string &msg);
int pmsg_command(const cmd_t &cmd, const string &nickname, string &msg);
int op_command(const cmd_t &cmd, const string &nickname, string &msg);
int kick_command(const cmd_t &cmd, const string &nickname, string &msg);
int topic_command(const cmd_t &cmd, const string &nickname, string &msg);
int quit_command(const string &nickname, string &msg);
```

This is our `main()` function. We start by declaring some variables for the sockets and threading.

```
/* main */
int main(int argc, char *argv[])
{
    struct sockaddr_in sAddr;
    int listensock;
    int newsock;
    int result;
    pthread_t thread_id;
    int flag = 1;
```

Next, we create our listening socket and set the socket option `SO_REUSEADDR`. This will keep us from getting "address in use" errors when we stop and start our server.

```
    listensock = socket(AF_INET, SOCK_STREAM, IPPROTO_TCP);
    setsockopt(listensock, IPPROTO_TCP, SO_REUSEADDR, (char *) &flag,
              sizeof(int));
```

Now we bind the socket to all available addresses and our listening port.

```
    sAddr.sin_family = AF_INET;
    sAddr.sin_port = htons(LISTEN_PORT);
    sAddr.sin_addr.s_addr = INADDR_ANY;
    result = bind(listensock, (struct sockaddr *) &sAddr, sizeof(sAddr));
    if (result < 0) {
        perror("chatsrv");
        return 0;
    }
```

We then set the socket to listening mode.

```
result = listen(listensock, 5);
if (result < 0) {
    perror("chatsrv");
    return 0;
}
```

If everything has succeeded so far, we go ahead an initialize our mutexes. This must be done only once and before any of the threads use them.

```
pthread_mutex_init(&room_topic_mutex, NULL);
pthread_mutex_init(&client_list_mutex, NULL);
```

This is our main loop. We accept incoming connections and start a new thread for each client.

```
while (1) {
    newsock = accept(listensock, NULL ,NULL);
    result = pthread_create(&thread_id, NULL, thread_proc, (void *) newsock);
    if (result != 0) {
        printf("could not create thread.\n");
        return 0;
    }
    pthread_detach(thread_id);
    sched_yield();
}

return 1;
}
```

Next, we define our thread procedure. We start by declaring some variables.

```
void* thread_proc(void *arg)
{
    int sock;
    char buffer[MAX_LINE_BUFF];
    int nread;
    int flag = 1;
    bool joined = false;
    bool quit = false;
    string nickname;
    struct cmd_t cmd;
    string return_msg;
```

```
map<string, client_t>::iterator client_iter;
int status;
string outstring;
```

Then we grab the socket that was passed to us by the main() function. Immediately, we turn off Nagle's algorithm and set the socket to nonblocking.

```
/* Retrieve socket passed to thread_proc */
sock = (int) arg;
/* Turn off Nagle's algorithm*/
setsockopt(sock, IPPROTO_TCP, TCP_NODELAY, (char *) &flag, sizeof(int));
/* Set socket to nonblocking */
ioctl(sock, FIONBIO, (char *) &flag);
```

> **NOTE** *Nagle's algorithm is enabled by default in Linux. It attempts to group undersized outgoing packets in order to send them out at once. This can introduce delays by forcing outgoing packets to wait, and it can really cause problems with a client-server application. Since our chat application will send many small packets, we turn off Nagle's algorithm to prevent those delays.*

This is our main thread loop. We basically check for commands from the client and then relay any waiting server commands back. We start by calling our readLine() function, which we describe later. It returns a negative value if an error occurred on the socket. If this happens, then we want to remove the client from the room.

```
while (!quit) {
    /* Get any commands that the client has sent */
    status = readLine(sock, buffer, MAX_LINE_BUFF);
    if (status < 0) {
        /* If we've lost the client then process it as a QUIT. */
        if (joined) {
            quit_command(nickname, return_msg);
        }
        return arg;
```

readLine() returns a positive value if a command was received. If so, then we check to see what the command was.

```
    } else if (status > 0) {
```

First, we call decodeCommand(), which we describe later. It fills our cmd_t structure to make it easier to determine what the client is requesting.

```
cmd = decodeCommand(buffer);
```

If the client has issued a command without joining the room, then we set the return message to an error.

```
if (!joined && cmd.command != "JOIN") {
    return_msg = "203 DENIED - MUST JOIN FIRST";
} else {
```

Otherwise, we check to see if they have already joined. They can't join twice, so if they have, we send an error.

```
if (cmd.command == "JOIN") {
    if (joined) {
        return_msg = "203 DENIED - ALREADY JOINED";
    } else {
```

If the preceding checks pass, then we send the command off to the join_command() function. It will check to make sure the nickname is unique and valid. If it accepts the join, then it returns a positive value and we set our joined flag and nickname. Each of the command handlers also sets the return message with the outcome of the command.

```
status = join_command(cmd, return_msg);
if (status > 0) {
    joined = true;
    nickname = cmd.op1;
}
}
```

Next, we have handlers for the remaining commands. Notice that on the QUIT command we set our joined flag to false and QUIT to true. This ends the main loop. For the KICK command, we can't do this. The reason is that the client doing the kicking is usually not the one being kicked. That is why we have the kicked flag in the global client list.

```
} else if (cmd.command == "MSG") {
    msg_command(cmd, nickname, return_msg);
} else if (cmd.command == "PMSG") {
    pmsg_command(cmd, nickname, return_msg);
```

```
    } else if (cmd.command == "OP") {
        op_command(cmd, nickname, return_msg);
    } else if (cmd.command == "KICK") {
        kick_command(cmd, nickname, return_msg);
    } else if (cmd.command == "TOPIC") {
        topic_command(cmd, nickname, return_msg);
    } else if (cmd.command == "QUIT") {
        quit_command(nickname,return_msg);
        joined = false;
        quit = true;
    } else {
        return_msg = "900 UNKNOWN COMMAND";
    }
}
```

Now we send the return message with the status of the command to the client.

```
    return_msg += "\n";
    send(sock, return_msg.c_str(), return_msg.length(), 0);
}
```

We send any pending server commands to the client. First, we make sure the client has joined the room. Otherwise, there won't be any server commands and we can skip the entire section.

```
/* Send any pending server commands to the client. */
if (joined) {
```

Before checking the client list for outgoing commands, we need to lock the client list mutex. This keeps two threads from modifying the list at the same time.

```
    pthread_mutex_lock(&client_list_mutex);
```

Once we have the mutex lock, we send any messages that are available and clear the list.

```
    for (int i = 0; i < client_list[nickname].outbound.size(); i++) {
        outstring = client_list[nickname].outbound[i] + "\n";
        send(sock, outstring.c_str(), outstring.length(), 0);
    }
    client_list[nickname].outbound.clear();
```

Here is where we checked to see if this client has been kicked out of the room. If it has, then we remove it from the client list and set quit to true.

```
if (client_list[nickname].kickflag == true) {
    client_iter = client_list.find(nickname);
    if (client_iter != client_list.end()) {
        client_list.erase(client_iter);
    }
    quit = true;
}
```

Since we are done with the client list, we unlock the mutex so that other threads may access it.

```
    pthread_mutex_unlock(&client_list_mutex);
}
```

With a tight loop like this, it is a good idea to voluntarily give up your time slice. This keeps any one thread from hogging the processor.

```
    sched_yield();
}
```

When the quit flag is set to true, we exit the loop, close the socket, and exit the thread.

```
close(sock);

return arg;
}
```

That's all there is to the main logic of the server. Now we'll go over the helper functions used in the preceding code.

First, let's look at the readLine() function. Commands from the client are terminated with a newline character. This function will read up to a newline and then return. First, we set up some needed variables.

```
int readLine(int sock, char *buffer, int buffsize)
{
    char *buffPos;
    char *buffEnd;
    int nChars;
    int readlen;
    bool complete = false;
```

```
fd_set fset;
struct timeval tv;
int sockStatus;
int readSize;
unsigned long blockMode;
```

Next, we check to see if there is even anything to read. If not, then we will return right away.

```
FD_ZERO(&fset);
FD_SET(sock, &fset);
tv.tv_sec = 0;
tv.tv_usec = 50;
sockStatus = select(sock + 1, &fset, NULL,  &fset, &tv);
if (sockStatus <= 0) {
        return sockStatus;
}
```

Otherwise, we initialize the supplied buffer and set pointers for the current buffer position and the end of the buffer.

```
buffer[0] = '\0';
buffPos = buffer;
buffEnd = buffer + buffsize;
readlen = 0;
```

This is the main loop for reading the data. First, we make sure that we aren't overrunning our buffer space. If not, then we set up to read a character.

```
while (!complete) {
    if ((buffEnd - buffPos) < 0) {
        readSize = 0;
    } else {
        readSize = 1;
    }
```

Now we call select() to make sure that there is something to read. This also allows us to escape if the client suddenly disconnects or if the client is sending data too slowly. We set a timeout of 5 seconds for getting data from the client.

```
FD_ZERO(&fset);
FD_SET(sock, &fset);
tv.tv_sec = 5;
tv.tv_usec = 0;
```

```
        sockStatus = select(sock + 1, &fset, NULL,  &fset, &tv);
        if (sockStatus < 0) {
            return -1;
        }
```

Next, we receive the character and check to see if it is a newline. If it is, then we are done. Otherwise, we add it to the buffer and loop.

```
        nChars = recv(sock, (char *) buffPos, readSize, MSG_NOSIGNAL);
        readlen += nChars;
        if (nChars <= 0) {
            return -1;
        }
        if (buffPos[nChars - 1] == '\n') {
            complete = true;
            buffPos[nChars - 1] = '\0';
        }
        buffPos += nChars;
    }
```

Finally, we return the size of the string we read.

```
    return readlen;
}
```

The next helper function decodes a string received from the client into our cmd_t structure. It basically separates the buffer based on the space being the delimiter. Since we can have at most two operands for a command, after it finds the second space it places the remaining text from the buffer into the second operand. This works perfectly for our commands such as PMSG, where the second operand can contain spaces. It also works well enough for the MSG command, which has only one operand. If the message contains spaces, we just concatenate the two operands, in the msg_command() function.

```
cmd_t decodeCommand(const char *buffer)
{
    struct cmd_t ret_cmd;
    int state;

    state = 0;
    for (int x = 0; x < strlen(buffer); x++) {
        if (buffer[x] == ' ' && state < 2) {
            state++;
        } else {
```

```
        switch (state) {
        case 0:    ret_cmd.command += toupper(buffer[x]);
                   break;
        case 1:    ret_cmd.op1 += buffer[x];
                   break;
        default:   ret_cmd.op2 += buffer[x];
        }
    }
}


    return ret_cmd;
}
```

This function handles the JOIN command and, if successful, adds the user to the client_list map.

```
int join_command(const cmd_t &cmd, string &msg)
{
    int retval;
    map<string, client_t>::iterator client_iter;
```

First, we do a preliminary check on the nickname. If the nickname has a space in it, then it will have been separated into op1 and op2. Therefore, if op2 is not an empty string, then the nickname is invalid.

```
    if (cmd.op1.length() == 0 || cmd.op2.length() > 0) {
        msg = "201 INVALID NICKNAME";
        return 0;
    } else {
```

Next, we check to make sure that a room member isn't already using the nickname. Before checking the client_list map, we need to lock the mutex. Otherwise, another thread could be looking at the same time for the same nickname, and both threads would think that the name isn't taken. The mutex ensures that only one thread may examine the client list at a time.

```
        pthread_mutex_lock(&client_list_mutex);
        client_iter = client_list.find(cmd.op1);
```

If the nickname isn't already in use, we add the client to the room. First, though, we check to see if this is the first user in the room. If so, then that user automatically becomes a room operator. Notice that we're implicitly adding the user to the room by taking advantage of the fact that an STL map will create a new entry for us if one doesn't exist.

```
    if (client_iter == client_list.end()) {
        if (client_list.size() == 0) {
            client_list[cmd.op1].opstatus = true;
        } else {
            client_list[cmd.op1].opstatus = false;
        }
        client_list[cmd.op1].kickflag = false;
```

Now we cycle through the other users in the room, if there are any. We do three things here. First, we tell the other users that a new person has joined the room. Second, we gather the names of the users already in the room to relay to the new user. Third, we tell the new user which existing users are room operators. Notice that the server commands are added to the clients' outbound message queues. They will then be sent to the client in the main loop.

```
        for (client_iter = client_list.begin();
             client_iter != client_list.end(); ++client_iter) {
            /* Tell other clients that a new user has joined */
            if ((*client_iter).first != cmd.op1) {
                (*client_iter).second.outbound.push_back("JOIN " + cmd.op1);
            }
            /* Tell the new client which users are already in the room */
            client_list[cmd.op1].outbound.push_back("JOIN " +
                                                (*client_iter).first);
            /* Tell the new client who has operator status */
            if ((*client_iter).second.opstatus == true) {
                client_list[cmd.op1].outbound.push_back("OP " +
                                                (*client_iter).first);
            }
        }
    }
```

Finally, we send the room's topic to the new user and return a success code.

```
        /* Tell the new client the room topic */
        pthread_mutex_lock(&room_topic_mutex);
        client_list[cmd.op1].outbound.push_back("TOPIC * " + room_topic);
        pthread_mutex_unlock(&room_topic_mutex);
        msg = "100 OK";
        retval = 1;
```

If the nickname is in use, then we send the failure notice.

```
    } else {
        msg = "200 NICKNAME IN USE";
```

```
            retval = 0;
        }
        pthread_mutex_unlock(&client_list_mutex);
    }

    return retval;
}
```

Next, we handle the MSG command. This is a simple function, because all it does is relay the message to all connected clients by adding it to their outbound queues.

```
int msg_command(const cmd_t &cmd, const string &nickname, string &msg)
{
    map<string, client_t>::iterator client_iter;

    pthread_mutex_lock(&client_list_mutex);
    for (client_iter = client_list.begin();
            client_iter != client_list.end(); client_iter++) {
        (*client_iter).second.outbound.push_back("MSG " + nickname + " " +
                                        cmd.op1 + " " + cmd.op2);
    }
    pthread_mutex_unlock(&client_list_mutex);
    msg = "100 OK";

    return 1;
}
```

Handling a private message is almost as easy. First, we check to make sure that the recipient exists and, if so, add the message to their outbound queue.

```
int pmsg_command(const cmd_t &cmd, const string &nickname, string &msg)
{
    map<string, client_t>::iterator client_iter;

    pthread_mutex_lock(&client_list_mutex);
    client_iter = client_list.find(cmd.op1);
    if (client_iter == client_list.end()) {
        msg = "202 UNKNOWN NICKNAME";
    } else {
        (*client_iter).second.outbound.push_back("PMSG " + nickname + " " +
                                        cmd.op2);
        msg = "100 OK";
    }
```

```
    pthread_mutex_unlock(&client_list_mutex);

    return 1;
}
```

Our next function handles the `OP` command.

```
int op_command(const cmd_t &cmd, const string &nickname, string &msg)
{
    map<string, client_t>::iterator client_iter;

    pthread_mutex_lock(&client_list_mutex);
    client_iter = client_list.find(nickname);
```

We first get the client list entry for the user issuing the `OP` command. If we can't find that entry, then something is wrong.

```
    if (client_iter == client_list.end()) {
        msg = "999 UNKNOWN";
    } else {
```

In this case, we first need to verify that the client issuing the command is a room operator.

```
        if ((*client_iter).second.opstatus == false) {
            msg = "203 DENIED";
        } else {
```

If the verification succeeds, we then check to make sure that the target of the `OP` command is valid.

```
            client_iter = client_list.find(cmd.op1);
            if (client_iter == client_list.end()) {
                msg = "202 UNKNOWN NICKNAME";
            } else {
```

Finally, we set the operator status flag on the recipient and notify the room members of the new room operator.

```
                (*client_iter).second.opstatus = true;
                for (client_iter = client_list.begin();
                        client_iter != client_list.end(); client_iter++) {
                    (*client_iter).second.outbound.push_back("OP " + cmd.op1);
                }
```

```
                  msg = "100 OK";
            }
        }
    }
    pthread_mutex_unlock(&client_list_mutex);

    return 1;
}
```

The `KICK` command causes a user to be forcibly removed from the room.

```
int kick_command(const cmd_t &cmd, const string &nickname, string &msg)
{
    map<string, client_t>::iterator client_iter;
```

We first get the client list entry for the user issuing the `OP` command. If we can't find that entry, then something is wrong.

```
    pthread_mutex_lock(&client_list_mutex);
    client_iter = client_list.find(nickname);
    if (client_iter == client_list.end()) {
        msg = "999 UNKNOWN";
    } else {
```

Next, we verify that the caller is a room operator.

```
        if ((*client_iter).second.opstatus == false) {
            msg = "203 DENIED";
        } else {
```

Then, we validate the target of the `KICK` command.

```
            client_iter = client_list.find(cmd.op1);
            if (client_iter == client_list.end()) {
                msg = "202 UNKNOWN NICKNAME";
            } else {
```

Finally, we set the kick flag on the user being removed and notify everyone in the room about what happened. The kick flag will be picked up in the main loop, and the client will be disconnected.

```
                (*client_iter).second.kickflag = true;
                for (client_iter = client_list.begin();
                        client_iter != client_list.end(); client_iter++) {
```

```
                        (*client_iter).second.outbound.push_back("KICK " + cmd.op1
                                                    + " " + nickname);
                }
                msg = "100 OK";
            }
        }
    }
    pthread_mutex_unlock(&client_list_mutex);

    return 1;
}
```

Room operators have the ability to set the topic for the room. This function handles the TOPIC command. It is very similar to the other operator-only commands.

```
int topic_command(const cmd_t &cmd, const string &nickname, string &msg)
{
    map<string, client_t>::iterator client_iter;

    pthread_mutex_lock(&client_list_mutex);
    client_iter = client_list.find(nickname);
    if (client_iter == client_list.end()) {
        msg = "999 UNKNOWN";
    } else {
        if ((*client_iter).second.opstatus == false) {
            msg = "203 DENIED";
        } else {
            pthread_mutex_lock(&room_topic_mutex);
            room_topic = cmd.op1;
            if (cmd.op2.length() != 0) {
                room_topic += " " + cmd.op2;
            }
            for (client_iter = client_list.begin();
                    client_iter != client_list.end(); client_iter++) {
                (*client_iter).second.outbound.push_back("TOPIC " + nickname
                                                    + " " + room_topic);
            }
            pthread_mutex_unlock(&room_topic_mutex);
            msg = "100 OK";
        }
    }
}
```

```
    pthread_mutex_unlock(&client_list_mutex);

    return 1;
}
```

Finally, we need to handle the QUIT command. We remove the client from the client_list map and notify the others in the room that the client has left.

```
int quit_command(const string &nickname, string &msg)
{
    map<string, client_t>::iterator client_iter;

    pthread_mutex_lock(&client_list_mutex);
    client_iter = client_list.find(nickname);
    if (client_iter == client_list.end()) {
        msg = "999 UNKNOWN";
    } else {
        client_list.erase(client_iter);
        for (client_iter = client_list.begin(); client_iter != client_list.end();
                    client_iter++) {
            (*client_iter).second.outbound.push_back("QUIT " + nickname);
        }
        msg = "100 OK";
    }
    pthread_mutex_unlock(&client_list_mutex);

    return 1;
}
```

The server can be compiled as follows:

```
g++ -o chatsrv chatsrv.cpp -lpthread
```

A good way to test the server is with the netcat application we talked about in Chapter 8. You can connect to the server and manually issue the commands to see how the server responds.

The Client

Figure 9-1 shows what our GUI client looks like.

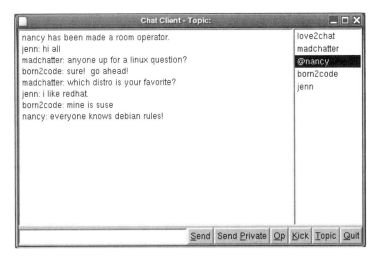

Figure 9-1. GUI client

For the client, we are using Trolltech's Qt GUI toolkit. Most Linux distributions install the noncommercial version of Qt, but you can download it from `http://www.trolltech.com`. Due to the nature of GUI programs, it is easier to split the source code among several files, unlike the server. We will have the following files:

- `chatcli.h`: This file will contain non-GUI declarations.

- `chatcli.cpp`: This file will contain our `main()` function, as well as functions for connecting and reading socket data.

- `logindlg.h`: This file will contain declarations for our login dialog box.

- `logindlg.cpp`: This file will contain the implementation for our login dialog box.

- `chatwin.h`: This file will contain the declarations for our main window.

- `chatwin.cpp`: This file will contain the implementation for our main window. The bulk of the GUI handling is in this file.

- `Makefile`: This is our makefile for building the client.

chatcli.h

We start our main header file off by including the STL string header and setting up our maximum line length.

```
/* chatcli.h */
#ifndef CHATCLI_H
#define CHATCLI_H

#include <string>

using namespace std;

/* #define's */
#define MAX_LINE_BUFF    1024
```

Next, we define our command structure. This is the same structure that the server used.

```
/* Structures */
struct cmd_t {
    string command;
    string op1;
    string op2;
};
```

Finally, we have prototypes for our functions in the main source file. Notice that we have a only few functions. The bulk of the communication functions will be in our main window class.

```
/* Function Declarations */
int connectAndJoin(string host, int port, string nickname);
int readLine(int sock, char *buffer, int buffsize);
cmd_t decodeCommand(const char *buffer);


#endif
```

chatcli.cpp

Our main source file starts by including all of the familiar system header files for
socket communication as well as header files needed by the Qt library. In addition, we include the classes used for our login dialog box and the main window.

```
/* chatcli.cpp */
#include <unistd.h>
#include <sys/ioctl.h>
#include <sys/types.h>
#include <sys/socket.h>
#include <netinet/tcp.h>
#include <netinet/in.h>
#include <arpa/inet.h>
#include <netdb.h>
#include <string>
#include <qapplication.h>
#include <qmessagebox.h>
#include "logindlg.h"
#include "chatwin.h"
#include "chatcli.h"

using namespace std;
```

Next, we declare a global variable for our client socket. This makes it easily
accessible from the GUI source files.

```
/* Global Variables */
int client_socket;
```

Our main() function starts by initializing the QApplication object.

```
int main(int argc, char **argv)
{
    cLoginDlg *logindlg;
    string host;
    int port;
    string nickname;

    QApplication app(argc, argv);
```

Next, we display the login dialog box so that the user may specify the host and
port of the chat server, as well as the nickname she'd like to use. If the user clicks

the Connect button, then we attempt to connect using our connectAndJoin()
utility function. If it fails, it displays the error and we display the login dialog
box again.

```
do {
    logindlg = new cLoginDlg(NULL);
    if (logindlg->exec() == QDialog::Rejected) {
        delete logindlg;
        return 0;
    }
    host = logindlg->hostEdit->text().ascii();
    port = atoi(logindlg->portEdit->text().ascii());
    nickname = logindlg->nickEdit->text().ascii();
} while (connectAndJoin(host, port, nickname) == 0);
```

If the connection succeeds, we initialize and display the chat window. Then
we enter Qt's main event loop.

```
cChatWin *chatwin = new cChatWin();
chatwin->client_socket = client_socket;
app.setMainWidget(chatwin);
chatwin->setCaption("Chat Test");
chatwin->show();
app.connect(&app, SIGNAL(lastWindowClosed()), &app, SLOT(quit()));
int res = app.exec();
return res;
}
```

Our first utility function accomplishes two tasks. First, it attempts to connect
to the chat server. Second, if the connection succeeds, it tries to join the chat
room with the provided nickname.

```
int connectAndJoin(string host, int port, string nickname)
{
    sockaddr_in sAddr;
    hostent *dotaddr = NULL;
    int flag = 1;
    string joinString;
    char buff[MAX_LINE_BUFF];
    cmd_t cmd;
```

Here we create our client socket.

```
client_socket = socket(AF_INET, SOCK_STREAM, IPPROTO_TCP);
```

Next, we initialize our sockaddr_in structure and use gethostbyname() in case the user provided us with a host name instead of an IP address. If the gethostbyname() function fails, we set the address to "0.0.0.0", which will surely fail to connect.

```
bzero(&sAddr, sizeof(sockaddr_in));
sAddr.sin_family = AF_INET;
sAddr.sin_addr.s_addr = INADDR_ANY;
sAddr.sin_port = htons(port);
dotaddr = gethostbyname(host.c_str());
if (dotaddr) {
    bcopy((const void *) dotaddr->h_addr_list[0],
            (void *) &sAddr.sin_addr.s_addr, dotaddr->h_length);
} else {
    sAddr.sin_addr.s_addr = inet_addr("0.0.0.0");
}
```

Once we have the IP address of the server, we try to connect.

```
/* Connect to server */
if (connect(client_socket, (const sockaddr *) &sAddr, sizeof(sAddr)) != 0) {
    QMessageBox::critical(NULL, "Connection Failed", "Unable to connect.");
    close(client_socket);
    return 0;
}
```

After connecting, we turn off Nagle's algorithm and set the socket to non-blocking. We left the socket as blocking until now because it simplifies the connect() call. Otherwise, we would need to call select() and poll the socket for connection success.

```
/* Turn off Nagle's algorithm*/
setsockopt(client_socket, IPPROTO_TCP, TCP_NODELAY, (char *) &flag,
            sizeof(int));
/* Set socket to nonblocking */
ioctl(client_socket, FIONBIO, (char *) &flag);
```

Now that we are connected and the socket options are set, we send our JOIN command to the server with the nickname the user specified.

```
joinString = "JOIN " + nickname + "\n";
send(client_socket, joinString.c_str(), joinString.length(), 0);
readLine(client_socket, buff, MAX_LINE_BUFF, 0);
cmd = decodeCommand(buff);
```

Next, we examine the response and return success or notify the user that the operation failed.

```
if (cmd.command == "100") {
    return 1;
} else if (cmd.command == "200") {
    QMessageBox::critical(NULL, "Nickname In Use",
                        "The nickname you've chosen is already in use.");
    close(client_socket);
    return 0;
} else if (cmd.command == "201") {
    QMessageBox::critical(NULL, "Invalid Nickname",
                        "The nickname you've chosen is invalid.");
    close(client_socket);
    return 0;
} else {
    QMessageBox::critical(NULL, "Unknown Error",
                        "An unknown error has occurred.");
    close(client_socket);
    return 0;
}

}
```

The next two functions should look familiar. They are nearly identical to those used in the server. We have made a slight modification to the readLine() function, though. In this version we've added a timeout parameter. Some of the calls to readLine() need to be blocking, and this lets us determine which ones are.

```
int readLine(int sock, char *buffer, int buffsize, int timeout)
{
    char *buffPos;
    char *buffEnd;
    int nChars;
    int readlen;
    bool complete = false;
    fd_set fset;
    struct timeval tv;
    int sockStatus;
    int readSize;
      unsigned long blockMode;

    FD_ZERO(&fset);
    FD_SET(sock, &fset);
```

```
            if (timeout > 0) {
              tv.tv_sec = 0;
              tv.tv_usec = timeout;
              sockStatus = select(sock + 1, &fset, NULL,  &fset, &tv);
            } else {
              sockStatus = select(sock + 1, &fset, NULL,  &fset, NULL);
            }
            if (sockStatus <= 0) {
                return sockStatus;
            }

            buffer[0] = '\0';
            buffPos = buffer;
            buffEnd = buffer + buffsize;
            readlen = 0;
            while (!complete) {
                if ((buffEnd - buffPos) < 0) {
                    readSize = 0;
                } else {
                    readSize = 1;
                }
                FD_ZERO(&fset);
                FD_SET(sock, &fset);
                tv.tv_sec = 5;
                tv.tv_usec = 0;
                sockStatus = select(sock + 1, &fset, NULL,  &fset, &tv);
                if (sockStatus < 0) {
                    return -1;
                }
                nChars = recv(sock, (char *) buffPos, readSize, MSG_NOSIGNAL);
                readlen += nChars;
                if (nChars <= 0) {
                    return -1;
                }
                if (buffPos[nChars - 1] == '\n') {
                    complete = true;
                    buffPos[nChars - 1] = '\0';
                }
                buffPos += nChars;
            }

            return readlen;
        }
```

```
cmd_t decodeCommand(const char *buffer)
{
    struct cmd_t ret_cmd;
    int state;

    state = 0;
    for (int x = 0; x < strlen(buffer); x++) {
        if (buffer[x] == ' ' && state < 2) {
            state++;
        } else {
            switch (state) {
            case 0:    ret_cmd.command += toupper(buffer[x]);
                       break;
            case 1:    ret_cmd.op1 += buffer[x];
                       break;
            default:   ret_cmd.op2 += buffer[x];
            }
        }
    }

    return ret_cmd;
}
```

logindlg.h

This is the header file for our login dialog box. It declares the derived class and
the edit controls that will hold the user's values.

```
/* logindlg.h */
#ifndef LOGINDLG_H
#define LOGINDLG_H


#include <qdialog.h>
#include <qlineedit.h>

class cLoginDlg : public QDialog
{
Q_OBJECT
public:
    cLoginDlg(QWidget *parent);
    ~cLoginDlg();
```

```
public:
    QLineEdit *hostEdit;
    QLineEdit *portEdit;
    QLineEdit *nickEdit;
};



#endif
```

logindlg.cpp

This file contains the implementation of the login dialog box. Here we add the widgets to the dialog box and set up signal handlers for the buttons.

```
/* logindlg.cpp */
#include <qvbox.h>
#include <qhbox.h>
#include <qlabel.h>
#include <qpushbutton.h>
#include "logindlg.h"

cLoginDlg::cLoginDlg(QWidget *parent) : QDialog(parent, "", true)
{
    this->setCaption("Connect");
    this->setMinimumHeight(110);
    this->setMinimumWidth(200);

    QVBox *main = new QVBox(this);
    main->setSpacing(3);
    main->setMargin(3);
    main->setMinimumHeight(104);
    main->setMinimumWidth(200);

    QHBox *row1 = new QHBox(main);
    row1->setSpacing(3);
    QLabel *hostLabel = new QLabel("Host", row1);
    hostEdit = new QLineEdit(row1);

    QHBox *row2 = new QHBox(main);
    row2->setSpacing(3);
    QLabel *portLabel = new QLabel("Port", row2);
    portEdit = new QLineEdit(row2);

    QHBox *row3 = new QHBox(main);
```

```
    row3->setSpacing(3);
    QLabel *nickLabel = new QLabel("Nickname", row3);
    nickEdit = new QLineEdit(row3);

    QHBox *row4 = new QHBox(main);
    row4->setSpacing(10);
    QPushButton *connButton = new QPushButton("Connect", row4);
    this->connect(connButton, SIGNAL(clicked()), this, SLOT(accept()));
    QPushButton *cancelButton = new QPushButton("Cancel", row4);
    this->connect(cancelButton, SIGNAL(clicked()), this, SLOT(reject()));
}
```

Finally, we have the destructor for the dialog box. Since Qt takes care of destroying all of the widget objects, we have an empty implementation.

```
cLoginDlg::~cLoginDlg()
{
}
```

chatwin.h

This file contains the declaration for our main chat window class. First, we include some Qt header files.

```
/* chatwin.h */
#ifndef CHATWIN_H
#define CHATWIN_H

#include <qmainwindow.h>
#include <qtextedit.h>
#include <qlineedit.h>
#include <qlistbox.h>
#include <qtimer.h>
```

Next, we subclass Qt's `QMainWindow` class.

```
class cChatWin : public QMainWindow
{
Q_OBJECT
public:
    cChatWin();
    ~cChatWin();
```

Our member variables include the socket we used to connect to the server, the window containing the room chat, the text widget the user will enter dialogue into, and the list of users in the room.

```
public:
    int client_socket;
    QTextEdit *chatEdit;
    QLineEdit *msgEdit;
    QListBox *userList;
```

Here we define event handlers for the window. We have functions to handle all of the button clicks as well as a timer that we use to check for commands from the server.

```
protected slots:
    void sendButtonClicked();
    void privButtonClicked();
    void opButtonClicked();
    void kickButtonClicked();
    void topicButtonClicked();
    void quitButtonClicked();
    void timerFired();

protected:
    QTimer *theTimer;
};

#endif
```

chatwin.cpp

This file contains all the code for the main chat window. It is the only means that the user has to interact with the server. We not only relay the user's commands, but also check with the server for commands that need to be displayed to the user. First, we include the necessary header files.

```
/* chatwin.cpp */
#include <sys/socket.h>
#include <qvbox.h>
#include <qpushbutton.h>
#include <qmessagebox.h>
```

```
#include <qapplication.h>
#include <qinputdialog.h>
#include "chatcli.h"
#include "chatwin.h"
```

Next, we have our constructor. Here, we create the chat window. Since this is specific to Qt, we won't go into the details.

```
cChatWin::cChatWin() : QMainWindow(0, "", WDestructiveClose)
{
    this->setCaption("Chat Client");

    QVBox *main = new QVBox(this);
    main->setSpacing(3);
    main->setMinimumHeight(300);
    main->setMinimumWidth(400);
    this->setCentralWidget(main);

    QHBox *row1 = new QHBox(main);
    row1->setMinimumHeight(280);
    chatEdit = new QTextEdit(row1);
    chatEdit->setMinimumWidth(300);
    chatEdit->setReadOnly(true);
    userList = new QListBox(row1);
    userList->setMinimumWidth(100);
    userList->setMaximumWidth(100);

    QHBox *row2 = new QHBox(main);
    msgEdit = new QLineEdit(row2);
    msgEdit->setMinimumWidth(250);
    QPushButton *sendButton = new QPushButton("&Send", row2);
    this->connect(sendButton, SIGNAL(clicked()), this,
                  SLOT(sendButtonClicked()));
    QPushButton *privButton = new QPushButton("Send &Private", row2);
    this->connect(privButton, SIGNAL(clicked()), this,
                  SLOT(privButtonClicked()));
    QPushButton *opButton = new QPushButton("&Op", row2);
    this->connect(opButton, SIGNAL(clicked()), this, SLOT(opButtonClicked()));
    QPushButton *kickButton = new QPushButton("&Kick", row2);
    this->connect(kickButton, SIGNAL(clicked()), this,
                  SLOT(kickButtonClicked()));
    QPushButton *topicButton = new QPushButton("&Topic", row2);
    this->connect(topicButton, SIGNAL(clicked()), this,
                  SLOT(topicButtonClicked()));
```

```
QPushButton *quitButton = new QPushButton("&Quit", row2);
this->connect(quitButton, SIGNAL(clicked()), this,
              SLOT(quitButtonClicked()));
```

In addition to building the main window, we set up a `QTimer`. We will use the timer to check if the server has sent any commands on a regular basis. In this case, we will check every 0.25 seconds.

```
theTimer = new QTimer(this);
this->connect(theTimer, SIGNAL(timeout()), this, SLOT(timerFired()));
theTimer->start(250, true);
}
```

Since Qt takes care of destroying its own widgets, our destructor is empty.

```
cChatWin::~cChatWin()
{
}
```

Here we have our first user-interface handler. This member function is called whenever the user clicks the Send button. We start off with some useful variable declarations.

```
void cChatWin::sendButtonClicked()
{
    string send_string;
    char buffer[MAX_LINE_BUFF];
    cmd_t cmd;
    int status;
```

Next, we check to make sure that the user entered some text to send. If not, then we return. We won't send an empty message.

```
if (msgEdit->text() == "") {
    return;
}
```

Now, we build our message string to send to the server. Notice that the command is terminated with a newline.

```
send_string = "MSG " + string::basic_string(msgEdit->text().ascii()) + "\n";
```

We send the command and wait for a reply. The next data from the server will be the success or failure of this command. Notice that we pass 0 as the last readLine() parameter. This tells the readLine() function to block until the server sends a reply. If we don't do this, there is a chance that this call could return nothing and our response will be picked up by the timer event. We need to handle the response here.

```
send(client_socket, send_string.c_str(), send_string.length(), 0);
status = readLine(client_socket, buffer, MAX_LINE_BUFF, 0);
if (status < 0) {
    theTimer->stop();
    QMessageBox::critical(NULL, "Lost Connection",
                          "The server has closed the connection.");
    this->close();
    return;
}
```

Once the server has sent a response, we decode the command and check for success. If an error occurred, we tell the user.

```
cmd = decodeCommand(buffer);
if (cmd.command != "100") {
    QMessageBox::critical(NULL, "Unknown Error",
                          "An unknown error has occurred.");
    return;
}
```

Finally, we clear the text box so the user can enter more text.

```
msgEdit->setText("");
}
```

The next member function is called when the user clicks the Send Private button. This is the private message command.

```
void cChatWin::privButtonClicked()
{
    string send_string;
    char buffer[MAX_LINE_BUFF];
    cmd_t cmd;
    int status;
    string username;
```

To send a private message, the user must enter some text and select a room member.

```
if (msgEdit->text() == "") {
    return;
}

if (userList->currentText() == "") {
    QMessageBox::critical(NULL, "Private Message",
                "You must select a user before sending a private message.");
    return;
}
```

Room operators are denoted in the room list with an at sign (@) prefix. If the user is sending a private message to a room operator, then we need to strip the leading @.

```
username = userList->currentText().ascii();
if (username[0] == '@') {
    username = username.substr(1);
}
```

Next, we build the PMSG command. In addition to the message, we also send the name of the user for whom the message is intended.

```
send_string = "PMSG " + username + " "
                + string::basic_string(msgEdit->text().ascii()) + "\n";
send(client_socket, send_string.c_str(), send_string.length(), 0);
status = readLine(client_socket, buffer, MAX_LINE_BUFF, 0);
if (status < 0) {
    theTimer->stop();
    QMessageBox::critical(NULL, "Lost Connection",
                        "The server has closed the connection.");
    this->close();
    return;
}
cmd = decodeCommand(buffer);
```

After decoding the response, we check for success or failure. If we succeeded, then we clear the text box. Otherwise, we report the error to the user.

```
if (cmd.command == "100") {
    msgEdit->setText("");
```

```
        return;
    } else if (cmd.command == "202") {
        QMessageBox::critical(NULL, "Unknown User",
                            "The user specified is not in the room.");
        return;
    } else {
        QMessageBox::critical(NULL, "Unknown Error",
                            "An unknown error has occurred.");
        return;
    }
}
```

Our next handler is called whenever the user clicks the Op button. This command promotes a user to operator status in the room.

```
void cChatWin::opButtonClicked()
{
    string send_string;
    char buffer[MAX_LINE_BUFF];
    cmd_t cmd;
    int status;
    string username;
```

Just like the previous function for the Send Private button, this command requires the user to select a room member from the list.

```
    if (userList->currentText() == "") {
        QMessageBox::critical(NULL, "Op Error",
                        "You must select a user before making them an operator.");
        return;
    }
```

Next, we save a call to the server by checking our list to see if the user is already an operator.

```
    username = userList->currentText().ascii();
    if (username[0] == '@') {
        username = username.substr(1);
        QMessageBox::critical(NULL, "Op Error",
                            "User is already a room operator.");
        return;
    }
```

Otherwise, we send the OP command.

```
send_string = "OP " + username + "\n";
send(client_socket, send_string.c_str(), send_string.length(), 0);
status = readLine(client_socket, buffer, MAX_LINE_BUFF, 0);
if (status < 0) {
    theTimer->stop();
    QMessageBox::critical(NULL, "Lost Connection",
                          "The server has closed the connection.");
    this->close();
    return;
}
cmd = decodeCommand(buffer);
```

After decoding the response, we check the return code. If it was successful, we simply return. Note that we do not need to update our member list to reflect the new operator. The server will send out a command to all clients (including us), informing them of the newly made operator. This will be handled in timerFired() function.

```
if (cmd.command == "100") {
    return;
```

If an error occurred, we report it to the user.

```
} else if (cmd.command == "202") {
    QMessageBox::critical(NULL, "Unknown User",
                          "The user specified is not in the room.");
    return;
} else if (cmd.command == "203") {
    QMessageBox::critical(NULL, "Denied",
                          "Only room operators may op other users.");
    return;
} else {
    QMessageBox::critical(NULL, "Unknown Error",
                          "An unknown error has occurred.");
    return;
}
}
```

This member function is called whenever the user clicks the Kick button.

```
void cChatWin::kickButtonClicked()
{
```

```
string send_string;
char buffer[MAX_LINE_BUFF];
cmd_t cmd;
int status;
string username;
```

Just like the previous two functions, we need the user to select a room member.

```
if (userList->currentText() == "") {
    QMessageBox::critical(NULL, "Kick Error",
                          "You must select a user before kicking them out.");
    return;
}
```

If the room member is an operator, then we need to strip out the leading @ in the username.

```
username = userList->currentText().ascii();
if (username[0] == '@') {
    username = username.substr(1);
}
```

Next, we send the KICK command.

```
send_string = "KICK " + username + "\n";
send(client_socket, send_string.c_str(), send_string.length(), 0);
status = readLine(client_socket, buffer, MAX_LINE_BUFF, 0);
if (status < 0) {
    theTimer->stop();
    QMessageBox::critical(NULL, "Lost Connection",
                          "The server has closed the connection.");
    this->close();
    return;
}
```

Finally, we decode the response from the server. If successful, we return. Just like the previous OP command handler, we don't need to remove the kicked-out user here. The server will relay a command to inform us that it has happened. We'll handle it in the timerFired() function.

```
cmd = decodeCommand(buffer);
if (cmd.command == "100") {
    return;
```

If an error occurred, then report it to the user.

```
} else if (cmd.command == "202") {
    QMessageBox::critical(NULL, "Unknown User",
                          "The user specified is not in the room.");
    return;
} else if (cmd.command == "203") {
    QMessageBox::critical(NULL, "Denied",
                          "Only room operators may kick out other users.");
    return;
} else {
    QMessageBox::critical(NULL, "Unknown Error",
                          "An unknown error has occurred.");
    return;
    }
}
```

Another command available to the user changes the topic of the room. The room topic is displayed in the chat window's title bar. When the user clicks the Topic button, this function is called.

```
void cChatWin::topicButtonClicked()
{
    string send_string;
    char buffer[MAX_LINE_BUFF];
    cmd_t cmd;
    int status;
    bool ok;
```

First, we ask the user to enter the new topic.

```
QString topic = QInputDialog::getText("Chat Client", "Enter the new topic:",
                          QLineEdit::Normal, QString::null, &ok, this );
```

If the user clicks Cancel or enters a blank topic, we simply return.

```
if (ok == false || topic.isEmpty()) {
    return;
}
```

Otherwise, we send the TOPIC command to the server.

```
send_string = "TOPIC " + string::basic_string(topic.ascii()) + "\n";
send(client_socket, send_string.c_str(), send_string.length(), 0);
```

```
status = readLine(client_socket, buffer, MAX_LINE_BUFF, 0);
if (status < 0) {
    theTimer->stop();
    QMessageBox::critical(NULL, "Lost Connection",
                            "The server has closed the connection.");
    this->close();
    return;
}
cmd = decodeCommand(buffer);
```

If the command succeeded, we return. Again, the server will send a command to tell all connected clients that the topic has been changed. We will retrieve that command in the timerFired() function.

```
if (cmd.command == "100") {
    return;
} else if (cmd.command == "203") {
    QMessageBox::critical(NULL, "Denied",
                            "Only room operators may change the topic.");
    return;
} else {
    QMessageBox::critical(NULL, "Unknown Error",
                            "An unknown error has occurred.");
    return;
}

}
```

Our final handler is called when the user clicks the Quit button.

```
void cChatWin::quitButtonClicked()
{
    string send_string;
    char buffer[MAX_LINE_BUFF];
    cmd_t cmd;
    int status;
```

The QUIT command requires no parameters. We send it all by itself.

```
send_string = "QUIT\n";
send(client_socket, send_string.c_str(), send_string.length(), 0);
status = readLine(client_socket, buffer, MAX_LINE_BUFF, 0);
if (status < 0) {
    theTimer->stop();
```

```
            QMessageBox::critical(NULL, "Lost Connection",
                                "The server has closed the connection.");
            this->close();
            return;
        }
        cmd = decodeCommand(buffer);
```

Whenever we don't receive a successful return code, we inform the user.

```
        if (cmd.command != "100") {
            QMessageBox::critical(NULL, "Unknown Error",
                                "An unknown error has occurred.");
        }
```

Either way, though, we close the chat window. Closing the main window will also end the program.

```
        this->close();
    }
```

Our final member function is called by a QTimer event. In it we process all commands that the server has sent us.

```
void cChatWin::timerFired()
{
    int status;
    char buffer[MAX_LINE_BUFF];
    cmd_t cmd;
    string str;
```

First, we set up a loop to read the command list line by line.

```
    /* Get any commands that the server has sent */
    while ((status = readLine(client_socket, buffer, MAX_LINE_BUFF, 100)) != 0) {
```

Since we could get many commands from the server, we call processEvents() to keep the GUI responsive to the user while we are processing.

```
        qApp->processEvents();
        if (status < 0) {
            QMessageBox::critical(NULL, "Lost Connection",
                                "The server has closed the connection.");
            this->close();
```

```
        return;
    } else if (status > 0) {
        cmd = decodeCommand(buffer);
```

If we successfully retrieve the next command, we start to match it against the list of commands that we support. If we get a JOIN command, then we add the name of the new room member to our member list.

```
    if (cmd.command == "JOIN") {
        userList->insertItem(cmd.op1.c_str());
        str = cmd.op1 + " has joined the room.\n";
```

The MSG command posts a message to the entire room. If we get one, we add it to the chat window along with the username of who sent it.

```
    } else if (cmd.command == "MSG") {
        str = cmd.op1 + ": " + cmd.op2 + "\n";
        chatEdit->append(str.c_str());
```

A private message is not sent to the whole room and is not added to the chat window. Instead, we inform the user through a message box.

```
    } else if (cmd.command == "PMSG") {
        str = cmd.op1 + " has sent you a private message:\n\n";
        str += cmd.op2;
        QMessageBox::information(NULL, "Private Message", str.c_str());
```

When a user has been made a room operator, we designate that in our room list by prefixing their username with @. In addition, we add the notification string to the chat window.

```
    } else if (cmd.command == "OP") {
        QListBoxItem *itm = userList->findItem(cmd.op1.c_str(),
                                               Qt::ExactMatch);
        if (itm != NULL) {
            userList->changeItem("@" + itm->text(),
                                 userList->index(itm));
        }
        str = cmd.op1 + " has been made a room operator.\n";
        chatEdit->append(str.c_str());
```

If a user has been kicked out of the room, we remove the user from our member list and add the notification to the chat window.

```
    } else if (cmd.command == "KICK") {
        QListBoxItem *itm = userList->findItem(cmd.op1.c_str(),
                                                Qt::ExactMatch);
        if (itm != NULL) {
            userList->removeItem(userList->index(itm));
        } else {
            str = "@" + cmd.op1;
            itm = userList->findItem(str.c_str(), Qt::ExactMatch);
            if (itm != NULL) {
                userList->removeItem(userList->index(itm));
            }
        }
        str = cmd.op1 + " was kicked out of the room by "
                + cmd.op2 + "\n";
        chatEdit->append(str.c_str());
```

When a room operator changes the topic, we add the notification to the chat window and change the title bar text.

```
    } else if (cmd.command == "TOPIC") {
        if (cmd.op1 != "*") {
            str = "The topic has been changed to \"" + cmd.op2
                    + "\" by " + cmd.op1 + "\n";
            chatEdit->append(str.c_str());
        }
        str = "Chat Client - Topic: " + cmd.op2;
        this->setCaption(str.c_str());
```

When a user leaves the room, we remove the user from the member list and add the notification to the chat window.

```
    } else if (cmd.command == "QUIT") {
        QListBoxItem *itm = userList->findItem(cmd.op1.c_str(),
                                                Qt::ExactMatch);
        if (itm != NULL) {
            userList->removeItem(userList->index(itm));
        } else {
            str = "@" + cmd.op1;
            itm = userList->findItem(str.c_str(), Qt::ExactMatch);
            if (itm != NULL) {
                userList->removeItem(userList->index(itm));
            }
        }
```

```
            str = cmd.op1 + " has left the room.\n";
            chatEdit->append(str.c_str());
        }
    }
}
```

After we process all of the pending messages, we start the timer again.

```
    theTimer->start(250, true);
}
```

Makefile

Here is the makefile used to build the chat client. Notice that we have to do
a couple of extra steps to preprocess our window classes so that the event-
handling mechanism is built.

```
CC = g++
INCDIR = -I $(QTDIR)/include
LDFLAGS = -L $(QTDIR)/lib -lqt-mt


all: chatcli

chatcli: chatcli.o chatwin.o logindlg.o    moc_chatwin.o moc_logindlg.o
    $(CC) -o chatcli $(LDFLAGS) chatcli.o chatwin.o logindlg.o moc_chatwin.o \
        moc_logindlg.o

chatcli.o: chatcli.cpp
    $(CC) -c $(INCDIR) chatcli.cpp

chatwin.o: chatwin.cpp chatwin.h moc_chatwin.cpp
    $(CC) -c $(INCDIR) chatwin.cpp

moc_chatwin.o: moc_chatwin.cpp
    $(CC) -c $(INCDIR) moc_chatwin.cpp

moc_chatwin.cpp: chatwin.h
    $(QTDIR)/bin/moc chatwin.h -o moc_chatwin.cpp

logindlg.o: logindlg.cpp logindlg.h moc_logindlg.cpp
    $(CC) -c $(INCDIR) logindlg.cpp
```

```
moc_logindlg.o: moc_logindlg.cpp
        $(CC) -c $(INCDIR) moc_logindlg.cpp

moc_logindlg.cpp: logindlg.h
        $(QTDIR)/bin/moc logindlg.h -o moc_logindlg.cpp

clean: FORCE
        rm -f *.o
        rm -f moc_*

FORCE:
```

To build the chat client, ensure that your `QTDIR` environment variable is set to point to the Qt directory. Then type

```
make
```

The client can be run by typing

```
./chatcli
```

Recommendations for Improvements

While we've built a working chat client and server, here are a few suggestions for further improvements:

- Convert the server to a daemon, put it in a `chroot()` jail, and implement system logging.

- When a user sends a private message, open a private chat window. This will allow the users to privately chat in a more fluid manner. Any messages sent in this window will be considered private messages. When the client receives a private message, you will need to determine if a private message window exists and send the message to it. If not, then open a new private message window.

- Use colors to dress up the messages in the chat window. Use different colors for server notifications and chat messages.

- Allow for multiple rooms to exist. This will require modifications to the protocol, server, and client. You might also have a configurable list of rooms that always exist in addition to allowing users to create rooms.

Summary

In this chapter, we implemented a working chat server and client using the protocol described in Chapter 6.

In Part Three of this book, we will look at security and authentication.

Part Three

Security

CHAPTER 10

Securing Network Communication

AT THE HEART OF NETWORK PROGRAMMING is the need to transfer information from one place to another. When this transfer is done between processes on the same host or between hosts on a private network, then we don't need to be so concerned about network security—the main considerations are general protocol design and endpoint security through authorization. However, with the rise of the Internet, it has become necessary to consider what happens to the information as it is passed between computers, routers, and other networks. The advent of semipublic networks has created a need for network security. Thus, protocol design has taken on a new dimension as it has become necessary to consider not only how the information should be packaged, transferred, and interpreted, but also how to ensure that only authorized parties can access the information.

Because of the physical design of current-day networks and the nature of the TCP/IP standard, any computer situated between the sender and recipient of a data packet on the network can see, or "sniff," that packet. A packet on the wire contains information intended to ensure proper delivery of itself to a host or address. However, it has no provisions to prevent someone from reading that information and the enclosed data. The TCP/IP standards even permit such data and information to be manipulated and changed in some circumstances. This potentially results in preventing the data from being received or altering information that could otherwise be used to verify the authenticity of the data enclosed.

There are many tools available for GNU/Linux dedicated to sniffing, all of which require root access, as the network device must be put into promiscuous mode. In nonpromiscuous mode (which is the default), a network adapter checks the address of each packet to determine whether it should read the whole packet or send it along, and it reads only those packets that are addressed to it. By contrast, putting the device into promiscuous mode causes the adapter to read each and every packet on the wire. Tools such as Ethereal (http://www.ethereal.com) make this a point-and-click process, providing easy-to-use filters, packet analysis, and even the ability to follow a session automatically. Using such a tool, it is possible for an unauthorized person to gain access to insecure data. For example, monitoring an entire telnet session, to see everything from the initial login and password to the commands and output of the session itself.

> **NOTE**   *It is important to note that sniffing has many legitimate uses for such things as fault analysis, network intrusion detection, etc.*

Capturing passwords from telnet sessions is bad enough, but extend the same process to sniffing web-browsing sessions at an online store where credit cards are processed or tax information is recorded, and it's easy to see how vital it is to have secure communication. We know that we have to secure our application somehow, but this seems like a rather big problem. The good news is that this isn't a new problem. There are several large projects and standards already in place to help. In this chapter, we'll examine the following options:

- Securing existing protocols using tunneling

- The Public Key Infrastructure standard and the concept of asymmetric cryptography

- Creating a secure network application using the OpenSSL library

Tunneling

Tunneling allows a secure connection between a client and server to be made first, then other network connections are forwarded, or "tunneled," over that single secure connection, as shown in Figure 10-1.

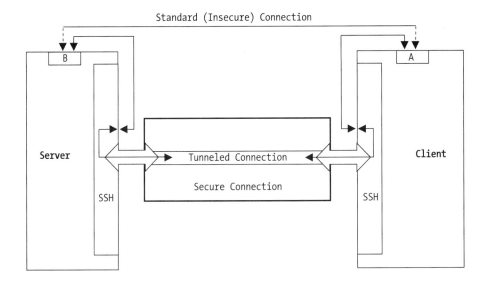

Figure 10-1. Tunneling over a secure connection

This is the first option in making communication secure and is a solution for applications, or protocols, that are already fully developed and widely used, as adding security at the program level, post design, is an extremely disruptive task. Tunneling is how most virtual private networks (VPNs) work. By employing tunneling, the application does not have to change, but the information is relayed inside a secure channel. The drawback is that the server and client must each connect to themselves to use the tunnel, which makes logging or filtering access by remote address much harder, if not impossible. Tunneling can be done in several ways, using either of two common packages: OpenSSH or Stunnel.

Tunneling with OpenSSH

The OpenSSH project (http://www.openssh.org) is an ongoing effort to implement the Secure Shell (SSH) protocol under a BSD license. The SSH protocol allows secure remote shell access and file transfer (similar to FTP), and was intended as a replacement for the older and insecure methods of remote administration and access such as RCP, RSH, and FTP. The SSH protocol allows automatic forwarding (meaning tunneling) of the X protocol, as well as tunneling of arbitrary TCP (and, just recently, UDP) connections. As a result of its design, the SSH protocol suite can be used to curb network attacks, prevent eavesdropping, and so on.

Once SSH is installed, tunneling a connection over SSH requires either a username/password pair or a predefined public/private-key pair for authentication on the server. Tunneling can be specified in the SSH configuration file or on the command line. The man page for SSH (from OpenSSH) says it best:

> -L port:host:hostport *Specifies that the given port on the local (client) host is to be forwarded to the given host and port on the remote side. This works by allocating a socket to listen to* port *on the local side, and whenever a connection is made to this port, the connection is forwarded over the secure channel, and a connection is made to* host *on port* hostport *from the remote machine. Port forwardings can also be specified in the configuration file. Only root can forward privileged ports. IPv6 addresses can be specified with an alternative syntax:* port/host/hostport.

The -R flag operates in the same manner; however, it tunnels the remote port to the local machine, which is the opposite of the -L flag.

Let's take an insecure application, for example telnet, and tunnel it over an SSH connection. Be sure that the SSH server is set up, and that a telnet server exists on the same machine. After verifying that we can connect to the server with SSH, we try the following command:

```
$ ssh username@server -L 6699:server:23
```

We replace username in the preceding command with our username and server with the fully qualified host name (or IP address) of our server. After logging in, we'll be given a prompt. Well, that's great, but to enjoy the benefits of port forwarding, or redirecting a local port to a remote port, we'll now have to open another terminal window and telnet to localhost:6699. What if we just wanted to forward the port and push it to the background for use at any time? By adding the -N and -f flags, we can accomplish just that. The -f option forces SSH into the background, and the -N flag tells it not to execute any remote commands after connecting and authenticating:

```
$ ssh username@server -L 6699:server:23 -N -f
```

We run the preceding command, and then run

```
$ telnet localhost 6699
```

We should now be able to log in over a telnet connection to the server. The benefit, now, is that the connection is secure, and despite the fact that we're using a plain-text client-server protocol, we're doing so over an encrypted connection that can't be sniffed.

 TIP *For it to be truly useful, we would configure our OpenSSH server to allow forwarding only particular ports and setup keys to allow passwordless forwarding for authorized individuals. While beyond the scope of this text, this technique is a well-documented method of configuration using the* authorized_keys *file and its configuration syntax.*

Tunneling with Stunnel

Stunnel (http://www.stunnel.org) is the second option used to implement tunneling. Stunnel uses the OpenSSL (http://www.openssl.org) libraries to implement a Secure Sockets Layer/Transport Layer Security (SSL/TLS) encrypted channel, thus tunneling arbitrary TCP (as yet, not UDP) connections between a client and server in much the same way (although through a different protocol) as SSH did in the previous example.

The major difference in using Stunnel is that its sole use is for forwarding an insecure connection over a secure channel, whereas SSH is capable of doing so in addition to its main functionality. An advantage to Stunnel's use of the SSL/TLS library is the availability of client software that already knows and speaks the SSL/TLS protocols. For instance, a common use of Stunnel is to provide SSL capabilities to an IMAP or POP e-mail server that otherwise could not support SSL. In this case, the e-mail server can do its job without worrying about encryption, while most available e-mail clients support SSL connectivity already.

Providing SSL encryption to a non-SSL-enabled IMAP mail service is as easy as this:

```
$ stunnel -d imaps -r localhost:imap
```

This command basically says "accept connections on port IMAPS (as listed in /etc/services), and send the decrypted data to port imap on server localhost."

Stunnel requires a signed SSL certificate, which can be generated and "self-signed" with the OpenSSL toolkit (as demonstrated later in this section), or a certificate can be purchased through several companies on the Internet.

Public Key Infrastructure

The Public Key Infrastructure (PKI) defines a standard for security using asymmetric encryption. This standard is at the core of most current-day secure communication methods. To understand its uses, we must first examine some key terms and concepts.

Symmetric Key Cryptography

Prior to the PKI standard, there was only one kind of encryption: *symmetric key cryptography* (also known as *secret key cryptography*). Symmetric key cryptography employs a mathematical function that uses a single unique key for both encryption and decryption. This operation results in obfuscated, or encrypted, data, making it necessary to reverse the process before the data can be used.

As the need for secure communication grew, a basic flaw in symmetric cryptography became clear: key distribution. Encrypted data, while statistically impossible to decrypt, was only as strong as the integrity, or security, of the key that was used to encrypt it.

This is best demonstrated, as is often the case in writing about cryptography and security, with an "Alice and Bob" example. Consider a real-world situation involving our key players, Alice and Bob. Alice has a message she wants only Bob to be able to read. She uses a mathematical function and a secret key (let's say she used the name of her dog, "Fido") to encrypt the message. She then sends the encrypted message to Bob. However, before Bob can read the message, he needs to know what key Alice used to encrypt it. Effectively, this brings us back to square one, Alice must somehow communicate her key to Bob in a way that prevents others from knowing it. Whether she conveys it to him verbally, sends him a registered letter, or gives it to him on a floppy disk, there is a chance that the key could be compromised and the message decrypted by someone else.

Asymmetric Key Cryptography

The answer to the key distribution problem is provided by *asymmetric key cryptography* (also known as *public key cryptography*). With this technique, two keys are used. One key, used to encrypt the data, is made public. This key can be used only to encrypt data, not to decrypt it. Therefore, this key can be shared with anyone or any program wishing to provide secure data. The second key, called the *private key*, is used for decryption of the data encrypted with the public key.

Asymmetrical key cryptography is at the core of the PKI standard. Using this method of cryptography, anyone can encrypt data, but only the intended recipient, who holds the correct private key, can read it. This makes secure communication much easier to handle. In the initiation of a PKI session, the host and client exchange public keys. Each encrypts a small handshake message with the other's public key, as a test, and decrypts the corresponding message from the other for verification.

Let's again consider our friend Alice's predicament. This time around she has learned her lesson, so she and Bob first trade public keys. Alice then encrypts her message with Bob's public key and sends the result along to Bob. Bob, being the only person who has the corresponding private key, can now decrypt the message safely. Likewise, Bob can respond by encrypting his own message with Alice's public key. In this way, the piece of information needed to read an encrypted message never has to be transmitted or endangered.

Asymmetric key cryptography makes it possible to share a public key without risk of compromising secure communication. However, an attack known as the *man-in-the-middle attack* exposes another problem: key-validity. In this attack, the attacker intercepts the first message and sends its own public key to each. By doing this, each person thinks that the attacker is the other person. The end result is a stream of decrypted traffic that the attacker can read, modify, and use.

In Alice and Bob's world, this means the introduction of a new character to our unfolding drama—let's call him Charlie. In the previous example, say that Charlie was to get a copy of both Alice and Bob's public keys. This in itself is no danger, as messages can't be decrypted by a public key. However, if Charlie then makes sure he's in a position to intercept messages being passed between Alice and Bob, then he can pretend to be Bob when speaking with Alice, and likewise he can pretend to be Alice when speaking with Bob. Figure 10-2 illustrates how the man-in-the-middle attack works.

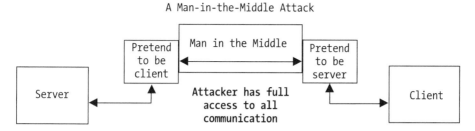

Figure 10-2. Man-in-the-middle attack

Certificates

To prevent a man-in-the-middle attack, the PKI standard includes the use of certificates. A certificate is used to confirm that certain data has been sent by the person or organization that claims to have sent it. It contains a digital signature that is applied and verified with asymmetric cryptography by a trusted third party. As a result, a client and server exchange public keys as well as certificates (often combined as a single item) when a session is initiated. These can then be verified by the trusted third party that signed them.

Let's return to Alice and Bob's story one more time to see the whole picture of the PKI standard. This time around, when Bob and Alice exchange their public keys, they also provide the name of a third person, Dan. Dan has received a copy of both Bob and Alice's public keys as well, he has taken other steps to verify their authenticity, and both Alice and Bob trust Dan. Now, when Alice receives Bob's public key, she looks at it and sees that Dan has also signed it, so she knows that Bob is who he says he is. Likewise, when Bob sees that Alice's key has been verified by Dan, he knows that she is in fact Alice, and not that annoying eavesdropper Charlie.

In this way, both a client and server can establish the other's authenticity with digital signatures, as well as guarantee, through asymmetric cryptography and certificates, that only the intended recipient can decrypt the encrypted data. The usual practice is that only servers provide certificates, to prove their identity, as typical client-server communication requires only that the client be assured of the server's identity. A common example is HTTPS, the HTTP-over-SSL standard that is used by many popular web servers and browsers. When connecting to a secure website, such as an e-commerce site, the browser will validate the server's certificate to ensure that any private data is being shared only with the intended server. In this case, the server that is used to verify certificates is typically one of a few trusted signing authorities known to both parties.

The decision to use client certificates or not is one of protocol and design. It really depends on the nature of the application and the usage thereof. A general rule of thumb is that if only particular clients are to connect, they should also use certificates, whereas if any number of clients are expected and allowed to connect, client certificates are unnecessary.

Creating Certificates

Some of the examples in this section make extensive use of PKI certificates. This requires that we have a certificate available for the example program. To create this certificate and provide a better introduction to PKI, let's examine how we can create a certificate using the OpenSSL toolkit (http://www.openssl.org).

Creating a Certificate Authority

A certificate is typically signed by a trusted third party known as a *certificate authority*, or CA. However, using the OpenSSL toolkit, it is possible to create our own CA while creating a self-signed certificate for use in testing. To do this, we must first create a root-level private key and a root certificate request. OpenSSL includes a command-line utility called openssl that functions as a tool for working with OpenSSL's cryptographic capabilities. We begin with the following:

```
$ openssl req -newkey rsa:2048 -keyout root_key.pem -out root_request.pem
```

This generates a new key using the RSA standard with a key size of 2048 bits, puts the private key into the file root_key.pem, and puts a certificate request into the file root_request.pem. The preceding commands should result in output similar to the following:

```
Generating a 2048 bit RSA private key
.........................................+++
............................+++
writing new private key to 'root_key.pem'
Enter PEM pass phrase:
Verifying - Enter PEM pass phrase:
-----
You are about to be asked to enter information that will be incorporated
into your certificate request.
What you are about to enter is what is called a Distinguished Name or a DN.
There are quite a few fields but you can leave some blank
For some fields there will be a default value,
If you enter '.', the field will be left blank.
-----
```

```
Country Name (2 letter code) [AU]:US
State or Province Name (full name) [Some-State]:Maine
Locality Name (eg, city) []:Portland
Organization Name (eg, company) [Internet Widgits Pty Ltd]:Somecompany Inc.
Organizational Unit Name (eg, section) []:IT/IS
Common Name (eg, YOUR name) []:Nathan
Email Address []:nate@yocom.org


Please enter the following 'extra' attributes
to be sent with your certificate request
A challenge password []:
An optional company name []:
```

We should choose a pass phrase to protect our private key, as without the pass phrase our private key cannot be used to sign anything. As we are creating a test certificate, the other fields may be left blank. To avoid entering a password to run your application later, be sure to leave the challenge password, under the extra attributes, blank.

We now have two files in our directory, root_key.pem, which holds the encrypted private key, and root_request.pem, which contains our certificate request. We go on to actually generate a certificate with the following:

```
$ openssl x509 -req -in root_request.pem -signkey root_key.pem \
 -out root_certificate.pem
```

This command uses the x509 processor to sign the key and output our root certificate as root_certificate.pem. Output from this should be similar to this:

```
Signature ok
subject=/C=US/ST=Maine/L=Portland
/O=SomecompanyInc./OU=IT/IS/CN=Nathan
/emailAddress=nate@yocom.org
Getting Private key
Enter pass phrase for root_key.pem:
```

 TIP   *x509 is a common standard for dealing with certificates.*

The pass phrase being requested is the one you assigned to the private key earlier. If you enter this incorrectly, you will get an error message stating "Unable to load private key," as your private key cannot be read without this pass phrase.

To keep things simple, we can now combine our information into a single file (OpenSSL is smart enough to handle files with multiple types of information in them).

```
$ cat root_certificate.pem root_key.pem > root.pem
```

This completes the first step in creating a certifying authority. We now have a root-level certificate that we can use to create and sign a CA certificate. The procedure now is similar to that used previously. First, we generate the CA's private key and certificate request:

```
$ openssl req -newkey rsa:2048 -keyout CA_key.pem -out CA_request.pem
```

Then we process the request with x509 and create our actual CA certificate:

```
$ openssl x509 -req -in CA_request.pem -CA root.pem -CAkey root.pem \
-CAcreateserial -out CAcert.pem
```

This time we provide root.pem as the certificate to use for signing, as well as the key, because we combined both these sets of data into one file. The output from both these commands should resemble those from the previous commands. We again combine our information into one file:

```
$ cat CAcert.pem CA_key.pem root_certificate.pem > CA.pem
```

We now have our CA certificate and can generate self-signed server and client certificates with it.

Creating a Server Certificate

In creating a private key and certificate request for our server certificate, we don't want to be prompted for a password on every connection, so we generate an unencrypted private key of length 2048 bits with the genrsa command:

```
$ openssl genrsa 2048 > server_key.pem
```

We then use this key and generate a certificate request as we have before:

```
$ openssl req -new -key server_key.pem -out server_request.pem
You are about to be asked to enter information that will be incorporated
into your certificate request.
```

```
What you are about to enter is what is called a Distinguished Name or a DN.
There are quite a few fields but you can leave some blank
For some fields there will be a default value,
If you enter '.', the field will be left blank.
-----
Country Name (2 letter code) [AU]:US
State or Province Name (full name) [Some-State]:California
Locality Name (eg, city) []:Almeda
Organization Name (eg, company) [Internet Widgits Pty Ltd]:Secure Servers Inc.
Organizational Unit Name (eg, section) []:
Common Name (eg, YOUR name) []:Joe Admin
Email Address []:

Please enter the following 'extra' attributes
to be sent with your certificate request
A challenge password []:
An optional company name []:
```

Note that this time we are not asked for a password, as the private key in server_key.pem is not encrypted. We now process the certificate request with the CA key and certificate:

```
$ openssl x509 -req -in server_request.pem -CA CA.pem -CAcreateserial \
-CAkey CA.pem -out server_certificate.pem
```

We will then be asked for the password we used to encrypt our CA's private key. We have all the information we need spread across several files. We combine things one last time:

```
$ cat server_certificate.pem server_key.pem CAcert.pem \
root_certificate.pem > server.pem
```

We can now use the server.pem file as a certificate for our OpenSSL example.

 CAUTION   *It is important to note that because we combined information and included a plain-text private key in the same file as our certificate, this file should remain accessible only to the process using it, as our private key is vital to the security of the application. Should another server get hold of the private key, it could effectively masquerade as us with no way for a client to tell the difference.*

Secure Network Programming Using OpenSSL

So you've seen how to secure existing, insecure applications with tunneling, but how do you design a secure network application so that you don't have to use tunneling? Again, you have several options. One of these options is to use the OpenSSL library, a cryptography toolkit, to secure your application. OpenSSL is based on the SSLeay library developed by Eric A. Young and Tim J. Hudson. In addition to SSL and TLS implementations, the OpenSSL library contains crypto-graphic routines, random number generators, and large number, or BIGNUM, math support. This all-in-one approach, combined with its open source nature, makes OpenSSL an easy to use library for securing any network application.

Using the OpenSSL library first requires an examination of the structures and functions that make the library work. Once you fully understand these, we'll continue on to discuss the methods used to create network servers and clients with the OpenSSL library. After we've created a couple of example servers and clients, it's important that we also look at the use of threading in conjunction with the OpenSSL library. The remainder of this chapter will deal with these issues in the order mentioned.

OpenSSL Functions and Structures

The OpenSSL libraries (`libcrypto` and `libssl`) adhere to a pretty standard Linux familiar method of naming functions and parameters. The library itself is written in a mix of C and assembler, and as such easily integrates into a C program. The library's well-defined and discrete functions also make it an easy candidate for wrapping in a simple C++ class for inclusion in C++ projects.

The library's main header files are `openssl/ssl.h` and `openssl/err.h`. These include the declarations for most of the functions that we will be concerned with in this section. Each function name includes a prefix that identifies the type of object the function operates on. `SSL_` functions deal with the `SSL *` structure and the SSL and TLS standards, `SSL_CTX_` functions deal with the `CTX *` structure that describes the context of a connection, and this continues. Each of these is described in the `openssl/ssl.h` header file.

The second header file, `openssl/err.h`, contains declarations for the built-in error handling and reporting capabilities of the library. This includes not only a host of defined errors and their descriptions, but also custom `ERR_` functions for converting the result of a library function into a human-readable string and even putting that string into different contexts, such as printing to a file. Let's walk through the steps necessary to use the library and the basic structures that are required.

Library Initialization

The first thing that an application using the OpenSSL library must do is initialize the internal state of the library. While it is possible to initialize only those parts pertaining to the algorithms and structures we are going to use, the library provides a simple one-call solution that will set things up regardless of how we choose to use the library: OpenSSL_add_all_algorithms(). By first calling this function, we can then safely continue and call other library functions, and use library structures.

While not required, it is also quite desirable to initialize the library's error-handling capabilities and strings. This is done through a one-time call to SSL_load_error_strings(). After calling this function, we can then use the ERR_ functions in the library to change an error number into a human-readable message.

Library Structures

The four main structures that our applications will deal with are SSL_METHOD, SSL_CTX, SSL, and BIO. In almost every case, we will use pointers to these structures to interact with the OpenSSL library. As such, an examination of where each structure applies is in order. Briefly, these structures are as follows:

- SSL_METHOD: Indicates the PKI encryption method to use for communication.

- SSL_CTX: Defines the context of a server's communication, including the SSL_METHOD of choice, applicable certificates, and so on.

- BIO: A stackable input/output interface for reading/writing data to/from multiple sources using multiple methods.

- SSL: This structure maintains the data necessary for the library to operate on a given connection securely. There is typically a 1:1 relationship between the number of SSL * structures in use and the number of open connections.

SSL_METHOD

The SSL_METHOD structure is used to set the internal state of the library for particular types of encryption methods. We will use this structure to indicate to

OpenSSL what standard of communication we want to use. The available standards correspond to the various standards for the SSL and TLS standards defined by RFC. As of this writing, the OpenSSL toolkit supports SSLv1, SSLv2, SSLv3, SSLv23 (version 3 with fallback to 2), and TLSv1. TLSv1 is the newest and is considered the safest.

Because the value we choose for our SSL_METHOD affects the library at a very basic level, it is important that we first define the method we want to use prior to any other connection setup or initiation. The following code example illustrates creating an SSL_METHOD structure variable and initializing it such that the OpenSSL library knows we want to communicate using a TLSv1 connection.

```
SSL_METHOD *my_ssl_method;
my_ssl_method = TLSv1_method();
```

SSL_CTX

It is our duty to provide OpenSSL with the information it may need later in the game by giving as much information about our configuration as possible. We provide this information through the SSL_CTX layer. After deciding what method and standard of communication we will use for encryption, we need to provide a context for what we are doing. This context essentially allows us to provide sane default values for many of the things the OpenSSL library must do.

The first piece of context we must provide is the SSL_METHOD we have chosen. This base information allows us to create a new context with

```
SSL_CTX *my_ssl_ctx;
my_ssl_ctx = SSL_CTX_new(my_ssl_method);
```

Now that we have created a base context, we can add more information for the library's use. In the case of a process that will act as a server, a common piece of information provided is the location of the private key and certificate files. To add this information to our context, we use SSL_CTX_use_certificate_file() and SSL_CTX_use_PrivateKey_file() and provide proper arguments for context, file location, and file type. These functions can also be used in client processes to add client certificates when needed.

The following example shows how to add the file server.pem from the current directory to our previously created context. In this example, the server.pem file is a PEM-encoded file that includes both our private key and server certificate.

```
SSL_CTX_use_certificate_file(my_ssl_ctx,"server.pem",SSL_FILETYPE_PEM);
SSL_CTX_use_PrivateKey_file(my_ssl_ctx,"server.pem",SSL_FILETYPE_PEM);
```

The context information can also be used in our program to verify information that may have been provided by the user. For instance, if the user had provided paths for certificate and key files that were added to the context in our previous example, we would want to verify that the private key the user gave does in fact match the certificate. The SSL_CTX interface gives us the ability to do this with SSL_CTX_check_private_key(). By calling this function and providing our context, we can verify that the private key works and won't fail on us when we communicate later:

```
if(SSL_CTX_check_private_key(my_ssl_ctx))
    // The key works
else
    // The key is wrong
```

This gives us the opportunity to catch errors before they occur, and prevent potentially dangerous security situations. Also note that all SSL_CTX structures created with SSL_CTX_new() should be released with a call to SSL_CTX_free(SSL_CTX *) when they are no longer of use.

BIO

The BIO structure is the base layer used for input and output. This can be the communication between a client and server process, reading an encrypted file from disk, or reading from and writing to a memory buffer. BIOs are stackable and flexible, allowing a programmer to create one BIO that does input/output to a socket, another that encrypts/decrypts with the 3DES algorithm, and yet another that reads from and writes to a file. By stacking these three BIOs, it is then possible, with a single read or write call, to have a 3DES-encoded file read directly from disk and over the socket in plain-text form or vice versa, as shown in Figure 10-3.

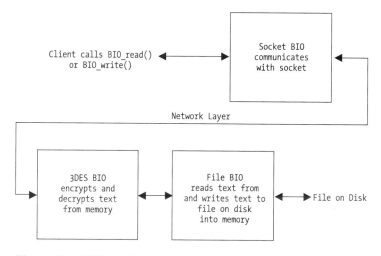

Figure 10-3. BIO stacking

> **NOTE** *A feature of the* BIO *layer worth noting is the ability to use one* BIO *for reading and another for writing, allowing for methods of communication that do not require a bidirectional pipe.*

SSL

The SSL structure abstracts some of the dirty work of connection handling for us. An SSL structure should be created for each connection within a context and is used to communicate on that connection, set connection options, and handle connection state.

The first step in creating an SSL structure is to associate it with a context. This allows the individual connections to inherit the default values and settings we associated with the context earlier. The SSL_new() function takes an SSL_CTX argument and returns a new SSL structure for use, as demonstrated here:

```
SSL *my_ssl;
my_ssl = SSL_new(my_ssl_ctx);
```

However, our newly created SSL structure is still not associated with any particular connection. We will explore other methods of doing this later in the chapter, but for now let's assume we already have a file descriptor, file_descriptor, which points to a socket connection. We can use the SSL_set_fd function to associate our SSL structure with this connection:

```
SSL_set_fd(my_ssl,file_descriptor);
```

It is now important that we handshake with the other side of the connection. This allows the SSL or TLS connection to be negotiated and established, ensuring that future communication with this SSL structure is secure. On the server side of the connection, we use SSL_accept(), which is analogous to the BSD socket call accept() in that it waits for either an error condition or the handshake from the client. On the client side, we use SSL_connect() to initiate the handshake with the server.

```
// Server Side
if(SSL_accept(my_ssl) <= 0)
    // Some error occurred
else
    // Connection is made and secure
```

```
// Client Side
if(SSL_connect(my_ssl) <= 0)
    // Some error occurred
else
    // Connection is made and secure
```

With the handshake process complete, we can now use the SSL structure to read and write data, report on connection status, and so forth. For instance, we can output the version of SSL and the type of cipher used on the connection with the SSL_get_version() and SSL_get_cipher() functions:

```
printf("[%s,%s]\n",SSL_get_version(my_ssl),SSL_get_cipher(my_ssl));
```

Similarly, we can use the SSL_write() and SSL_read() functions to read and write data on the connection. These functions follow the semantics and definition of their socket-level counterparts read() and write() nearly identically. The exception is that the SSL_ functions require an SSL structure as the first argument.

Closing a connection requires another handshake process initiated by the SSL_shutdown() function. Both ends of the connection must make this call before the connection can be cleanly severed. It is important to check any error conditions returned by calls to SSL_read() or SSL_write() (as well as other data input/output functions) to see if a read/write error occurred because the other side requested a shutdown handshake. This can be done as follows:

```
if( SSL_get_shutdown(my_ssl) & SSL_RECEIVED_SHUTDOWN )
    SSL_shutdown(my_ssl);  // Make our handshake call to close cleanly
else
    // Some other error occurred
```

The SSL_get_shutdown() function checks the current state of the SSL structure and uses the logical AND operation to evaluate whether an SSL_shutdown() call was made from the other side of the connection, thereby allowing us to cleanly close the connection. Once you are done with an SSL structure, it is important that it be released before being reused or going out of scope. Releasing the SSL structure is done by calling SSL_free(SSL *). Note that this function decrements a reference count on the structure and only releases the underlying memory if that count reaches zero.

With an understanding of the basic steps and structures necessary, we can move on to creating a server that uses the OpenSSL library's functions and structures. First, we will examine the use of a method called *file descriptor association*.

File Descriptor Association

One of the easiest ways to incorporate OpenSSL into the design of an application is through file descriptor association. With this technique, you create, open, and connect sockets using the common methods, obtaining a file descriptor that references the connected socket. You can then initialize and create an SSL reference on top of that file descriptor. Because this does not change the method you make a connection with, it is the easiest and fastest method to implement for beginners, as well as to modify an existing code base. Examination of a simple server/client example will help to make this clearer.

The Server

We will start with a simple server example. Our server will listen for a single connection at a time and will respond to each connection by writing the text "Hello there! Welcome to the SSL test server." to the client.

We start by defining the different variables we will need, including one for each of the three basic SSL structures, and initializing the OpenSSL library as we discussed in our overview previously. Note that we also put our message into a memory buffer here.

```
int my_fd,client_fd;
struct sockaddr_in server, client;
int client_size;
int error = 0, wrote = 0;
char buffer[] = "Hello there! Welcome to the SSL test server.\n\n";
SSL_METHOD *my_ssl_method;
SSL_CTX *my_ssl_ctx;
SSL *my_ssl;

OpenSSL_add_all_algorithms();
SSL_load_error_strings();
```

Following the outline provided in our overview, we now decide to use the TLSv1-encrypted communication standard and set up our context with a server certificate. Note the call to ERR_print_errors_fp(), which outputs the last error from the OpenSSL library to the given file handle, in this case standard error. After our context is initialized and set up, we check the private key chosen to ensure it and the certificate match with SSL_CTX_check_private_key().

```
my_ssl_method = TLSv1_server_method();

if( ( my_ssl_ctx = SSL_CTX_new(my_ssl_method) ) == NULL ) {
```

```
        ERR_print_errors_fp(stderr);
        exit(-1);
}


if( !SSL_CTX_check_private_key(ssl_ctx) ) {
        fprintf(stderr,"Private key does not match certificate\n");
        exit(-1);
}
```

We then use standard socket library calls to bind() to port 5353 and listen for new connections, entering an endless listen loop and accepting new connections one at a time.

```
myFd = socket(PF_INET, SOCK_STREAM, 0);
server.sin_family = AF_INET;
server.sin_port = htons(5353);
server.sin_addr.s_addr = INADDR_ANY;
bind(my_fd, (struct sockaddr *)&server, sizeof(server));
listen(my_fd, 5);
for( ;; ) {
        client_size = sizeof(client);
        bzero(&client,sizeof(client));
        client_fd = accept(my_fd, (sockaddr *)&client, (socklen_t *)&client_size);
```

CAUTION   *To keep the code sparse and readable in our examples, the return values from socket calls such as* bind() *and* accept() *are not evaluated or checked for correct behavior. In a real-world scenario, you should always check these values to prevent potentially insecure, if not unhealthy, behavior.*

For each connection established, we create a new SSL structure within the program's context.

```
    if((my_ssl = SSL_new(my_ssl_ctx)) == NULL) {
        ERR_print_errors_fp(stderr);
        exit(-1);
    }
```

We can now associate the newly created SSL structure with our client socket and file descriptor using SSL_set_fd(). Following that, we make a call to SSL_accept() to handle the server side of our initial SSL handshake. Finally, we output to standard out the version and cipher in use by the connection that has

been established. To do this, we use the functions SSL_get_version() and
SSL_get_cipher().

```
SSL_set_fd(my_ssl,client_fd);
if(SSL_accept(my_ssl) <= 0) {
    ERR_print_errors_fp(stderr);
    exit(-1);
}
printf("[%s,%s]\n",SSL_get_version(my_ssl),SSL_get_cipher(my_ssl));
```

Now we enter a for loop and write the contents of buffer, which contains
our welcome string, out to the client using SSL_write(). We check the return
value of SSL_write() for errors and simply shut down and move to the next connection if there are any problems. Note the call to SSL_free() to ensure we have
released any underlying memory retained by the SSL structure, followed by a call
to close the client socket connection.

```
for(wrote = 0; wrote < strlen(buffer); wrote += error) {
    error = SSL_write(my_ssl,buffer+wrote,strlen(buffer)-wrote);
    if(error <= 0)
        break;
}
SSL_shutdown(serverSSL);
SSL_free(my_ssl);
close(client_fd);
```

We close our outside (and infinite) loop, and although execution will never
get there, we call SSL_CTX_free() to ensure that we release any used memory.
This is simply good programming practice and has no effect on the actual performance of the server as it stands. However, if we were to change things to not
use an infinite loop, having this already in would eliminate a lot of time hunting
down a memory leak.

```
}
SSL_CTX_free(my_ssl_ctx);
```

The server is now put together and working, but before we can test it, we
need a client.

The Client

The client side of this pair is quite simple. Much of the SSL code is the same,
regardless of which side of the connection you are on, which is yet another

feature of OpenSSL programming. Again, we begin with the declaration of the variables we will need for our socket operations, as well as our triumvirate of OpenSSL structures. We clear space in the buffer we want to read into, initialize OpenSSL, choose our TLSv1 method, and create a context and SSL structure.

```
SSL_METHOD *my_ssl_method;
SSL_CTX *my_ssl_ctx;
SSL *my_ssl;
int my_fd;
struct sockaddr_in server;
int error = 0, read_in = 0;
char buffer[512];

memset(buffer,'\0',sizeof(buffer));

OpenSSL_add_all_algorithms();
SSL_load_error_strings();

my_ssl_method = TLSv1_client_method();

if((my_ssl_ctx = SSL_CTX_new(my_ssl_method)) == NULL) {
    ERR_print_errors_fp(stderr);
    exit(-1);
}

if((my_ssl = SSL_new(my_ssl_ctx)) == NULL) {
    ERR_print_errors_fp(stderr);
    exit(-1);
}
```

Note the lack of any certificate-handling code. As our server model is one in which any client can connect, we do not need to load any client certificates. A public/private-key pair will be generated on the fly for our client process when the connection is established to ensure bidirectional security.

We now move on to creating our socket, connecting to the server, and associating our SSL connection with SSL_set_fd(). Once associated, we can initiate the secure handshake process with the call to SSL_connect() and output some information about the connection with SSL_get_version() and SSL_get_cipher().

```
my_fd = socket(AF_INET, SOCK_STREAM, 0);
bzero(&server,sizeof(server));
server.sin_family = AF_INET;
server.sin_port = htons(5353);
```

```
inet_aton("127.0.0.1",&server.sin_addr);
bind(my_fd, (struct sockaddr *)&server, sizeof(server));
connect(my_fd,(struct sockaddr *)&server, sizeof(server));

SSL_set_fd(my_ssl,my_fd);

if(SSL_connect(my_ssl) <= 0) {
    ERR_print_errors_fp(stderr);
    exit(-1);
}

printf("[%s,%s]\n",SSL_get_version(my_ssl),SSL_get_cipher(my_ssl));
```

Next is the task of using SSL_read() to read data from the server into our memory buffer. Notice that we check the return value of SSL_read() on a continual basis to ensure that a read error has not occurred during the process of reading any data from the server.

```
for( read_in = 0; read_in < sizeof(buffer); read_in += error ) {
    error = SSL_read(my_ssl,buffer+read_in,sizeof(buffer) - read_in);
    if(error <= 0)
        break;
}
```

As we are not looking for any particular end of string, and we know our server sends SSL_shutdown() when it has sent everything it has to send, we know that our for loop used for reading will break out when the server sends SSL_shutdown(), which causes our SSL_read() to return an error. As a result, we need to handle our half of the shutdown handshake by calling SSL_shutdown() ourselves, then releasing the memory used by our context, SSL structure, and finally, closing the socket connection. The last things we do are print the message the server sent and close the process itself.

```
SSL_shutdown(my_ssl);
SSL_free(my_ssl);
SSL_CTX_free(my_ssl_ctx);
close(my_fd);

printf("%s",buffer);
```

This finishes out the code necessary to connect to a TLS-aware server and read a string of text as sent by that server.

At this point, it is important to understand that we could use a different method for creating our server and client—a method that relies on the OpenSSL structure BIO for the connection handling rather than the socket-level calls used by our file descriptor method. Let's examine the BIO method.

BIO Connection Handling

While using the file descriptor association method may be easy to incorporate into an existing code base, or as a means of transition, there exists another way of connection handling. By using the underlying BIO framework of the OpenSSL library, it is possible to create both a client and a server that require no standard socket code (although this still happens at a lower level).

This is a major advantage when writing an application that will communicate only with a SSL or TLS counterpart, and it has the added benefit of being cross-platform. Code that does all connection handling with the OpenSSL library will work on any platform for which the OpenSSL library is available, including the many varying types and forms of Linux, UNIX, and other operating systems, such as Windows and Mac OS X. A modification of the previous examples, substituting the use of BIO structures for socket functions, helps us clarify this.

The Server

Using the BIO layer to handle incoming connections is very similar in style to that of the standard BSD bind() and accept() functions. We start by declaring our variables and setting up our SSL context, certificates, and so forth. Note that we impart only new information here to keep the discussion as clean as possible.

```
BIO *server_bio,*client_bio;
```

Now, where we would have begun the process of creating a socket and binding it to a port and so on, we do the same with the BIO functions provided by OpenSSL, namely BIO_new_accept() and BIO_do_accept(). The former sets up a socket on the given port and prepares the process to listen on that port. The latter has two functions. The first time it is called, it results in the process being bound, similar to the bind() function call. The second time we call BIO_do_accept(), it acts as the accept() function call would, by blocking until the next incoming connection is present and available. This is shown in our code by the fact that the second call is inside the server's for loop.

```
if((server_bio = BIO_new_accept("5353")) == NULL) {
    ERR_print_errors_fp(stderr);
    exit(-1);
}
```

```
if(BIO_do_accept(server_bio) <= 0) {
    ERR_print_errors_fp(stderr);
    exit(-1);
}

for(;;) {
    if(BIO_do_accept(server_bio) <= 0) {
        ERR_print_errors_fp(stderr);
        exit(-1);
    }
```

One thing that becomes apparent is that there is no return from our call to
BIO_do_accept() that would provide a way to manipulate the connection. This
is because the call results in a new BIO structure being created and placed on a
stack in the passed BIO structure. To get a "handle" to the incoming connection,
we need to pop a BIO off of the stack with BIO_pop().

```
client_bio = BIO_pop(server_bio);
```

We then create a new SSL structure to communicate on this connection with
SSL_new() and use SSL_set_bio() to associate the new SSL structure with our new
connection. Note that we provide the same BIO for both the read and write portions of the SSL connection.

```
if((my_ssl = SSL_new(my_ssl_ctx)) == NULL) {
    ERR_print_errors_fp(stderr);
    exit(-1);
}

SSL_set_bio(my_ssl,client_bio,client_bio);
```

Now that we have an SSL structure that corresponds to our connection, the
remaining code is identical to that of our file descriptor example. Note that a
new BIO structure was created when we accepted the incoming connection, but
we do not have to explicitly release that structure. This is handled instead by the
SSL_free() function, which releases all underlying structures associated with the
given connection. However, should the server ever exit the infinite for loop, we
do need to release the BIO structure we created with BIO_new_accept() by calling
SSL_BIO_free().

```
SSL_BIO_free(server_bio);
```

As the implementation details of a connection are abstracted from us,
regardless of whether we use a method such as is provided by the BIO layer or the

previously discussed file descriptor association, it is possible to test this server with the previous section's client. However, we can also create a client that uses BIO functions for connection handling.

The Client

Much like its server counterpart, the client uses BIO functions to connect instead of using socket functions. These functions are BIO_new_connect() and BIO_do_connect(). Once we have initialized OpenSSL and so forth, we make successive calls to these functions to create a new connection with our BIO * my_bio. We then associate the resulting BIO with our SSL structure and commence communicating exactly as in the file descriptor example.

```
if((my_bio = BIO_new_connect("127.0.0.1:5353")) == NULL) {
    ERR_print_errors_fp(stderr);
    exit(-1);
}

if(BIO_do_connect(my_bio) <=0) {
    ERR_print_errors_fp(stderr);
    exit(-1);
}

SSL_set_bio(my_ssl,my_bio,my_bio);
```

This shows what minimal changes are necessary to move from a file descriptor and socket–based framework to one using the more cross-platform BIO layer handling.

Thread-safe Programming with OpenSSL

While we now have at our disposal a couple of different methods for setting up and using the OpenSSL library in a server or client process, it is important that we not dive right into the creation of a real-world example. First, we must examine the issues that arise when using OpenSSL in the real world, for instance, with threading.

The use of OpenSSL in a multithreaded program is possible—however, a set of callbacks must be initialized for OpenSSL to ensure thread safety. By using callbacks like this, the OpenSSL library remains cross-platform by not requiring a specific threading framework be used. Also, by using these callbacks, OpenSSL can manage its own internal thread safety and we will not have to worry about protecting calls into the library with our own thread-management code.

The required callbacks include a set each for static and dynamic thread allocation. The choice of which to use is highly dependent on the library itself and how it was compiled. It is recommended that callbacks for both methods be provided to produce code that is compatible with both older and newer versions of the OpenSSL library.

 TIP *A callback is a function defined in our program that is provided for use by a library. The library can then call our function to perform tasks that only we know how to do.*

Static Allocation

In providing callbacks for static allocation, we know that OpenSSL will use only a set number of threads for mutual exclusion. This being the case, we create a linear array of mutexes, and only two callback functions are necessary. The OpenSSL library tells us that it will use no more than `CRYPTO_num_locks()` mutexes, so we can initialize our mutex array with that many values.

```
pthread_mutex_t *mutex_buffer;
mutex_buffer = (pthread_mutex_t *) malloc(CRYPTO_num_locks() *
          sizeof(pthread_mutex_t));
for(i=0; i<CRYPTO_num_locks(); i++)
    pthread_mutex_init(&mutex_buffer[i],NULL);
```

We can then take a look at the two callback functions needed. These are defined as follows:

```
static unsigned long (callback)(void);
static void (callback)(int mode, int id, const char *file, int line);
```

The first of these returns an `unsigned long` number that should uniquely identify the calling thread from all other threads. The second is a callback for locking and unlocking the given thread. For us, implementing the first function is a simple matter of returning the result of a call to `pthread_self()`.

```
static unsigned long thread_id_function(void) {
    return ((unsigned long) pthread_self());
}
```

The second callback is a bit more involved, as it performs two actions. If the first argument, `mode`, logically ANDed with the OpenSSL-defined `CRYPTO_LOCK` evaluates as true, then we should lock the id[th] thread in our linear array. Otherwise, we should unlock the same thread. This behavior is easily captured with an if...else structure as follows:

```
static void locking_function(int mode, int id, const char *file, int line) {
    if(mode & CRYPTO_LOCK)
        pthread_mutex_lock(&mutex_buffer[id]);
    else
        pthread_mutex_unlock(&mutex_buffer[id]);
}
```

Note that we make no use of the third or fourth parameters to this function. These are provided by OpenSSL so that we can log from where the call to this callback takes place to better troubleshoot potential problems. As our implementation is relatively simple, we ignore these parameters.

All that remains now is to actually register the callbacks with the library. To register our functions, we use CRYPTO_set_id_callback() and CRYPTO_set_locking_callback(). Note that deregistering callbacks simply requires calling these functions again and providing a NULL parameter.

```
CRYPTO_set_id_callback(thread_id_function);
CRYPTO_set_locking_callback(locking_function);
```

Dynamic Allocation

Unlike when using static allocation, in dynamic allocation we are not provided with a maximum for the number of mutexes that may be used by the library. As a result, the library requires that we create a structure to hold a mutex, thereby providing the library a method for receiving, storing, and passing any given mutex. This structure is called CRYPTO_dynlock_value, and we define it as follows:

```
struct CRYPTO_dynlock_value {
    pthread_mutex_t mutex;
};
```

We now have to provide three callback functions for the library, one each for creation, destruction, and modification of any given mutex. In the same order, these are defined as follows:

```
static struct CRYPTO_dynlock_value * (callback) (const char *, int);
static void (callback) (struct CRYPTO_dynlock_value *, const char *, int);
static void (callback) (int, struct CRYPTO_dynlock_value *, const char *, int);
```

As with the static allocation callbacks, the const char * and last int parameters to these functions are the filename and line number of the calling functions in the OpenSSL library, thus we ignore them.

The first function we implement is responsible for creating and initializing a new mutex, and then returning that mutex in the form of a CRYPTO_dynlock_value structure. We first allocate memory for the structure, initialize the mutex it contains, and then return a pointer to the freshly allocated memory, thereby completing the implementation of our first callback:

```
static struct CRYPTO_dynlock_value *dyn_create_func(const char *file, int line)
{
    struct CRYPTO_dynlock_value *value;

    value = (struct CRYPTO_dynlock_value *) malloc(sizeof(struct
CRYPTO_dynlock_value));

    pthread_mutex_init(&value->mutex,NULL);
    return value;
}
```

Next, we implement the function responsible for destroying a mutex. In our case, this simply takes the form of calling pthread_mutex_destroy() on the mutex and releasing any allocated memory back to the heap:

```
static void dyn_destroy_func(struct CRYPTO_dynlock_value *l,
    const char *file, int line)
{
    pthread_mutex_destroy(&l->mutex);
    free(l);
}
```

The last function that we require is nearly identical to the locking function in our static allocation. The only difference is in how it references the mutex that should be (un)locked. Instead of using an offset into a linear array, we are given the CRYPTO_dynlock_value containing the mutex. We again check the mode for the CRYPTO_LOCK flag and take the appropriate action:

```
static void dyn_lock_func(int mode, struct CRYPTO_dynlock_value *l,
    const char *file, int line)
{
    if(mode & CRYPTO_LOCK)
        pthread_mutex_lock(&l->mutex);
```

```
    else
        pthread_mutex_unlock(&l->mutex);
}
```

Our last step is to register our callbacks with the library. Again, this involves a call per callback:

```
CRYPTO_set_dynlock_create_callback(dyn_create_func);
CRYPTO_set_dynlock_lock_callback(dyn_lock_func);
CRYPTO_set_dynlock_destroy_callback(dyn_destroy_func);
```

Removing these callbacks also requires recalling each with a NULL argument. By registering the callbacks for both the dynamic and static allocation methods, we can be assured that the OpenSSL library functions we use will operate in a thread-safe manner.

Compiling and Running the Example

All the client and server examples in this chapter have been compiled and tested with OpenSSL 0.9.7c and GCC 3.3.1-r5, although there is nothing that technically requires these versions over others. Compilation requires that the crypto and ssl libraries from the OpenSSL kit be linked in with

```
$ gcc -o server server.c -lcrypto -lssl
$ gcc -o client client.c -lcrypto -lssl
```

Running the server examples requires a PEM-style certificate. Details on generating such a certificate can be found in the earlier section "Creating Certificates." Running the examples requires that the certificate be in the same directory as the server executable. Execution should begin with the server:

```
$ ./server
```

to be followed by running the client (doing so in another terminal is recommended) with

```
$./client
```

An example using the thread-safety code discussed in the last section, as well as proper error-condition handling, is included as part of Chapter 13 when we bring everything together into a single real-world example.

Summary

Looking back, you can see that you now have at your disposal several methods of enhancing the security of your programs. In this chapter, we discussed the various methods of tunneling existing protocols over an encrypted connection and the role of PKI in encrypting communication. We put together server and client programs that used two different methods of secure communication provided through the OpenSSL library. Lastly, we discussed some caveats, such as thread safety.

Looking ahead, we move on in the next chapter to discuss methods of user authentication and data verification.

CHAPTER 11

Authentication and Data Signing

THE PREVIOUS CHAPTER SHOWED you some of the basics of secure communication and how to keep data secure while it is being transmitted and received. However, how do you verify the authenticity of a person on either side of the equation? Public Key Infrastructure handles this when you are talking about a server or client that anyone can use, but to restrict access to a resource, you need to also be able to verify that a person is who they say they are.

The solution to this problem has been around in one form or another since the Internet was first comprised of a few computers connected over local cable: authentication. This is also possible with PKI in that a person or entity will have two pieces of information. One piece will be semipublic, in that it is not passed around left and right, but it is well known and verifiable. The other piece is a token that only one person will know or have access to. In PKI, these are known as a *public key and private key pair*; in authentication terms, these are known as *username and password*.

The Old Scenario

The /etc/passwd method of user authentication is still the most prevalent and accepted method of checking a user's identity while logging into a Linux system locally. In this method, user information is stored in plain-text format using the file /etc/passwd. This information includes username, home directory, user ID, group ID, shell, and sometimes password (otherwise the password is in /etc/shadow). When a user logs in, the system encrypts the password he's attempted to use and compares it with the encrypted password on the system. If they match, the user is granted access. If they don't match, the user is provided with a set number of opportunities to fix any mistakes. Encryption of passwords is through a one-way hash function, and then on some systems, an MD5 sum is calculated to make comparisons even faster.

As networks have expanded, computer usage has changed, and it has become necessary to maintain a list of users and their tokens in a method accessible to multiple machines. Otherwise, users would have to keep track of usernames and passwords for every machine they used, which is difficult and, let's face it, more work than any user wants to do (or should be expected to do in a secure manner).

As a result, Sun Microsystems created Sun Yellow Pages (YP) and later renamed it as Network Information Services (NIS) for trademark reasons. An NIS server stores information known to all machines on the network, such as login names, passwords, home directories, etc. An NIS server can serve "maps" to clients. One of these maps can be an /etc/passwd-style file. When a user attempts to log onto a client machine, the client checks the username and password against the local /etc/passwd file and, transparently, against the NIS server's /etc/passwd map. This allows an administrator to concentrate her work on a single resource while allowing access to multiple machines.

The Present-Day Scenario

The growth of networks has continued and, as a result, businesses, schools, and organizations often have to manage several thousand accounts at a time. This increase in size, in addition to the call for integration with things like web pages, has called for some innovations in the storage of user accounts and data. Many administrators find themselves replicating data into multiple locations and formats to account for all the applications and uses of account data. Others have begun working on consolidated solutions.

Central directory storage has taken a few forms, the most prevalent being Lightweight Directory Access Protocol (LDAP). Servers such as OpenLDAP (http://www.openldap.org) that support this protocol are in use for companywide directories, e-mail services, class registries and, of course, as authentication sources. Being open source and easily available makes OpenLDAP a popular choice for adding LDAP functionality to applications. Applications written for the Web in PHP or Perl, or stand-alone applications in C/C++, can use LDAP to provide a sign-on or login service. This is popular for institutions wishing to provide integrated and easy-to-use account management features. It is through services like LDAP that an administrator can provide a website for account creation, password changing, and account and password deletion, and have changes reflected instantaneously across multiple systems.

The creation of new storage methods and services created a need to revamp the login process to account for new authentication methods. From this effort came Pluggable Authentication Modules (PAM). By writing the authentication process so that the back-end used a set of plug-ins that could be individually stacked and configured, the developers who created PAM provided a flexible manner for future generations of authentication management. It is now possible for developers to link against the PAM library and have an application that authenticates users in the same manner, transparently, that the operating system itself would use—whether this is using the /etc/passwd file, LDAP, NIS, or anything else. It is also possible to develop custom PAM modules that provide everything from custom login and logout functionality to strong password choice enforcement. PAM modules for LDAP, Oracle, MySQL, and others already exist and are actively maintained and developed.

The PAM Library

Using the PAM library to create an application that uses PAM for authentication is relatively straightforward. By making an application PAM-aware, it is possible to harness the power of PAM authentication, session management, and password handling. Using a combination of the SSL code from the previous chapter and the following PAM sample, it is possible to create a server that can authenticate clients using any means that PAM allows, including LDAP.

Most GNU/Linux distributions today include PAM by default. The configuration of PAM is fairly simple, as everything is typically maintained in a single file, /etc/pam.conf. While it is beyond the scope of this book to discuss the configuration of PAM, it is necessary to have PAM installed and working for the examples to compile and run correctly.

The Conversation Function

Using the PAM library in an application is a little different than some libraries, as not only will we make calls into the library, but also the library will call a function in our code. This function is called a *conversation function*. PAM uses this function as a method of communicating with our program. This facilitates the ability to provide information in the form of usernames, passwords, and so forth, without PAM having to know how to interact with the user directly. Figure 11-1 shows how our application interacts with PAM.

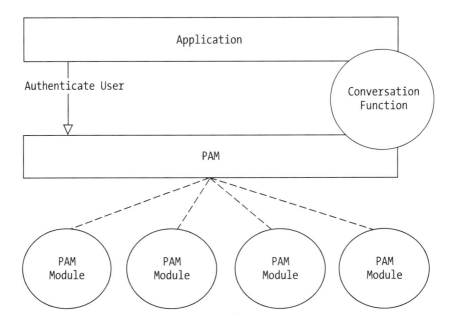

Figure 11-1. An application interacts with PAM through a callback conversation function.

To use the functionality provided by PAM, it is necessary to first include the PAM application header file `security/pam_appl.h`.

```
#include <security/pam_appl.h>
```

We can then move on to examining the conversation function definition:

```
int (callback)(int, const struct pam_message **, struct pam_response **, void *);
```

The first argument functions as a counter, indicating the number of entries in the `pam_message` array that is given as the second parameter.[1] The `pam_response` array will contain our 1:1 reply to each message in the second parameter. The last parameter is provided so that we can pass our own data through to the conversation function. This last parameter is often used to pass a username and password so that a visual prompt need not be made.

---

1. Documentation on all the messages and the PAM architecture in general is available at
    `http://www.kernel.org/pub/linux/libs/pam/Linux-PAM-html`.

As it is possible that we would want different conversations to be called, PAM provides a structure that we must use to give it the conversation functions. We first define our own conversation definition, and then we create a pam_conv structure to hold it:

```
int my_conv(int, const struct pam_message **, struct pam_response **, void *);
static struct pam_conv conv = {
    my_conv,
    NULL
};
```

We can now examine the implementation of my_conv. First, we make sure we have something to process. This involves two steps: checking to see that there is at least one message to handle and then allocating enough memory for our responses. If either of these steps should fail, we will return one of two errors: PAM_CONV_ERR to indicate there were no messages or PAM_SYSTEM_ERR if we do not have enough memory.

```
int my_conv(int num_msg,const struct pam_message **msg,
    struct pam_response *response, void *appdata_ptr) {
    struct pam_response *reply_with = NULL;
    int num_replies;
    char buffer[80];

    if (num_msg <= 0)
        return PAM_CONV_ERR;

    reply_with = (struct pam_response *)calloc(num_msg,
            sizeof(struct pam_response));

    if (reply_with == NULL)
        return PAM_SYSTEM_ERR;
```

If we get this far without any errors, then we can begin handling messages from PAM. We do this by looping over the passed messages using the passed number as a limit:

```
    for( num_replies = 0; num_replies < num_msg; num_replies++ ) {
```

Inside this loop, we need to determine which type of message we are dealing with. For this example, the only two types we are concerned with are PAM_PROMPT_ECHO_OFF and PAM_PROMPT_ECHO_ON. In the former case, we should prompt the user for a password, and in the latter case we are to prompt the user for her username. To maintain simplicity for this example, we will not actually turn the echo off. If the message type is not one of these two, we clean up the memory allocated and return an error indicating we don't know how to handle whatever PAM has given us with PAM_CONV_ERR. Note that the result of our actions is stored in the response array we allocated previously, ordered identically to that of the requests.

```
if( msg[num_replies]->msg_style == PAM_PROMPT_ECHO_OFF ) {
        reply_with[num_replies].resp_retcode = PAM_SUCCESS;
        printf("What is your password? ");
        scanf("%s",buffer);
        reply_with[num_replies].resp = (char *)strdup(buffer);
    } else if( msg[num_replies]->msg_style == PAM_PROMPT_ECHO_ON ) {
        reply_with[num_replies].resp_retcode = PAM_SUCCESS;
        printf("What is your username? ");
        scanf("%s",buffer);
        reply_with[num_replies].resp = (char *)strdup(buffer);
    } else {
        free(reply_with);
        return PAM_CONV_ERR;
    }
}
```

It is important to note that in this example we have not done any strong checking to be sure that buffer is not overrun or that the responses are within valid range, both of which could be used as attacks against an application. For a truly robust system, these exploits must be guarded against. The last thing we need to do in the conversation function is supply the responses we have formatted and return PAM_SUCCESS:

```
*response = reply_with;
return PAM_SUCCESS;
}
```

Creating a PAM-Aware Application

In this example application, we will use PAM to authenticate a username and password pair through whatever means the PAM "login" service dictates.

```
int main(int argc, char *argv[]) {
    pam_handle_t *pamh=NULL;
    int ret;
    int authenticated = 0;
```

Using the previous section's conversation function, our application has what
we need for PAM to communicate with us, but we have not yet done anything to
tell PAM that, or to perform the actions we want. Thus we begin our main function by calling

```
if( (ret = pam_start("login", NULL, &conv, &pamh)) == PAM_SUCCESS )
    if( (ret = pam_authenticate(pamh, 0)) == PAM_SUCCESS )
        if( (ret = pam_acct_mgmt(pamh, 0)) == PAM_SUCCESS )
            authenticated = 1;
```

The call to pam_start initializes the PAM library, having it read /etc/pam.conf
and set things up. The first argument is the name of the service we want to use
(this is any valid service from pam.conf), the second should be NULL, the third is
a pointer to the pam_conv structure that holds our conversation function, and the
last is a pam_handle_t structure, which we will need for future calls into the
library. As long as this call returns PAM_SUCCESS, we can continue.

We then call pam_authenticate, which does exactly what its name implies.
PAM first calls our conversation function to retrieve the username and password
of the user to authenticate, and then issues calls in each of the modules in the
stack according to the rules in /etc/pam.conf. If the username and password are
authenticated, pam_authenticate returns PAM_SUCCESS.

While we could stop at this point, knowing that the user has provided a username and password that are valid on this system, we call pam_acct_mgmt. This
gives PAM the opportunity to ensure that the authenticated account is not only
valid, but also allowed to access this system. Situations such as expired accounts
can result in successful authentication but a failure from pam_acct_mgmt. If this
also returns PAM_SUCCESS, then we know the user has provided a valid username
and password, and that the user is allowed access to this system. We then set our
authenticated flag to indicate that the user is valid and is allowed access to the
system. Using that flag, we can indicate our results to the user:

```
if(authenticated)
    printf("Authenticated\n");
else
    printf("Not Authenticated\n");
```

The last thing a PAM-aware application needs to do is end the PAM session
with a call to pam_end. We call pam_end and supply the PAM session handle and the
last known return status of PAM, exiting with the return value of pam_end:

```
if( pam_end(pamh,ret) != PAM_SUCCESS ) {
    pamh = NULL;
    printf("Failed to release pam...\n");
    exit(1);
```

```
    }

    if( ret == PAM_SUCCESS )
        return 0;
    else
        return 1;
}
```

Compiling and Running the Program

The sample PAM-aware application can be compiled using gcc with the following command:

```
$ gcc -o pamtest pamtest.c -lpam
```

The resulting binary, pamtest, must be run as root to work and have access to the appropriate modules in PAM. Upon execution, it should prompt for a username and password and state whether or not that account is authenticated (as dictated by the rules in /etc/pam.conf).

Public Key Authentication

Using the PAM library as shown in the previous section allows us to verify a user based on his username and password. However, it is sometimes necessary and desirable to access a resource without having to provide a password every time. In this case, it is possible to apply the same concepts of PKI that we used for data transmission authentication to the authentication of a person. For example, the OpenSSH utility allows a user to generate a public and private key, and upload the public key to the server. Once the key is uploaded, when the user connects to the server, SSH sees both keys and attempts to verify whether they match. If they do, then the user is authenticated. Although this can be seen as reducing security to the same level as that of the private key (unless the private key is itself encrypted), this is a common compromise between security and accessibility.

 TIP *By using the* ssh-agent *tool included with OpenSSH, it is possible to create encrypted private keys, yet only require the user to enter his password once in order to use them, thereby mitigating the security concerns of an unencrypted private key while allowing a mostly passwordless method of accessing resources.*

Using Signed Data for Authentication

One method used to verify that a public and private key match is to use a known piece of data. We first use the private key to sign a piece of known data. Once signed, the corresponding public key can be used to verify that signature mathematically (due to the tightly coupled relationship between the two). If the signature is verifiable, then the keys are a pair and the holder of the private key may be considered authenticated.

To look at this in further detail, we revisit the OpenSSL library, which provides PKI functions for key management, storage, and data signing. We will use RSA keys for the purpose of our examples; however, it should be noted that DSA and other formats are possible with similar, if not the same, library functions. In all cases, the general methodology is the same.

Creating and Destroying Keys

When working with RSA keys in the OpenSSL library, we need to ensure that we have included the necessary library header file, `openssl/rsa.h`.

We can then look at creating a key using the library function `RSA_generate_key()`. As defined in the library, this function looks like this:

```
RSA *RSA_generate_key(int num, unsigned long e,
    void (*callback)(int,int,void*),void *cb_arg);
```

The modulus used to create the key is passed as the first argument, and the public exponent used is the second argument. The third and fourth arguments are used should we want OpenSSL to call back into our code during the creation of a key (as it can be a time-consuming task) to report progress. The third argument specifies the callback, and the fourth gives us the chance to pass arbitrary data we may want during a callback. For our purposes, we will not use these arguments, so we pass NULL for each.

The result of a call to this function is an RSA structure containing the new RSA keys, both public and private. While we can access the individual members of this structure, it is better practice to treat this as a "black box" structure and instead use the key-handling functions provided by OpenSSL. We finish by creating a key with a 2048-bit modulus, using the well-known F4 public exponent:

```
RSA *new_key = RSA_generate_key(2048,RSA_F4,NULL,NULL);
```

Now that we have a key, it is important to verify that some inherent weaknesses do not exist and that the key stands up to some internal tests. This is easily done using the RSA_check_key() function, which returns 1 if the key passes and an error otherwise:

```
if(RSA_check_key(new_key) == 1)
  // Key is Good
else
  // Key failed
```

It is also important that we properly destroy this key when we are no longer using it. We will discuss storage of the key on disk in the next section, but we should not allow the key to remain in memory any longer than necessary. This prevents other processes running with the same or higher permission from discerning key values by examining our process's stack and heap. Destruction of a key involves a single call to

```
RSA_free(this_key);
```

Key Storage

Storing keys on disk involves changing the format that the key is in. Once again, the OpenSSL library comes to our rescue with several functions that do this for us. We use a common format called PEM (derived from its original intention, and standing for, Privacy Enhanced Mail). The PEM interface to OpenSSL is kept in the openssl/pem.h include. We will use one function each for writing private keys, reading private keys, writing public keys, and reading public keys. Following the OpenSSL standard, functions that return an integer value return 0 on error and nonzero otherwise.

Public Keys

As public keys require no extra security, all we have to do is provide OpenSSL with a file pointer with which to write the PEM data:

```
int PEM_write_RSA_PUBKEY(FILE *,RSA *);
```

While reading the same data back from disk, we simply provide the file to read from and call

```
RSA * PEM_read_RSA_PUBKEY(FILE *, RSA **, (void)(callback),void *);
```

As we don't need the password callback in the third argument, or the application data in the last argument, we specify NULL for both. We also have the option of providing NULL as the second argument and the function will create, populate, and return a new RSA structure for us, making our call look like this:

```
RSA *my_key = PEM_read_RSA_PUBKEY(my_file_p,NULL,NULL,NULL);
```

Private Keys

Private keys require a little more security than their public counterparts, as anyone or any process that can read the private key file can effectively impersonate the user who owns that key. This added security is applied in the form of a password that is required to both encrypt and decrypt the data as it is written to or read from disk. When using the OpenSSL private key functions, this password can be supplied as an argument to the function, with the use of a callback function, or it can be ignored completely to create an unencrypted key file.

When writing a private RSA key, we use the PEM_write_RSAPrivateKey() function:

```
int PEM_write_RSAPrivateKey(FILE *, RSA *, const EVP_CIPHER *,
    unsigned char *, int, (password callback), void *);
```

The first and second arguments are familiar, as they are identical to the public key function counterpart. The third argument allows us to choose a specific encryption format, and the fourth is a buffer where we could provide the password. The fifth argument is needed to specify the number of bytes in the previous argument's string, followed by the callback function parameter and the application data parameter. If we specify NULL for the type of encryption, the remaining arguments are ignored and the key is written unencrypted:

```
PEM_write_RSAPrivateKey(my_file_p,my_key,NULL,NULL,0,NULL,NULL);
```

Alternatively, if we wanted to use the Blowfish cipher to encrypt the data on disk, with the password "mypass," we would call

```
PEM_write_RSAPrivateKey(my_file_p,my_key,EVP_bf_ecb(),"mypass",7,NULL,NULL);
```

 TIP *A full list of* EVP_CIPHER *types is available in the* openssl/evp.h *file.*

If we wanted to use the callback function, we would define it as

```
int pass_callback_function(char *buffer, int length, int rwflag, void *args);
```

Our implementation of this would require that we place the password as provided by the user into `buffer`, ensuring not to overwrite its boundary (specified by `length`). The `rwflag` indicates whether we are reading or writing PEM data—0 for reading and nonzero for writing. Finally, we would have to return a 0 value on error and nonzero otherwise.

Reading a RSA private key from disk involves calling `PEM_read_RSAPrivateKey()`, defined as follows:

```
RSA * PEM_read_RSAPrivateKey(FILE *, RSA **, (callback), void *);
```

In similar fashion to the public key counterpart, this function can create and populate a new RSA key if the second argument is `NULL`. The third and fourth arguments again provide us with a chance to give either a callback and user data or a password to OpenSSL. If the callback parameter is `NULL`, then the fourth argument is assumed to be a `NULL`-terminated C-style string, which will be used as the password for decryption.

To read the first key we wrote, which we did without encryption, we can simply do this:

```
RSA *my_key = PEM_read_RSAPrivateKey(my_file_p,NULL,NULL,NULL);
```

We could make the same call to open our encrypted file as well, and OpenSSL would provide its own default password prompt. Or, we can provide the password we used as such:

```
RSA *my_key = PEM_read_RSAPrivateKey(my_file_p,NULL,NULL,"mypass");
```

 CAUTION   *It is important to note that when reading a private key from disk, a new RSA key structure is created; however, the public key members of that structure are invalid. We need to either provide this object when reading a public key to have those members initialized or avoid using functions that operate on its public key members.*

Transmitting Keys

The use of PKI would be severely limited without the ability to transmit keys between processes. Doing this over the network is possible in a couple of different ways. OpenSSL provides a method for doing so through a BIO (and therefore through a BIO stack), or we can encode and transmit the data ourselves. The former is probably the easiest, but it doesn't allow us to transmit the keys over a TLS/SSL connection we may have established with the methods we examined in the previous chapter, and while the latter involves some custom code, it allows for us to be more flexible.

Transmitting keys through a BIO stack involves using a set of functions that are nearly identical to those used for reading keys from and writing keys to disk:

```
RSA * PEM_read_bio_RSAPrivateKey(BIO *bp, RSA **x, pem_password_cb *cb, void *u);
int PEM_write_bio_RSAPrivateKey(BIO *bp, RSA *x, const EVP_CIPHER *enc, unsigned
                        char *kstr, int klen, pem_password_cb *cb, void *u);
RSA * PEM_read_bio_RSA_PUBKEY(BIO *bp, RSA **x, pem_password_cb *cb, void *u);
int PEM_write_bio_RSA_PUBKEY(BIO *bp, RSA *x);
```

Other than the addition of _bio_ to the name, and the first argument being a BIO structure, these functions are equivalent to their FILE * counterparts as described in the previous section.

Transmitting keys through a custom method allows us a bit more flexibility, but it requires that we do some handling of the key itself first. While we could conceivably use the members of the RSA structure and send each member individually, this creates a dependency on a single definition of the structure and may invalidate our code if future versions of OpenSSL do things differently. Instead, we need to encode the RSA structure for transmission. We could encode to the plain-text format PEM, which is how we stored the structure on disk previously. However, to save ourselves overhead, we can instead encode to a format called DER, which is a binary-level format. This allows us to send the minimum amount of data necessary.

TIP   *It is also possible to use DER coding when reading or writing keys to disk with the* _read_ *and* _write_ *functions, such as* DER_write_RSA_PUBKEY().

NOTE *We do not discuss transmitting a private key using custom methods. While it is possible to do so with a similar algorithm, the concept of PKI cryptography relies on the safety and security of the private key, which should, in a perfect world, never be broadcast or transmitted by any means.*

We encode an RSA public key using the i2d_RSAPublicKey() function:

```
int i2d_RSAPublicKey(RSA *, char **);
```

The first argument is the key we want to encode, followed by the buffer we want to encode into. To provide a buffer of sufficient size, we first need to know how large the encoded key will be. Providing a NULL buffer causes this function to return that size in bytes:

```
int buffer_size = i2d_RSAPublicKey(my_key,NULL);
char *buffer = malloc(buffer_size);
```

Now that we have a buffer of sufficient size, we encode with a second call, providing the buffer to write the result into:

```
i2d_RSAPublicKey(my_key,&buffer);
```

We can now transmit our buffer however we would like, according to our own protocol. It is important that we provide both the buffer and the buffer's size to whatever process is responsible for decoding, however, as the reverse process requires both as arguments. To decode a DER-encoded buffer, we use d2i_RSAPublicKey():

```
RSA * d2i_RSAPublicKey(RSA **, char **, int);
```

We have the option of providing an existing RSA key structure (perhaps one we already had the private key in) as the first argument or specifying NULL and having the function return a new structure. The second argument is a pointer to the buffer containing the DER-encoded key, and the last argument is the size of that buffer in bytes. We can now decode our RSA key with

```
RSA *decoded_key = d2i_RSAPublicKey(NULL,&buffer,buffer_size);
```

Signing Data

With the ability to create and manage keys, we can now examine the use of keys for authentication purposes. The first step is to agree upon some piece of known data. Often this is something as simple as the user's login name or perhaps a constant string of text. For our example, we will use a null-terminated ASCII string: `"Known Data"`.

 CAUTION   *Using known data for signature verification is sufficient when we are already communicating over an encrypted and secure link. However, if we were to perform the same verification over a plain-text link, or if we did not trust the link we have created, then it is more advisable that the server provide a random value that the client must then encrypt with the private key for verification. This prevents an attacker from replaying the encrypted form of our known data after watching a single session.*

To sign and verify data with our key, we use the EVP interface provided by OpenSSL and defined in `openssl/evp.h`. This interface is an abstraction of the details involved in signature handling for any type of key structure. Use of this interface is predicated on two structures: EVP_MD_CTX and EVP_PKEY.

The first of these structures is similar in function to the SSL_CTX structure we used it handling the context of an SSL connection. We use the EVP_MD_CTX structure to describe the context of a generic operation on a key using the EVP family of functions. The second structure, EVP_PKEY, is an abstraction of a PKI key. Rather than having to use a different set of functions for each family of key structures (RSA, DSA, etc.), we instead use this structure to provide our key in its current form to the EVP_ family of functions.

We create a new EVP_PKEY with the EVP_PKEY_new() function:

```
EVP_PKEY *pkey = EVP_PKEY_new();
```

We then associate our RSA key with the EVP_PKEY with this function:

```
int EVP_PKEY_set1_RSA(EVP_PKEY *,RSA *);
```

The first argument is the EVP_PKEY structure to be associated with the key provided in the second argument. Assuming we had already created an RSA key structure called `my_rsa_key`, we call this function to associate the two:

```
EVP_PKEY_set1_RSA(pkey,my_rsa_key);
```

CAUTION *As with most other OpenSSL library functions, the EVP_PKEY_set1_RSA() function returns an integer value. This value is 0 if an error has occurred and is nonzero otherwise. For the sake of clarity in our examples, we do not check these return values. However, it is vital to the security of your software that you do so in real-world code. Demonstration of handling errors raised by these and other functions in the OpenSSL library is included in Chapter 13.*

Unlike the EVP_PKEY structure, our EVP_MD_CTX does not require its own initialization. Instead, this is taken care of when we call the Init function for the operation we want to perform. In our case, this is the function:

```
int EVP_SignInit(EVP_MD_CTX *, const EVP_MD *);
```

The first argument we supply is our EVP_MD_CTX which, after a successful call, will be initialized. The second argument defines what method of hashing we want to use. The processes of signing and verification are actually performed on a hash of the original. Our example uses the EVP_md5() hash. Also available are EVP_md2(), EVP_md4(), EVP_sha(), EVP_sha1(), EVP_dss(), and many others. So we begin the process of data signing by calling

```
EVP_MD_CTX my_evp;
EVP_SignInit(&my_evp, EVP_md5());
```

Now we can begin passing in data that is to be signed. We use the function

```
int EVP_DigestUpdate(EVP_MD_CTX *, const void *, int);
```

The first argument is the context we initialized with EVP_SignInit(), followed by a buffer containing the data to sign. The last argument tells the function how many bytes are in the data buffer we provide. We could call this function as many times as necessary to provide all the data (should it be from multiple sources, formats, or buffers) for signing. In our case, a single call with the constant string "Known Data" will suffice:

```
EVP_SignUpdate(&my_evp,"Known Data",10);
```

We need to create a buffer to place the signed data in. The size of this buffer is different depending on the type of key in use, and in our case it is guaranteed to be no larger than RSA_size(RSA *) bytes, so we create a buffer with a call to malloc():

```
unsigned char *signed_buffer = (unsigned char *) malloc(RSA_size(my_rsa_key));
```

We can now call the function:

```
int EVP_SignFinal(EVP_MD_CTX *, unsigned char *, unsigned int *, EVP_PKEY *);
```

Again, the first argument is the context we started with. The second argument is where we provide our buffer for the results of the signing. The third argument gives the function the size of the buffer when it is called, and upon return this will hold the actual number of bytes written to the buffer. The final argument is the EVP_PKEY structure that contains the key we want to sign the data with. We finish out the process by signing our data, reporting the number of bytes in the signed data, and freeing the EVP_PKEY structure we created with EVP_PKEY_new() earlier:

```
unsigned int signed_length;
signed_length = RSA_size();
EVP_SignFinal(&my_evp,signed_buffer,&signed_length,pkey);
printf("There are %d bytes in the signed data",signed_length);
EVP_PKEY_free(pkey);
```

Verifying Signed Data

The verification process for signed data is very similar to that of signing. Again, we use the EVP_ interface provided by OpenSSL, and again we need a context and an EVP_PKEY abstraction layer. Given the signed buffer and its size in signed_buffer and signed_length, respectively, the only difference in process is in which EVP_ functions we use. We start with

```
int EVP_VerifyInit(EVP_MD_CTX *, EVP_MD *);
```

which is identical in structure to its EVP_SignInit() counterpart, although it sets up the EVP interface to do the reverse of the signing process to verify a signature. Once initialized, we provide the signed data to

```
int EVP_VerifyUpdate(EVP_MD_CTX *, const unsigned char *, unsigned int);
```

This function also takes the same type of arguments as its EVP_SignUpdate() counterpart and updates the internal buffer of the EVP interface for later verification. As with its counterpart, we could call this function as many times as necessary to provide all the signed data we may have created. And finally, we call

```
int EVP_VerifyFinal(EVP_MD_CTX *, const unsigned char *, unsigned int, EVP_PKEY *);
```

This function takes our context, unsigned (known) data and length, and the key to use for verification. The return value of this function indicates whether the signature is successfully verified or not. Unlike other OpenSSL functions, a return value of 1 indicates success, while anything else indicates an error.

Putting this all together, we use the following code:

```
EVP_VerifyInit(&my_evp,EVP_md5());
EVP_VerifyUpdate(&my_evp,u_signed,u_length);
if(EVP_VerifyFinal (&my_evp,signd,s_length,pkey))
    // Signature verified, user authenticated
else
    // Signature failed
```

And we now have a method at our disposal that can be used independent of passwords for positive identification of a user. We will use this method in Chapter 13 when we examine a real-world example in detail.

With our examination of authentication methods and styles in this chapter, it is important to understand why centralization is an underlying theme in each. While it would be easy for an application to design and maintain its own user base, it seems that administrators are always seeking to centralize this information in an effort to achieve single sign-on.

Single Sign-on

The concept of *single sign-on* is to permit network users to use a single username and password (or similar authentication tokens) to access different machines and resources available on the network. While single sign-on across multiple protocols became possible with the development of PAM and services like LDAP, they were only feasible within the *nix platform. Institutions that maintained systems running the Microsoft Windows operating system in addition to various *nix platforms had to maintain two sets of usernames and passwords. As heterogeneous setups, or environments where multiple operating systems and platforms are being used, have become more common, the GNU/Linux and open source software (OSS) community has come onto the scene with software that provides true single sign-on capabilities. We describe some of these in this section.

The Samba project (http://www.samba.org), which began as an implementation of the Common Internet File System (CIFS) protocol for file sharing with the Microsoft Windows operating system, has expanded to include code allowing it to appear as a Windows Domain Server to a Windows network. This allows Linux machines to be integrated into a Windows Domain or Active Directory structure, as well as allowing Windows machines to be integrated into a Linux framework.

The pGina project (`http://pgina.xpasystems.com`) provides an alternative to Samba by replacing the login portion of the Microsoft Windows NT/2000/XP operating system. The replacement login code makes use of a framework similar in intention to PAM in that it uses plug-ins to provide limitless authentication possibilities. Also like PAM, the framework for creating plug-ins for pGina is open source and freely available. Currently, the most prevalent use of pGina, using an LDAP plug-in, is to authenticate a machine running Microsoft Windows against a non-Microsoft LDAP server. Plug-ins have also been created for PAM, NIS, POP, RSA SecurID, and Slashdot, and the list appears to be growing.

AcctSync (`http://acctsync.sourceforge.net`) is a little different, as it doesn't perform authentication itself, but it does attempt to automatically synchronize account information between an LDAP server and a local Microsoft Windows account registry. As stated by the group's website,

> *The LDAP Account Sync Project's goal is create a user and group account system synchronized between Windows and UNIX Systems. This is not authorization, but rather synchronization of the account information and passwords.*

Summary

Our examination in this chapter has taken us through past, current, and future methods of user authentication; coverage of the uses of the PAM library; and an in-depth look at PKI key management code. We looked at creating an application that can use PAM to do user authentication for us, and we covered creating code that would let us verify a user's authenticity through RSA keys.

In the next chapter, we will break from our examination of third-party libraries and authentication, and instead take a look at practices and methodologies for safe programming used to help avoid insecure code.

CHAPTER 12

Common Security Problems

LET'S TAKE A STEP BACK for a moment and move away from our discussion and analysis of things at the API level. Instead, let's look at our programming practices, how to include security as a priority, and what choices are available to us.

It's important to remember that programming is very much an expressive art, allowing the same functionality or goal to be achieved through many different methods and means. While there's no single method that's definitively considered secure, there are a series of guidelines we can follow to ensure we've taken all possible precautions. Before examining those guidelines, let's examine the common attacks we're protecting against.

Common Attacks

Attacks on a system or program are often separated into different categories:

- Information retrieval

- Network mapping

- Denial of service

- Exploitation

The first two are often attacks against a system at the operating system and TCP/IP stack level. The goal of these attacks is to use information gathered during the attack to determine potentially sensitive information for future attacks in the denial of service or exploitation category. This includes the type of operating system running, the existence of network services which are attached to open ports and their versions, the existence of trust level networks or other machines which may be potential targets and so on.

The *denial of service* attack, often referred to as DoS or DDoS (for *distributed denial of service*), is intended to flood the victim with a large number of requests, packets, connections, and so on, in such a manner as to prevent proper access to the system. Under certain situations, DoS attacks expose security flaws that arise through the mismanagement of high volumes of activity. While this type of attack is also usually at the operating system and TCP/IP stack level, it can also take the form of persistent connections, malformed client messages, and other things that network servers must handle properly to prevent the attack from succeeding.

The last category of attacks is the most dangerous. As its name infers, an *exploitation* attack attempts to exploit a mistake in a network server's code and gain control over the program or system. Gaining control of a program in this manner is typically done through a method called a *buffer overflow*. A buffer overflow is the most prevalent exploitation attack.

Buffer Overflow

The prevalence of the buffer overflow is in direct correlation to the prevalence of its cause: bounds checking errors. When a program fails to adequately check the boundaries for array operations, such as string copying, expansion, etc., it is possible that data will be written beyond the end of the array and into the programs stack, where through some creativity it could be executed.

When a C program calls a function, the arguments as well as the address to return execution to when the function returns are all pushed onto the stack. If that return address is overwritten with a new address during execution, the program will dutifully return from the function right into execution of the data that was written to the stack by an attacker. While this doesn't seem it would be very simple (and it isn't), careful examination of a server's code, combined with the execution environment properties, makes this kind of attack very much possible and extremely effective.

Secure Coding Practices

Thankfully, there are some steps we can take to mitigate the risk of these attacks being successful against our server code. In this section, we will show that some of these steps are direct responses to attack scenarios (such as protocol design), while others are simply guidelines that prevent us from falling into a situation where mistakes can happen.

Functions to Avoid and Their Alternatives

The first and best method for ensuring you do not fall into the buffer overflow trap is proper bounds checking. This seems at first to be relatively simple, until you consider the number of library functions you use throughout your code without considering their behavior in out-of-bounds conditions. The most common area for these functions to show up is in string handling, including functions such as gets(), sprintf(), vsprintf(), strcpy(), and so on.

None of these functions has an argument to specify the size of the buffer they are operating on. As such, consider the following code:

```
char buffer[10];
strcpy(buffer,"This is much longer than 10 bytes");
```

Although buffer is only 10 bytes in size, the strcpy() function will continue to write data into buffer[11], buffer[12], and so on. While this example may only cause our code to crash when run, it is not all that different from the method many network servers use to copy strings sent by a client into a buffer. This opens the door for the client to overflow the buffer, overwrite the stack, and gain control of the server.

The solution to this is to use the strncpy() function instead. The function, defined as

```
char *strncpy(char *dest, const char *src, size_t n);
```

allows us to specify the maximum size in bytes that should be copied. If the maximum is reached before a NULL character is found in the src string, then copying stops and the call returns.

NOTE   *When using* strncpy(), *if a* NULL *character is not encountered, the destination buffer may not be null terminated, which can cause problems if you use other string functions later. You should always leave an extra byte at the end of the buffer to be set to* NULL *to prevent these problems from arising.*

Other string handling functions also have alternatives that let you specify a boundary condition in bytes. Table 12-1 shows some of the common functions and their safer alternatives.

Table 12-1. Unsafe Functions and Their Safe Alternatives

UNSAFE FUNCTION	SAFE FUNCTION
sprintf()	snprintf()
strcpy()	strncpy()
strcmp()	strncmp()
strcasecmp()	strncasecmp()
scanf()	fscanf()

When an alternative function doesn't exist already, it's worth considering creating your own. For instance, if a safe version of strcpy() didn't exist, creation of our own wouldn't be overly complicated:

```
size_t our_strncpy(char *dest, const char *src, size_t bytes) {
    size_t x = 0;
    if(!dest || !src) return 0;
    for(x=0;x<bytes;x++) {
        dest[x] = src[x];
        if(src[x] == '\0')
            return x;
    }
    return x;
}
```

This simple function copies data one byte at a time from the source buffer to the destination, returning the total number of bytes copied when finished. The for loop inside this function is limited by the byte parameter, which ensures that we do not go beyond the end of the destination buffer.

 TIP *Using our custom* strcpy() *function still poses a risk if the source buffer is not null-terminated and is smaller than the destination. In this case, we will read beyond the limits of the source buffer. While this may result in abnormal termination or other problems, it is not likely to result in a security exploit. We could add a fourth parameter that limits the length of the source buffer to prevent this or simply ensure that all strings provided are null-terminated.*

Another common function used by developers is the strcmp() function used for string comparison. While safer versions that limit length like strncmp() exist, the return of these functions is actually one of three cases. When the strings are identical, the function will return 0, but if there is a difference, the function will return either –1 or 1 depending on which string's ASCII value is higher. It is easy to make the mistake of writing a string comparison function like this:

```
if(!strcmp(password_buffer,"mypassword")) { // password is correct }
```

This will work when the strings are equivalent. However, if the strcmp() function was to return a –1 this would still evaluate to true. As a result, a properly crafted (or guessed) invalid password may work as if it was the correct password.

To avoid this, we can implement our own bounds-safe function, which returns true (1) if the strings are equal and false (0) if they are not:

```
int is_strequal(const char *a, int a_len, const char *b, int b_len,int limit) {
    int x=0;
    if(limit) {
        if(limit > a_len || limit > b_len)
            return 0;
    } else {
        if(a_len != b_len)
            return 0;
    }
    if(limit) {
        for(x=0;x<a_len && x<b_len && x<limit;x++)
            if(a[x] != b[x]) return 0;
    } else {
        for(x=0;x<a_len && x<b_len;x++)
            if(a[x] != b[x]) return 0;
    }
    return 1;
}
```

We accept five arguments into our function, only the last of which is optional. The first four arguments provide the strings we are comparing and each string's buffer length. The last argument allows us to limit the comparison to a subset of characters. If the limit value is 0, then our function will compare the entire strings as well as their length (we make the assumption that if we are comparing full strings and the lengths are different, then they are not equal). We could now replace our strcmp() call with this:

```
if(is_strequal(password_buffer,strlen(password_buffer),
    "mypassword",10,0))) { // password is correct }
```

As these examples have shown, it is not overly difficult to implement safe replacements for commonly used functions. Should the safety of a library function ever be in question, we should always consider whether implementing the same functionality (or at least the portion we need) is worth the added effort and support. For instance, the memcpy() function has no "safe" alternative, which means that our only option is to ensure its proper use, perhaps via a wrapper, or to implement our own function.

The danger with memcpy() is mostly in proper use of the third parameter, which indicates the number of bytes to copy from the source buffer into the destination. So long as we always use a value that is less than or equal to the size of our destination buffer, we are safe. For instance, a safe use of the function is as follows:

```
char dest_buff[1024];
char source_buff[2048];
memcpy(dest_buff,source_buff,1024);
```

This will copy the first 1024 bytes from source_buff into dest_buff. However, a potentially unsafe usage is

```
memcpy(dest_buff,source_buff,strlen(source_buff));
```

This is intended to copy the entire string in source_buff, but if that string is larger than 1024 bytes, we have just overflowed our destination buffer and provided a potential means for exploitation. In this case, it is probably better to ensure the proper use of the function throughout the code, or to wrap the function. Implementing our own function would not be too difficult, but the memcpy() function in the library is written at a low enough level that we may be sacrificing some significant performance improvements should we choose not to use it.

Error Handling

Another place we can modify our coding practice to proactively prevent security problems is in error handling. Almost all socket and glibc library functions provide some method for determining whether they succeeded or not—usually through a return value. Additionally, we have full control over our internal function design, so we can make sure we design our functions so that they can do the same.

The rule with error handling is simple: always do it. We need to check every return value, parameter, and result to ensure that calls to library functions are succeeding, that our data is conformant to our protocol, and that we are always working with the expected type of data. The best method to make error handling easier is to use wrapper functions.

For each library function that we call, we will actually call our own wrapper function, in which we can handle all the dirty work of verifying things. This way, our main code remains readable, while ensuring that any errors are caught right away and not left to wreak havoc later in our program.

For example, first we define a function for reporting an error condition to the user. We call this function report_error() and define it as follows:

```
void report_error(const char *msg, const char *file, int line_no,
    int use_perror, int exit);
```

We will display the message provided in msg, along with the file and line number the error occurs on, which are given in the file and line_no arguments. If the use_perror flag is set, then we will use the standard library function perror(const char *) to display the error; otherwise, we will output just the text provided. Lastly, if the exit flag is set, then we exit the program instead of returning. Our implementation then looks like this:

```
void report_error(const char *msg, const char *file,
  int line_no, int use_perror, int exit) {
     if(!use_perror) {
         fprintf(stderr,"[%s:%d] %s\n",file,line_no,msg);
     } else {
         fprintf(stderr,"[%s:%d] ",file,line_no);
         perror(msg);
     }
     if(exit) {
         exit(-1);
     }
}
```

TIP   *If we were using a multithreaded program, we might consider using the* pthread_exit() *call instead of the system call* exit() *in our* report_error() *function. This would allow us to quit the active thread instead of causing the entire program to exit.*

Now that we can tell the user what has happened, let's look at wrapping some library functions to use this. For instance, let's wrap the socket() function with our own wrapper called w_socket(). Our function takes the same arguments that the library function takes making its definition:

```
int w_socket(int domain, int type, int protocol);
```

Then, when implementing this function, we check the result of the call to the library function socket(). If the return value is −1, then an error has occurred and the error is stored in the errno standard used by perror(). If an error occurs, then we call our error notification function report_error() and have it exit. If no error occurs, then we pass the return from the library function back, and our program can continue. In this way, our program can simply call w_socket() and expect that any error conditions are handled safely.

```
int w_socket(int domain, int type, int protocol) {
    int socket_return;
    socket_return = socket(domain,type,protocol);
    if(socket_return == -1)
        report_error("socket error:",__FILE__,__LINE__,1,1);
    else
        return socket_return;
}
```

By writing wrappers like this for each of our library calls, we can better manage erroneous situations without obfuscating our code beyond a readable state.

NOTE *We can extend this concept further by using macros. For the sake of simplicity, our examples do not do this; however, we could rename our* w_socket *function to* w_socket_func, *add parameters for the* __FILE__ *and* __LINE__ *arguments, and use this:*

```
#define w_socket(domain,type,protocol)
(w_socket_func((domain),(type),(protocol),__FILE__,__LINE__))
```

This would result in the actual line of code that called w_socket() *being used for the* report_error() *call, rather than always being the same.*

Memory Management

Another area that can benefit greatly from custom wrapper functions is memory management. Many programmers do not check the return value from function calls like malloc(), nor do they track the amount of memory that is currently in use. While we could go as far as to implement our own garbage collection, our major concern is avoiding error conditions, so we concentrate on doing so with special wrappers.

Our main goal is to check the return from all memory allocation attempts. Our secondary goal is to monitor the amount of memory being used to simplify identifying memory leak conditions.

The first wrapper we write is to allocate memory. Although we use the two-argument calloc() internally for its ability to zero memory, we require only a single argument indicating the amount of memory needed in bytes. If allocation succeeds, we return a pointer to the memory allocated, and we increment a

global counter of memory in use. If allocation fails, we use the report_error()
function we wrote in the last section to tell the user what has happened and exit
our process.

```
void * w_malloc(size_t bytes) {
    void *memory = NULL;
    memory = calloc(bytes,1);
    if(memory) {
        global_memory_counter += bytes;
        return memory;
    } else {
        report_error("Memory allocation error, out of memory.",
            __FILE__,__LINE__,0,1);
    }
}
```

This wrapper function helps us to ensure that we won't be operating on
invalid or nonallocated pointers, allowing us to allocate memory throughout our
program without having to worry about further error checking. However, where
this wrapper falls short is when we go to free the allocated memory. As the man
page for the free() library call states, a call to free() on memory not allocated
with malloc() or calloc(), or on memory previously free()'d, results in "undefined behavior."

To avoid this situation, which can also be the cause of security vulnerabilities
if not only stability problems, we extend our wrapper to include the maintenance
of a list of addresses that have been allocated. This way, when we go to free the
memory, we can first verify that it was actually allocated by us and has not
already been freed.

To accomplish this maintenance, we add a simple linked list based on a
structure memory_list defined as follows:

```
typedef struct memory_list {
void *address;
size_t size;
memory_list *next;
memory_list *prev;
} memory_list;
```

As we allocate memory, we create a new memory_list item, and then add it
to the list of allocated items using its built-in next pointer. We maintain the
start of the list in a global pointer memory_list_head, which is NULL when there are

no items in the list. Our allocation wrapper with the added list management looks like this:

```
void * w_malloc(size_t bytes) {
    void *memory = NULL;
    memory_list *new_item = NULL;
    memory = calloc(bytes,1);
    new_item = calloc(1,sizeof(struct memory_list));
    if(memory) {
        if(new_item == NULL) {
            report_error_q("Memory allocation error, no room for memory list item."
            ,__FILE__,__LINE__,0);
        }
        global_memory_counter += bytes + sizeof(struct memory_list);
        new_item->address = memory;
        new_item->size = bytes;
        new_item->next = NULL;
        new_item->prev = NULL;
        if(memory_list_head) {
            new_item->next = memory_list_head;
            memory_list_head->prev = new_item;
            memory_list_head = new_item;
        } else {
            memory_list_head = new_item;
        }
        return memory;
    } else {
        report_error_q("Memory allocation error, out of memory.",
    __FILE__,__LINE__,0);
        return NULL;
    }
}
```

This version of our wrapper is significantly more complex, and actually consumes more memory than we need allocated for the normal operation of our program. However, we gain the simplicity of not needing any additional code to check for error conditions or zero memory, or deal with double frees.

We can now move on to our wrapper for the free() function. The only error condition possible here is that we are given an invalid address to free. An invalid address is an address that does not exist in our linked list of memory addresses, or a NULL address. We first ensure that the address is valid, and then we can free the memory used by that address and remove its entry from our list while updating our global count of allocated memory. Our implementation takes the following form:

```
void w_free(void *f_address) {
    memory_list *temp = NULL,*found = NULL;
    if(f_address == NULL)
        return;

    for(temp=memory_list_head;temp!=NULL;temp = temp->next) {
        if(temp->address == f_address) {
            found = temp;
            break;
        }
    }

    if(!found) {
        report_error_q("Unable to free memory not previously allocated",
        __FILE__,__LINE__,0);   // Report this as an error
    }

    global_memory_count -= found->size + sizeof(struct memory_list);

    free(f_address);

    if(found->prev)
        found->prev->next = found->next;
    if(found->next)
        found->next->prev = found->prev;
    if(found == memory_list_head)
        memory_list_head = found->next;

    free(found);
}
```

TIP *Both of our wrapper functions operate on a global list. If our code was multithreaded, it would be important to ensure exclusive access to the list when adding or removing items using some sort of mutex (such as* pthread_mutex*).*

Worst-Case Scenarios

Other than being careful to avoid buffer mishaps, and wrapping functions to provide full error and return type checking, there are only a few things we can do in our code to bolster security. However, we can take a few steps to ensure that even a successful attack will not result in a compromise of an entire system (although it may mean a compromise in our ability to provide the service our program is for).

Changing Permissions

The first step we can take is to change who we are running as. If the only reason our program needs to be run as root is to open privileged ports, or perform some initialization, then after the ports are open or the initialization is complete we no longer need to be operating as root. We can use the system calls setuid() and setgid() to change the user ID and group ID we are running as, allowing us to shed root privileges. This way, should our program be compromised and execute arbitrary code, the operating system itself will prevent our process from doing anything overly nasty. This topic is discussed in finer detail in Chapter 7.

These functions are defined as

```
int setuid(uid_t uid);
int setgid(gid_t gid);
```

Each returns 0 when successful and –1 when not, and each accepts a single argument that indicates the desired uid or gid number to change to. This lends itself well to using our report_error() function to let the user know if something has gone wrong.

CAUTION   *We do not use the* seteuid() *or* setegid() *functions, as each of these allows for returning to the previous privilege level, which does not provide much in the way of security should an attacker manage to exploit our code.*

Changing Root

Another way that we can prevent damage from an exploit is by changing root. Also called chroot (as the function name chroot() would imply), this action results in the root path / being redefined. For instance, if we wanted all disk I/O to take place in the /etc/myprogram/ directory and its subdirectories, we could chroot() to /etc/myprogram/. From that point forward, all paths would be resolved with /etc/myprogram/ acting as /. So the path /etc/passwd would actually be /etc/myprogram/etc/passwd. This topic is discussed in finer detail in Chapter 7.

The system function chroot() is defined as

```
int chroot(const char *path);
```

and is available on most Linux systems. The function takes the path to chroot() to as an argument, and returns 0 on success and –1 on error. This function also conforms to the errno standard, and we could use report_error() to output any error information.

 CAUTION   *The process calling* chroot() *should always use the* chdir() *function to change to the new root first. Otherwise, the process can escape the* chroot() *by using relative paths to* "**.**".

Using chroot(), we avoid what is known as a *directory transversal* attack, whereby the attacker uses a flaw in the logic of the program or otherwise provides a path intended to result in an exploit or information retrieval. For instance, if our program was responsible for file transfers, and we were told to read the file /etc/passwd, we could code against this by not allowing paths that start with "/". But what about the path "./../etc/passwd"? If our program was run in a commonly known location, parsing all possible paths safely could be difficult. By running in a chroot() jail, we prevent the ability to access anything above the base directory we specify.

Shared Memory and Variable Scope

A major security concern comes into play when we first consider the design of our server. We have many options, as discussed earlier in our text, but we always have to decide which of the three methods of processing we will use: single process, forking, or multithreading. While the first method poses little more risk than we have already discussed, the latter two introduce another level of concern.

Anytime we decide to delegate processing to multiple tasks, whether they be forked or threaded, we must also consider what, if any, communication or data needs to be shared between them. For instance, do we need to collect statistics in our child processes or threads? Do we need information that only sibling processes or threads will have? Do we need to modify our parent process or master thread's state at all?

If the answer to any of these questions is yes, then we need to deal with some method of sharing data between processes and threads. While it is beyond the scope of this humble text to describe all the available methods, we should examine a very important aspect of a shared data situation.

Consider a forking process that uses a shared memory segment. A *shared memory segment* is a single address in memory shared by more than one process, usually created with a system call similar to shmget(). Now, if we intended the use of this shared data segment as a method of updating some common statistical information—say, the number of connections we had serviced—then we can look at some pseudo-code to see where a race condition may exist:

```
child process 1 reads shared memory to get current tally
child process 2 reads shared memory to get current tally
child process 2 increments tally and writes it to shared memory
child process 1 increments tally and writes it to shared memory
```

In the end, despite having serviced two connections, our tally is incremented by only one. Expand this type of problem into one where the shared memory is used for something like process management, authentication, or string handling in general, and you can see that we have once again opened the door for a potential buffer overflow, if not DDoS, attack. The same problem and potential race condition exists with data shared globally between threads.

To avoid these problems, it is best to first consider carefully each use of shared memory, including variables at the global scope. While this may often be the most convenient method of handling some things, if it puts us in a dangerous situation that we could avoid simply by changing our design to use things at a more localized scope, then we must consider that more work may be in order. If we cannot avoid the complications of shared memory by design, then we must consider alternative solutions. The most popular solutions are semaphores for forking and mutexes for threading.

Both semaphores and mutexes embody a concept called *mutual exclusion*. In other words, each can be consider an atomic (uninterruptible) operation that can be used to ensure that all other processes or threads are excluded from entering a critical section of code until there is no other process or thread in that section. In both cases, a process or thread makes a function call that blocks if there is another process or thread in the critical section and returns when access to the critical section is safe.

The mutex method most commonly available is in the pthread threading library. From this library, included via pthread.h, we can access a set of functions and data types meant for mutex handling:

```
int pthread_mutex_init(pthread_mutex_t *,const pthread_mutex_attr_t *);
int pthread_mutex_lock(pthread_mutex_t *);
```

```
int pthread_mutex_trylock(pthread_mutex_t *);
int pthread_mutex_unlock(pthread_mutex_t *);
int pthread_mutex_destroy(pthread_mutex_t *);
```

Each function returns 0 on success and a nonzero error code on error. The only exception to this is the pthread_mutex_init() function, which always returns 0. All the functions accept a common data type, pthread_mutex_t, which represents the mutex that we want to operate on. We first create a default mutex and initialize it with pthread_mutex_init():

```
pthread_mutex_t my_mutex;
pthread_mutex_init(&my_mutex,NULL);
```

Although there are several types of mutexes available to us, the default type is more than sufficient, so we pass a NULL as the second argument to pthread_mutex_init(). For more information on the different available attributes and their effect, see the man page for pthread_mutex_init(). Now that we have initialized the mutex, we can use it to implement critical sections of code. To take our pseudo-code from earlier as an example, it would translate to something like this in each process:

```
pthread_mutex_lock(&my_mutex);
shared_tally++;
pthread_mutex_unlock(&my_mutex);
```

When we call the pthread_mutex_lock(), it will try to lock the mutex. If the mutex is already locked, then it will block until it can unlock the mutex. This way, only one thread at a time is allowed to execute the increment statement at a time, thereby ensuring that the shared data is correctly managed. Once we are done in the critical section, we unlock the mutex with pthread_mutex_unlock(), allowing other threads to gain access. Once we are done with the mutex, or as our program is exiting, we destroy the mutex with pthread_mutex_destroy():

```
pthread_mutex_destroy(&my_mutex);
```

If we want to do something while we wait for a critical section to be free, we can use the pthread_mutex_trylock() function to determine whether or not the mutex is locked. The function returns immediately with a value of EBUSY if the mutex is already locked; otherwise, it locks the mutex exactly as pthread_mutex_lock(). This allows us to "busy loop" on the mutex, rather than blocking:

```
while(pthread_mutex_trylock(&my_mutex) == EBUSY) {
    // do something while we wait
```

```
}
// Our critical section starts here
shared_tally++;
pthread_mutex_unlock(&my_mutex);
```

Unless absolutely necessary, this method of handling is not recommended, as it requires that the thread continue to use valuable CPU and system resources. It is instead recommended that a one-time action take place before blocking. This allows us to take some action should we recognize we are going to block, but it does not require that we loop on a potentially infinite value. For instance, if we were trying to trace the source of a deadlock, we could use code like the following:

```
if(pthread_mutex_trylock(&my_mutex) == EBUSY)
    fprintf(stdout, "my_mutex is currently locked, waiting for lock.\n");
pthread_mutex_lock(&my_mutex);
fprintf(stdout,"achieved lock on my_mutex\n");
shared_tally++;
pthread_mutex_unlock(&my_mutex);
```

This allows us to note when we will have to block, but it is much less intensive than doing the same thing within a while loop.

Random Number Generation

To truly represent good security and reduce the risk of someone penetrating the encryption used in our examples, it is important to have a good source of randomness, or entropy. OpenSSL provides for this with its RAND_* interfaces. By using data from things like the local file system, user input, and network activity, the *pseudo-random number generator*, or PRNG, within OpenSSL needs to be seeded. To seed the PRNG, you must provide some data that OpenSSL will assume to contain entropy. You can do this in several ways:

```
RAND_load_file(const char *filename, long bytes);
RAND_seed(const void *buf, int num);
```

The RAND_seed() function allows you to specify a buffer of any type and size for entropy, while RAND_load_file() allows you to specify a file that contains entropy. In recent years, /dev/random has become increasingly popular in *nix systems as a file that the kernel maintains with as much entropy gathered from the system as possible. So to read 2048 bytes from /dev/random and seed the PRNG with the result requires only a single line:

```
RAND_load_file("/dev/random",2048);
```

If our code was to require random number generation without the added weight of the OpenSSL library, there are some system calls available on Linux systems that provide pseudo-random number generation. These are namely rand() and srand(), although many other derivatives such as srand48() and drand48() also exist depending on the precision necessary. While these functions can be useful for some applications, it is important to note that they do not provide enough statistical randomness to be considered "secure" when used for encryption.

TIP *You must ensure when you use the system call* rand() *or its derivatives to retrieve a random number that you initialize and seed the random number generator at least once. Without a seed, or if we were to always use the same seed, the generator would pump out the same list of numbers each time. A common method for seeding is to call* srand(time(NULL)); *to seed on the current time.*

Tools of the Trade

Although we may take all the necessary precautions and review our code carefully, we are but human after all, and mistakes happen. As a result, we also look to the tools of our trade to help us spot potential weaknesses and problems in our code.

The first place we see this is in the compiler. If our code does not compile without warnings, then we need to examine those sections of code called into question carefully. Similarly, we can look to several available tools and projects that do some extended checking, both for common and less common mistakes we may make, as well as tools that try to ensure extended safety through other methods.

Compiler Add-ons

When RedHat Linux 5.1 came out, buffer overflow attacks had become a prevalent method of attack on network daemons. As a result, Immunix (http://www.immunix.com) created a patch for the GCC compiler that manipulated the method of data storage, changed the order of variable declarations, and performed other such actions, each intended to make buffer overflow attacks less effective. While still only available for the 2.*x* series of GCC, a patch for the latest compilers that builds on these ideas is now available from IBM at http://www.trl.ibm.com/projects/security/ssp. Once the patch is installed, compiling your code with the -fstack-protector option results in code that is much more resistant, if not totally so, to buffer overflow and stack smashing–style attacks.

Code Analysis Tools

In addition to tools that enable the compiler to do some automatic protection, there are tools available that scan code looking for known security vulnerabilities, commonly misused functions, and other potentially unsafe situations. While none of these tools can (or does) claim 100 percent accuracy, it simply cannot hurt to have another opinion (if you can call the output of a program an "opinion") as to where things may be unsafe.

NOTE   *We will use one of these analysis tools in the following chapter to examine our practical example.*

Flawfinder

The first tool we will examine is called Flawfinder
(http://www.dwheeler.com/flawfinder). This tool scans C/C++ source code for commonly misused functions (strcpy(), strcat(), etc.) as well as for common argument-passing mistakes (passing bytes instead of character count, for instance). Recursive scanning is built in, so running the tool on a directory will cause it to recursively scan all files and directories in the given directory. Flawfinder outputs a list (in either plain-text or HTML format) of potential *hits*, where a hit is a potential misuse or unsafe section of code. The results are ranked by severity and output from the highest severity down.

Splint

Splint (http://www.splint.org) is an extended version of the popular source code–auditing tool Lint. As with Flawfinder, Splint scans C/C++ source code for common mistakes, potentially unsafe string manipulation, and other potential security problems. Splint also supports annotation, allowing you to modify Splint's behavior by commenting your code in particular ways. This allows you to ignore what you know to be false positives, to always report particular types of problems, and so on.

Summary

Keep in mind that there is no single method of programming or design that eliminates all potential security vulnerabilities, and no piece of software should ever be considered 100-percent secure. Network-aware software is built from extremely complex state machines incorporating not just the code we write, but also the libraries we depend on, the operating system, and the ever-unknown third party that uses the network itself. However, given the proper tools and knowledge of where and how security comes into play, you can take a proactive approach to ensuring data and software security.

In this chapter, we have shown that the following basic steps, at least, help in such an effort:

- Know the common methods of attack.

- Know the commonly misused or dangerous functions and their alternatives.

- Use proper error handling and return value management.

- Use memory management techniques to reduce or eliminate leakage or overflows.

- Don't retain privileges or disk access that is not needed (chroot()/setuid()).

- Use proper mutual exclusion handling for global scope and shared data.

- Ensure a minimum of entropy for pseudo-random numbers when using encryption.

- Make use of common analysis tools and add-ons to spot mistakes.

Case Study: A Secure Networked Application

AN EXAMINATION OF ALL THE CONCEPTS in this section is best supported by a single example that uses those concepts in a real-world context. Let's look at a networked application that requires the utmost security: an authentication server.

Our server will listen for incoming connections, negotiate a TLSv1 compliant encrypted connection, and then authenticate a user by one of two means, PAM or PKI. If the connecting user requests PAM authentication, then she sends her username and password, which are then checked using the server-side PAM implementation. If authentication is successful, the client will generate a PKI key pair and send the public portion to the server for future authentication. After the user is authenticated once by PAM, all future authentication attempts will be processed using PKI signature verification and the keys generated during the PAM authentication.

First, we will lay out the decisions we make in creating such an application, and then we will walk through the design of our code and finally through the code itself. To close out the chapter, we will examine improvements that could be made, and present the output from some security-auditing tools and explain how they apply to our security plan.

The Necessary Decisions

As with any networked program, we have a variety of decisions to make before we can even begin developing code. These decisions come about as the answers to several questions, such as "What process model will the server use?" and "How will we ensure communication security?"

Process Method

We have the option of writing any variation on a forking or multithreaded server—however, only a subset of these options actually falls within reasonable consideration. We must consider that we will be calling into and, even more important, be called back into from, the PAM library. The PAM library documentation (for Linux PAM) indicates that the library itself can be considered thread-safe so long as a single thread operates on a single PAM handle at a time. The documentation goes on to warn, though, that individual PAM modules may themselves not be thread-safe. This tells us that while it might be possible to interact with PAM in a threaded application, it may be safest to avoid the potential issues, which limits our options to those of the forking variety.

The rest of the decision lies in design. We could choose to create a preforking server that handles its own connection pool dynamically in a model similar to that adopted by the Apache Web Server, or we could choose to go with the simpler 1:1 use of a postforking server. For the sake of clarity, we choose the latter, forking a single process to handle each incoming connection. This has the drawback of not scaling overly well, but our requirements are slim, and the benefit of clarity in process handling can be seen as a sufficient enough gain to outweigh the added performance of a preforking design.

Security Model

Because we have the luxury of designing this application from the ground up, we can include in that design certain decisions that affect how security is handled as part of the big picture. This addition to the design is called a *security model*.

We start our model by stating some of the decisions we have made to ensure as safe a code base as is reasonable:

- We will use wrapper functions for memory management to ensure proper allocation and deallocation in a safe and secure manner.

- We will check the return of all possible API functions, especially those in the OpenSSL and network libraries, to ensure proper behavior. If a return value indicates an error condition, the calling process will report the error and exit to avoid potentially harmful conditions.

- We will use, whenever possible, "safe" versions of the commonly known "unsafe" functions, including strncpy() in place of strcpy() and others like it.

- We will use the open source tool Flawfinder to audit and review our code once we have written it.

With these items in mind and laid out as part of our design, we will move on to the remainder of our code design before finally starting to create the code for our program.

Code Design and Layout

With our security model in place, we can examine more mundane things, such as how and where we will store our code, how we will compile and test, and how we will run our final program.

File Layout

The layout we have selected is relatively simple, which is mostly the result of the simplicity of the application itself. We have chosen to use a simple directory layout, including a directory each for the client code, the code common to both the server and client, and the server code itself. This allows us to share code between the server and client, and to avoid the unnecessary complication of rewriting and adapting the same code multiple times.

In the common directory are three files: common.c, common.h, and Makefile. The first file contains all the common code that will be used by both the server and client, including the PKI management, wrapper functions, and so on. The second file includes declarations for each available function and is included in both the server and client code. In the client and server directories are three files that follow the same convention but for client- and server-specific code. Structuring the directory in this way allows us to simply type **make** in the top-level directory and automatically build the client, server, and common code.

The Protocol

As discussed in earlier chapters, it is important that we have thought out and designed our protocol ahead of time. In our example, this is relatively simple. We define our control messages as follows:

- REQUEST_KEY_AUTH

- REQUEST_PASS_AUTH

- SERVER_AUTH_SUCCESS

- SERVER_AUTH_FAILURE

Each of these will be an unsigned integer. The message REQUEST_KEY_AUTH is sent by the client at the start of a session to indicate that it would like to authenticate the user with the PKI signature verification. This is followed by sending the username, the size of the signed data in bytes, and the signed data itself.

The server then responds with either SERVER_AUTH_SUCCESS or SERVER_AUTH_FAILURE according to the result of the verification.

The message REQUEST_PASS_AUTH is sent by the client at the start of the session to indicate that it would like to authenticate the user via PAM. This is followed by sending the username and password of the user. The server will then respond with SERVER_AUTH_SUCCESS or SERVER_AUTH_FAILURE according to the result of the authentication. If the result is successful, the client then sends the public portion of a new RSA key by first sending the number of bytes in the DER-encoded key and then sending the encoded key itself.

Encapsulation

The last item in our design is related to encapsulation. While we are not using object-oriented programming (OOP), in that we are using the C language and not C++, we can benefit from some of the concepts incorporated by OOP. As we design our code, we try to encapsulate each "task" that we determine must be performed into its own independent function. For instance, we can list some of the functions our code will have to perform already:

- Authenticate a username and password with PAM.

- Verify signed data with PKI signature verification.

- Send data over a TLSv1 connection.

For each of these tasks, we will create a single function that does not require any of the others whenever possible. Some interdependence is a given; however, the more independent each function is, the more likely it is that we will be able to benefit from it later on.

The Code

With our design completed, we move on to writing the code itself. Developing a network server and client pair can seem a little like the chicken and the egg—which should we do first? We will start by writing the client utility in full, and then test it incrementally as we begin to implement the server.

Common Code Library

The common code is stored in the common/ subdirectory in both common.c and common.h. Other than the inserted commentary, these files are shown in their entirety. Note that for the sake of clarity, all in-code comments have been removed. A fully commented copy of the code is available electronically as described in the introduction to this text.

common.h

These first lines of code are a commonly used trick to prevent a recursive #include directive:

```
#ifndef COMMON_CODE_H
#define COMMON_CODE_H
```

By first checking for the definition of something and then immediately defining it, we can ensure that the contents of this file are included only once.

```
#include <stdlib.h>
#include <stdio.h>
#include <string.h>
#include <openssl/ssl.h>
#include <openssl/err.h>
#include <openssl/evp.h>
#include <openssl/rand.h>
#include <sys/types.h>
#include <sys/socket.h>
#include <netdb.h>
#include <ctype.h>
#include <arpa/inet.h>
#include <termios.h>
#include <unistd.h>
#include <pwd.h>
```

Both our server and client use many of the same system libraries and APIs, including the standard string-handling functions, the OpenSSL libraries, and the socket APIs. This lends itself to including each of these in the common code.

```
#define ENTROPY_SIZE 512
#define byte_t char
#define REQUEST_KEY_AUTH        10
#define REQUEST_PASS_AUTH       11
#define SERVER_AUTH_SUCCESS      1
#define SERVER_AUTH_FAILURE      2
#define SSL_ERROR                0
```

Next, we define the number of bytes our processes should seed the pseudo-random number generator (PRNG) with using ENTROPY_SIZE. We then define a custom data type, byte_t, to be synonymous with the built-in char. Often this type of definition is generated automatically with scripts or build tools. This allows code to operate on the byte level without having to maintain custom data type information on a per-platform basis. Lastly, we define a set of unsigned integers that we will use for our protocol messages.

```
void report_error_q(const char *msg, const char *file,
    int line_no, int use_perror);
void report_error(const char *msg, const char *file, int line_no, int
use_perror);

typedef struct memory_list {
    void *address;
    size_t size;
    struct memory_list *next;
    struct memory_list *prev;
} memory_list;

void *w_malloc(size_t bytes);
void w_free(void *f_address);
void w_free_all(void);
void w_memory_init(void);
memory_list *memory_list_head;
unsigned long global_memory_count;

void openssl_init(void);
void openssl_destroy(void);

char *ssl_read_string(SSL *my_ssl,size_t limit);
void ssl_write_string(SSL *my_ssl,const char *message);
unsigned int ssl_read_uint(SSL *my_ssl);
void ssl_write_uint(SSL *my_ssl,unsigned int value);
byte_t ssl_read_byte(SSL *my_ssl);
int ssl_read_bytes(SSL *my_ssl,void *buf,unsigned int limit);
void ssl_write_byte(SSL *my_ssl,byte_t this_byte);
void ssl_write_bytes(SSL *my_ssl, void *message, unsigned int length);

const char *network_get_ip_address(SSL *my_ssl);

RSA * key_create_key(void);
void key_destroy_key(RSA *);
```

```
unsigned int key_buffer_size(RSA *);
unsigned int key_sign_data(RSA *,const char *,unsigned int,char *,unsigned int);
int key_write_priv(RSA*, char *);
RSA *key_read_priv(char *);
void key_net_write_pub(RSA *,SSL *);
int key_verify_signature(RSA *, char *,unsigned int,char *,unsigned int);
int key_write_pub(RSA*, char *);
RSA *key_net_read_pub(SSL *);
RSA *key_read_pub(char *);
#endif
```

We then finish the file by declaring the report_error_q() and report_error() functions that we will use to report erroneous conditions and exit the program, as well as each of our memory wrapper functions, the wrapper functions for management of the OpenSSL library, the wrapper functions we will use to send and receive data, and finally the wrapper functions we will use for our PKI key management.

common.c

We begin our common code by including the common header file with

```
#include "common.h"
```

The first function we implement in our common code is report_error(). This function reports the given message, filename, and line number either by outputting them to the stderr file descriptor or by using the perror() function. This function is identical to that discussed in the previous chapter, except this function does not exit. Instead, we also implement a function called report_error_q(), which is a wrapper for report_error() that also exits. This eliminates the need for another argument and allows us to report potentially dangerous conditions without having to exit.

```
void report_error(const char *msg, const char *file, int line_no, int use_perror)
{
    fprintf(stderr,"[%s:%d] ",file,line_no);
    if(use_perror != 0) {
        perror(msg);
    } else {
        fprintf(stderr, "%s\n",msg);
    }
}
```

```
void report_error_q(const char *msg, const char *file, int line_no, int use_perror) {
    report_error(msg,file,line_no,use_perror);
    exit(EXIT_FAILURE);
}
```

We continue with our implementations of wrappers for the `malloc()` and `free()` calls. These are identical to those we looked at in the previous chapter and require no further explanation.

```
void * w_malloc(size_t bytes) {
    void *memory = NULL;
    memory_list *new_item = NULL;
    memory = calloc(bytes,1);
    new_item = calloc(1,sizeof(struct memory_list));
    if(memory) {
        if(new_item == NULL) {
            report_error_q("Memory allocation error, no room for memory list item.",
            __FILE__,__LINE__,0);
        }
        global_memory_count += bytes + sizeof(struct memory_list);
        new_item->address = memory;
        new_item->size = bytes;
        new_item->next = NULL;
        new_item->prev = NULL;
        if(memory_list_head) {
            new_item->next = memory_list_head;
            memory_list_head->prev = new_item;
            memory_list_head = new_item;
        } else {
            memory_list_head = new_item;
        }
        return memory;
    } else {
        report_error_q("Memory allocation error, out of memory.",
        __FILE__,__LINE__,0);
        return NULL;
    }
}
void w_free(void *f_address) {
    memory_list *temp = NULL,*found = NULL;
    if(f_address == NULL)
        return;
```

```
    for(temp=memory_list_head;temp!=NULL;temp = temp->next) {
        if(temp->address == f_address) {
            found = temp;
            break;
        }
    }

    if(!found) {
        report_error_q("Unable to free memory not previously allocated",
     __FILE__,__LINE__,0);   // Report this as an error
    }

    global_memory_count -= found->size + sizeof(struct memory_list);

    free(f_address);

    if(found->prev)
        found->prev->next = found->next;
    if(found->next)
        found->next->prev = found->prev;
    if(found == memory_list_head)
        memory_list_head = found->next;

    free(found);
}
```

To complete our collection of memory management wrappers, we add two more functions. First, we add the function w_free_all(), which walks the list of allocated memory and deallocates the memory itself as well as the associated memory in the list. This provides us with a catchall function we can call to ensure that memory we may have neglected to free is returned to the heap. The next function, w_memory_init(), is to be called prior to using any of the other memory wrapper functions. This function initializes the global variables that the w_malloc() and w_free() functions use and registers the w_free_all() function to be called at program termination by using the atexit() system call. After a call to w_memory_init(), anytime our program exits normally, by either returning 0 or calling exit(EXIT_SUCCESS), the w_free_all() function is called to ensure we clean up all allocated memory.

```
void w_free_all(void) {
    memory_list *temp = NULL;

    while(memory_list_head) {
        free(memory_list_head->address);
```

```
            temp = memory_list_head->next;
            free(memory_list_head);
            memory_list_head = temp;
        }
    }
    void w_memory_init(void) {
        static int state = 0;

        if(state != 0)
            return;

        state = 1;
        memory_list_head = NULL;
        global_memory_count = 0;
        atexit(w_free_all);
    }
```

The next wrapper functions we implement are openssl_init() and openssl_destroy(). These functions allow us to encapsulate the necessary steps in loading and unloading the OpenSSL library, as we discussed in Chapter 10. The openssl_init() function also takes on the process of seeding the PRNG within OpenSSL by reading ENTROPY_SIZE bytes from the kernel device /dev/random. We also register the openssl_destroy() function with a call to atexit() to ensure that our process cleans up after itself upon exiting.

```
void openssl_init(void) {
    static int state = 0;
    int bytes_read = 0;

    if(state != 0)
        return;

    state = 1;
    atexit(openssl_destroy);
    OpenSSL_add_all_algorithms();
    SSL_load_error_strings();

    printf("Seeding PRNG with /dev/random, this may take a moment... ");
    fflush(stdout);
    if((bytes_read = RAND_load_file("/dev/random",ENTROPY_SIZE)) != ENTROPY_SIZE)
    {
        report_error_q("Seeding PRNG failed",__FILE__,__LINE__,0);
    }
    printf("Done\n");
```

```
        fflush(stdout);
}
void openssl_destroy(void) {
    EVP_cleanup();
    ERR_free_strings();
}
```

In our quest to encapsulate things, the process of sending and receiving data is an easy target. We implement the functions ssl_read_string() and ssl_write_string() as wrappers for the code necessary to read and write a NULL-terminated character string over our encrypted connection using the OpenSSL library.

The ssl_read_string() function takes the connection to read from and a maximum limit for the number of characters to read as arguments, and returns a newly allocated character array containing the result of the read. If the limit is reached, or an error occurs, the string is truncated with a NULL character and returned as is; otherwise, the string is read until a terminating NULL character is read from the connection. We need to ensure that the string returned is later freed with a call to w_free() by the calling function.

```
char *ssl_read_string(SSL *my_ssl,size_t limit) {
    char * buffer = NULL;
    char this_one;
    int error = 0, read_in = 0;

    buffer = w_malloc(limit);

    while(read_in < limit) {
        error = SSL_read(my_ssl,&this_one,1);
        if(error > 0) {
            buffer[read_in++] = this_one;
            if(this_one == '\0') return buffer;
        } else {
            return buffer;
        }
    }
    buffer[limit-1]='\0';
    return buffer;
}
```

Our ssl_write_string() function takes the connection to write to and the string to write as arguments, and returns nothing. We walk over the string we are writing, sending as much as we can with each call to SSL_write().

```
void ssl_write_string(SSL *my_ssl,const char *message) {
    int ret_val = 0, bytes_written = 0;
    int bytes_to_write;

    bytes_to_write = strlen(message) + 1;

    while(bytes_written < bytes_to_write) {
        ret_val = SSL_write(my_ssl, message + bytes_written,
          bytes_to_write - bytes_written);
        if(ret_val <= 0) {
            break;
        } else {
            bytes_written += ret_val;
        }
    }
}
```

We continue by wrapping more functions around the SSL_write() and
SSL_read() functions, for reading and writing unsigned integer values, as well as
raw data. We will use these functions for our protocol, for which we need to be
able to send and receive unsigned integers, as well as for our PKI code, as we will
need to be able to send and receive the raw DER-encoded keys and signed data.

```
unsigned int ssl_read_uint(SSL *my_ssl) {
    unsigned int value = 0;

    if(ssl_read_bytes(my_ssl,&value,sizeof(unsigned int)) != -1) {
        value = ntohl(value);
        return value;
    } else
        return 0;
 }
void ssl_write_uint(SSL *my_ssl,unsigned int value) {
    unsigned int to_write = 0;
    to_write = htonl(value);
    ssl_write_bytes(my_ssl,&to_write,sizeof(unsigned int));
}
byte_t ssl_read_byte(SSL *my_ssl) {
    byte_t this_byte;
    if(SSL_read(my_ssl,&this_byte,sizeof(byte_t)) != 1)
        return '\0';
    else {
        return this_byte;
    }
```

```
}
int ssl_read_bytes(SSL *my_ssl,void *buf,unsigned int limit) {
    byte_t *my_buf = NULL;
    unsigned int x = 0;

    my_buf = (byte_t *)buf;

    for(;x<limit;x++) {
        my_buf[x] = ssl_read_byte(my_ssl);
    }
    return 0;
}
void ssl_write_byte(SSL *my_ssl,byte_t this_byte) {
    SSL_write(my_ssl,&this_byte,1);
}
void ssl_write_bytes(SSL *my_ssl, void *message, unsigned int length) {
    int ret_val = 0, bytes_written = 0;
    byte_t *buffer = NULL;

    buffer = (byte_t *)message;

    while(bytes_written < length) {
        ret_val = SSL_write(my_ssl,
                            buffer + bytes_written,
                            length - bytes_written);

        if(ret_val <= 0)
            break;
        else
            bytes_written += ret_val;
    }
}
```

With our SSL wrappers complete, we move on to wrapping other things. The network_get_ip_address() function takes an SSL connection as an argument and returns the IP address of the connected client as a character string. This function is used only by the server, but it is of general enough use that we put it here in our common code library.

```
const char *network_get_ip_address(SSL *my_ssl)  {
    struct sockaddr_in addr;
    int sizeof_addr = 0;
    int clientFd = 0;
```

```
    clientFd = SSL_get_fd(my_ssl);
    sizeof_addr = sizeof(addr);
    getpeername(clientFd, (struct sockaddr *) &addr, &sizeof_addr);

    return(const char *) inet_ntoa(addr.sin_addr);
}
```

The last set of wrappers in our common code base encapsulates the actions we will need to perform to fulfill the PKI portion of our goal. We begin by creating the function key_create_key(), which will create and validate a new RSA key. Afterward, we move on to create the complementary method key_destroy_key(), which will destroy and free the associated memory for a given RSA key. The last of the general-purpose PKI functions is key_buffer_size(), which wraps the RSA_size() OpenSSL function, returning the number of bytes necessary to store data signed with the given key.

```
RSA * key_create_key(void) {
    RSA *new_key = NULL;

    new_key = RSA_generate_key(2048,RSA_F4,NULL,NULL);

    if(new_key) {
        if(RSA_check_key(new_key) == 1)
            return new_key;
        else
            return NULL;
    }
    return NULL;
}
void key_destroy_key(RSA *this_key) {
    if(this_key)
        RSA_free(this_key);
}
unsigned int key_buffer_size(RSA *this_key) {
    return RSA_size(this_key);
}
```

With the general wrappers out of the way, we move on to wrap the code necessary to perform the PKI signature and verification processes. The first of these, key_sign_data(), performs the signing process on the given data with the provided key and returns the result in the provided buffer that is passed by reference. The unsigned integer that is returned indicates the number of bytes in the signature itself.

```
unsigned int key_sign_data(RSA *this_key,const char *original,
    unsigned int orig_size,char *signd,unsigned int signd_length) {
    EVP_MD_CTX my_evp;
    EVP_PKEY * pkey;
    unsigned int signed_length = 0;

    if(this_key == NULL)
        return 0;

    pkey = EVP_PKEY_new();
    EVP_PKEY_set1_RSA(pkey,this_key);
    signed_length = signd_length;

    EVP_SignInit(&my_evp, EVP_md5());
    EVP_SignUpdate (&my_evp,original, orig_size);
    EVP_SignFinal (&my_evp,signd, &signed_length,pkey);
    EVP_PKEY_free(pkey);
    return signed_length;
}
```

The signature verification process is encapsulated in the function, key_verify_signature(), which takes both a signed and an unsigned buffer as arguments. If the signature is verified with the passed key, then the function returns 0; otherwise, it returns –1.

```
int key_verify_signature(RSA *this_key, char *signd,unsigned
    int s_length,char * u_signed,unsigned int u_length) {
    EVP_MD_CTX my_evp;
    EVP_PKEY * pkey;
    int retval = 0;

    if(this_key == NULL)
        return -1;

    pkey = EVP_PKEY_new();
    EVP_PKEY_set1_RSA(pkey,this_key);
    EVP_VerifyInit(&my_evp,EVP_md5());
    EVP_VerifyUpdate(&my_evp,u_signed,u_length);
    retval = EVP_VerifyFinal (&my_evp,signd,s_length,pkey);
    EVP_PKEY_free(pkey);

    if(retval)
        return 0;
```

```
        else
            return -1;
    }
```

We finish our common code with a few more key management wrapper
functions. These functions handle reading and writing both the public and private portions of keys to and from both disk and the network (with the exception
of private keys, which should not be transmitted over the network). When public
keys are transmitted over the network, they are encoded in the DER format and
decoded at the receiving end of the connection. When stored on disk, both the
public and private keys are stored in the PEM format.

```
int key_write_priv(RSA *this_key, char *filename)  {
    FILE *store_file = NULL;
    int retval = 0;

    store_file = fopen(filename,"w");

    if(!store_file)
        return -1;

    retval = PEM_write_RSAPrivateKey(store_file,this_key,NULL,NULL,0,NULL,NULL);

    fclose(store_file);

    if(retval)
        return 0;
    else
        return -1;
}
RSA *key_read_priv(char *filename) {
    FILE *store_file = NULL;
    RSA *this_key = NULL;
    store_file = fopen(filename,"r");

    if(!store_file)
        return NULL;

    this_key = PEM_read_RSAPrivateKey(store_file,NULL,NULL,NULL);

    fclose(store_file);
    return this_key;
}
void key_net_write_pub(RSA *this_key,SSL *my_ssl) {
```

```
    unsigned int buf_size;
    unsigned char *buf,*next;

    buf_size = i2d_RSAPublicKey(this_key,NULL);
    ssl_write_uint(my_ssl,buf_size);
    buf = next = (unsigned char *)w_malloc(buf_size);
    i2d_RSAPublicKey(this_key,&next);
    ssl_write_bytes(my_ssl,buf,buf_size);
    w_free(buf);
}
RSA *key_net_read_pub(SSL *my_ssl) {
    RSA *this_key = NULL;
    unsigned int len = 0;
    unsigned char *temp = NULL,*buff;

    len = ssl_read_uint(my_ssl);
    buff = temp = (unsigned char *)w_malloc(len);
    ssl_read_bytes(my_ssl,temp,len);
    this_key = d2i_RSAPublicKey(NULL,&temp,len);
    w_free(buff);
    return this_key;
}
int key_write_pub(RSA *this_key, char *filename ) {
    FILE *store_file = NULL;
    int retval = 0;

    store_file = fopen(filename,"w");

    if(!store_file)
        return -1;

    retval = PEM_write_RSA_PUBKEY(store_file,this_key);
    fclose(store_file);

    if(retval)
        return 0;
    else
        return -1;
}
RSA *key_read_pub(char *filename)  {
    FILE *store_file = NULL;
    RSA *this_key = NULL;

    store_file = fopen(filename,"r");
```

```
    if(!store_file)
        return NULL;

    this_key = PEM_read_RSA_PUBKEY(store_file,NULL,NULL,NULL);
    fclose(store_file);

    return this_key;
}
```

With the conclusion of our key management wrappers, our common code base is complete. All of the code remaining is highly specific to one side of the connection or the other and should therefore be implemented in the corresponding file. We continue by looking at the code for the client process.

The Client

The code for the client process is stored in the client/ directory in both auth_client.h and auth_client.c.

auth_client.h

This file declares all of the functions we will use within the client that are specific to the client and are defined in auth_client.c.

```
#ifndef AUTH_CLIENT_H
#define AUTH_CLIENT_H
SSL * ssl_client_connect(const char *host, const char *port);
const char *getUsername(void);
const char *getUsersHome(const char *username);
int haveServerKey(const char *host,const char *username);
RSA *getServerKey(const char *host,const char *username);
void writePrivKey(const char *host, const char *username, RSA *my_key);
const char *getUserPassword(void);
#endif
```

auth_client.c

This file contains all of the code specific to the client. When compiled, the binary auth_client begins execution at the main() function defined herein:

```
#include "common.h"
#include "auth_client.h"
```

The function `ssl_client_connect()` takes a host name and port as arguments, and if it is successful, it returns a new SSL connection to that host on the specified port. This encapsulates all the code necessary to initiate and negotiate that connection, such that upon successful return, communication can begin immediately over the returned connection. We implement this function using the `BIO` method of connection handling, making our code slightly easier to read and more portable.

```
SSL * ssl_client_connect(const char *host, const char *port) {
    SSL_METHOD *my_ssl_method;
    SSL_CTX *my_ssl_ctx;
    SSL *my_ssl;
    BIO *my_bio;
    char *host_port;

    host_port = w_malloc(strlen(host) + strlen(port) + 2);
    sprintf(host_port,"%s:%s",host,port);
    my_ssl_method = TLSv1_client_method();

    if((my_ssl_ctx = SSL_CTX_new(my_ssl_method)) == NULL) {
        return NULL;
    }
    if((my_ssl = SSL_new(my_ssl_ctx)) == NULL) {
        SSL_CTX_free(my_ssl_ctx);
        return NULL;
    }
    if((my_bio = BIO_new_connect(host_port)) == NULL) {
        SSL_free(my_ssl);
        w_free(host_port);
        return NULL;
    }
    if(BIO_do_connect(my_bio) <=0) {
        SSL_free(my_ssl);
        BIO_free(my_bio);
        w_free(host_port);
        return NULL;
    }
    SSL_set_bio(my_ssl,my_bio,my_bio);
    if(SSL_connect(my_ssl) <= 0) {
        SSL_free(my_ssl);
```

```
        w_free(host_port);
        return NULL;
    }
    w_free(host_port);
    return my_ssl;
}
```

When providing a username to the server, we could simply prompt the user for the username. However, for our purposes it would seem that assuming the username of the person who ran the client would provide for an interesting divergence into extending an application. As a result, we implement the function getUsername(), which uses the glibc functions getpwent() and getuid() to locate and return our username in the NSS passwd database.

```
const char *getUsername(void) {
    static char *username_buffer = NULL;
    uid_t my_uid;
    struct passwd *current_pwent = NULL;

    my_uid = getuid();
    current_pwent = getpwent();

    if(username_buffer != NULL)  {
        w_free(username_buffer);
        username_buffer = NULL;
    }

    while(current_pwent && !username_buffer) {
        if(current_pwent->pw_uid == my_uid) {
            username_buffer = (char *)w_malloc(strlen(current_pwent->pw_name) + 1);
            strncpy(username_buffer,current_pwent->pw_name,
                strlen(current_pwent->pw_name) + 1);
        }
        current_pwent = getpwent();
    }

    endpwent();
    return username_buffer;
}
```

We need a place to store the private portion of generated PKI keys. We have decided to implement this by storing the files in the user's home directory. As a result, we also need a way to determine the user's home directory path. We could examine the environment for the HOME variable, but this is unreliable. Instead, we

take the same approach as our `getUsername()` function and create a function
`getUsersHome()` that searches the `passwd` database for our user's home directory.

```
const char *getUsersHome(const char *username) {
    static char *home_buffer = NULL;
    struct passwd *current_pwent = NULL;

    current_pwent = getpwent();
    if(home_buffer != NULL) {
        w_free(home_buffer);
        home_buffer = NULL;
    }

    while(current_pwent) {
        if(strcasecmp(username,current_pwent->pw_name) == 0) {
            home_buffer = (char *)w_malloc(strlen(current_pwent->pw_dir) + 1);
            strncpy(home_buffer,current_pwent->pw_dir,
                strlen(current_pwent->pw_dir) + 1);
        }
        current_pwent = getpwent();
    }
    endpwent();
    return home_buffer;
}
```

Now that we have a method for finding the user's home directory and for
getting the user's username, we need a function to write a given private key to
the user's home directory. We wrap our call to `key_write_priv()` from our common code with our `writePrivKey()` function, which first builds the path to the
private key by concatenating the user's home directory, a dot (.) to make it a
hidden file, and the host name we are connected to.

```
void writePrivKey(const char *host, const char *username, RSA *my_key) {
    char *file_path = NULL;
    const char *user_home = NULL;

    if((user_home = getUsersHome(username)) == NULL) {
        report_error_q("Unable to find user's home directory",__FILE__,__LINE__,0);
    }

    file_path = (char *)w_malloc(strlen(host) + strlen(user_home) + 15);

    strncpy(file_path,user_home,strlen(user_home));
    strncat(file_path,"/.",2);
```

```
        strncat(file_path,host,strlen(host));
        strncat(file_path,".priv",strlen(".priv"));

        if(key_write_priv(my_key,file_path) != 0) {
            report_error_q("Unable to write private key to file",__FILE__,__LINE__,0);
        }
    }
```

When our client first starts, it needs to decide whether it should authenticate via PAM (password) or with PKI. This is done by first checking to see if we have a private key corresponding to the server we are connected to. To do this check, we implement the function haveServerkey(), which returns 0 if we do and –1 if we do not have a private key for use with the given host.

```
int haveServerKey(const char *host,const char *username) {
    char *file_path = NULL;
    const char *user_home = NULL;
    FILE *key_file = NULL;

    if((user_home = getUsersHome(username)) == NULL) {
        report_error_q("Unable to find user's home directory",__FILE__,__LINE__,0);
    }

    file_path = (char *)w_malloc(strlen(host) + strlen(user_home) + 15);

    strncpy(file_path,user_home,strlen(user_home));
    strncat(file_path,"/.",2);
    strncat(file_path,host,strlen(host));
    strncat(file_path,".priv",strlen(".priv"));

    if((key_file = fopen(file_path,"r")) == NULL) {
        w_free(file_path);
        return -1;
    }
    else {
        fclose(key_file);
        w_free(file_path);
        return 0;
    }
}
```

With the ability to determine whether or not we have a key for the current host, we also need to read that key from disk. We do this through the getServerKey() function, which returns an RSA key whose private structures are instantiated with our private key data and is sufficient for data signing.

```
RSA *getServerKey(const char *host, const char *username) {
    char *file_path = NULL;
    const char *user_home = NULL;
    RSA *my_key = NULL;

    if((user_home = getUsersHome(username)) == NULL) {
        report_error_q("Unable to find user's home directory",__FILE__,__LINE__,0);
    }

    file_path = (char *)w_malloc(strlen(host) + strlen(user_home) + 15);

    strncpy(file_path,user_home,strlen(user_home));
    strncat(file_path,"/.",2);
    strncat(file_path,host,strlen(host));
    strncat(file_path,".priv",strlen(".priv"));
    my_key = key_read_priv(file_path);
    w_free(file_path);
    return my_key;
}
```

The last bit of functionality we want to encapsulate before we begin implementing the main() function is the ability to prompt the user for a password. Prompting a user for input can be relatively easy; however, when a user types a password, we should turn off the echo in his terminal (or at least attempt to), so that his password is not shown on the screen for any passing eyes to see. Therefore, we combine turning off the terminal echo and the prompt into a single function, getUserPassword(), which returns the password the user enters.

```
const char *getUserPassword(void) {
    struct termios terminal_setup, old_terminal_setup;
    static char *password_buffer[2048];
    char *newline = NULL;

    memset(password_buffer,'\0',2048);

    tcgetattr(STDIN_FILENO, &terminal_setup);
    old_terminal_setup = terminal_setup;

    terminal_setup.c_lflag &= ~ECHO;
    terminal_setup.c_lflag |= ECHONL;
    tcsetattr(STDIN_FILENO, TCSAFLUSH, &terminal_setup);
```

```
    printf("Password: ");
    fflush(stdout);
    fgets((char *)password_buffer, 2048, stdin);
    tcsetattr(STDIN_FILENO, TCSANOW, &old_terminal_setup);

    while((newline = strstr((char *)password_buffer,"\n")) != NULL) {
        *newline = '\0';
    }
    return (char *)password_buffer;
}
```

Between the common code base and the encapsulation functions before this, we can now implement the body of the client fairly quickly. We have decided to implement our client in the main() function rather than as another wrapper as follows:

```
int main(int argc, char *argv[]) {
    SSL *ssl_connection = NULL;
    const char *host = NULL, *port = NULL;
    const char *username = NULL;
    char *response = NULL;
    char *signed_data_buffer = NULL;
    unsigned int signed_data_buffer_size = 0;
    RSA *my_rsa_key = NULL;
```

First, we check to ensure that we were given two arguments at runtime, one for the host name and one for the port:

```
    if(argc != 3) {
        fprintf(stderr, "Usage: %s host port\n",argv[0]);
        exit(EXIT_FAILURE);
    }
```

We then call our initialization wrappers for memory management purposes and for the OpenSSL library:

```
    w_memory_init();
    openssl_init();
```

Next, we store the arguments given to us on the command line, and then call getUsername() to get the user's username. We make sure to validate the username before continuing by checking to ensure it is not NULL:

```
host = argv[1];
port = argv[2];
username = getUsername();

if(username == NULL) {
    report_error_q("Unable to determine the username of this process.",
  __FILE__,__LINE__,0);
}
```

With our arguments stored and the necessary (up to this point) information gathered, we can try to connect to the server. We call our wrapper function `ssl_client_connect()` and verify that it returns a valid SSL pointer. If it does not, we report the error as reported by the OpenSSL library and quit:

```
if((ssl_connection = ssl_client_connect(host,port)) == NULL) {

report_error_q(ERR_error_string(ERR_get_error(),NULL),__FILE__,__LINE__,0);
    }
```

At this point, we have connected to the server successfully, so we now need to determine which course of action to take. Either we have a private key and do PKI verification or we prompt the user for his password and do PAM authentication. We call our `haveServerKey()` function to determine which of these actions to take. If we are to do PKI authentication, we first send the control message `REQUEST_KEY_AUTH`, followed by the username. We then read the private key from disk, sign a data buffer containing our username, and send the result. Once the server has received all this, it will attempt to verify the signed data and will return either `SERVER_AUTH_SUCCESS` or `SERVER_AUTH_FAILURE`, which we read with `ssl_read_uint()`.

If we are to do password authentication, we first send the control message `REQUEST_PASS_AUTH`, followed by the user's username and password (retrieved with a call to `getUserPassword()`). We then read the server's response with `ssl_read_uint()`. If the response is `SERVER_AUTH_SUCCESS`, we generate and send the public portion of a new RSA key, and then write the private portion to disk for future authentication.

```
if(haveServerKey(host,username) == 0) {
    ssl_write_uint(ssl_connection,REQUEST_KEY_AUTH);
    ssl_write_string(ssl_connection,username);
    my_rsa_key = getServerKey(host,username);
    if(my_rsa_key == NULL) {
        report_error_q("Key file exists, but data is invalid",
```

```
                __FILE__,__LINE__,0);
            }

            signed_data_buffer = (char *)w_malloc(key_buffer_size(my_rsa_key));
            signed_data_buffer_size =
        key_sign_data(my_rsa_key,username,strlen(username),signed_data_buffer,
        key_buffer_size(my_rsa_key));
            ssl_write_uint(ssl_connection,signed_data_buffer_size);

    ssl_write_bytes(ssl_connection,signed_data_buffer,signed_data_buffer_size);

            if(ssl_read_uint(ssl_connection) == SERVER_AUTH_SUCCESS) {
                printf("Server responded with SERVER_AUTH_SUCCESS\n");
            } else {
                printf("Server responded with SERVER_AUTH_FAILURE\n");
            }
            w_free(response);
        } else {
            ssl_write_uint(ssl_connection,REQUEST_PASS_AUTH);
            ssl_write_string(ssl_connection,username);
            ssl_write_string(ssl_connection,getUserPassword());

            if(ssl_read_uint(ssl_connection) == SERVER_AUTH_SUCCESS) {
                printf("Server responded with SERVER_AUTH_SUCCESS, sending PKI Key\n");
                my_rsa_key = key_create_key();
                if(!my_rsa_key) {
                    report_error("Error creating RSA key.",__FILE__,__LINE__,0);
                }
                key_net_write_pub(my_rsa_key,ssl_connection);
                writePrivKey(host,username,my_rsa_key);
            } else {
                printf("Server responded with SERVER_AUTH_FAILURE\n");
            }
        }
    }
```

We finish by closing the connection with the server, freeing the memory used by the connection, and returning 0. Remember that at initialization we registered a couple of things to be called at exit time that will now run and ensure OpenSSL and our memory wrapper list are destroyed properly.

```
    SSL_shutdown(ssl_connection);
    SSL_free(ssl_connection);
    return 0;
}
```

With our client code complete, we need to implement a large portion of the server before we can begin testing. We continue by examining the code specific to the server.

The Server

Our server code resides in the server/ directory, and consists of the files auth_server.c and auth_server.h. These files contain the code that is specific to the server portion of our example and build into the binary executable auth_server.

auth_server.h

We begin our server code by preventing circular #includes and including the main PAM header with

```
#ifndef AUTH_SERVER_H
#define AUTH_SERVER_H

#include <security/pam_appl.h>
```

Remember that our server will be using the PAM library in addition to the OpenSSL library. As a result, we need to make sure we include the pam_appl.h file from the PAM project.

```
SSL *get_connection(char *port);
int pam_authenticate_user(const char *,const char *);
int auth_conv(int, const struct pam_message **, struct pam_response **, void *);
void child_process(SSL *my_ssl);
int auth_conv(int num_msg,const struct pam_message **msg,
    struct pam_response **response, void *appdata_ptr);

typedef struct auth_struct {
    const char *username;
    const char *password;
} auth_struct;
#endif
```

In addition to our conversation function (declared as auth_conv() previously), we define the auth_struct structure as a means by which we can pass our conversation function the username and password for the user we are trying to authenticate. As a result of the conversation function being a callback, we do not have access to any data not defined in the local scope of the callback itself. PAM resolves this by allowing us to pass a void *, which is then provided unchanged as an argument to the callback, giving us a chance to access something in our own heap from the callback function.

auth_server.c

We begin our server code by including both the common header file and our server specific header with

```
#include "common.h"
#include "auth_server.h"
```

The function pam_authenticate_user() is our wrapper function for PAM authentication. We pass it a username and password, and it will return either 1 for success or –1 for failure. This function takes care of setting up the interface with PAM, calling into PAM, and verifying the results PAM provides.

```
int pam_authenticate_user(const char *username,const char *password) {
  struct auth_struct buffer;
  static struct pam_conv myauthconv = {
    auth_conv,
    NULL
  };
  pam_handle_t *pamh=NULL;
  int ret = 0, authenticated = 0;

  buffer.username = username;
  buffer.password = password;
  myauthconv.appdata_ptr = &buffer;

  if(username && password)    {
    authenticated =
    (ret = pam_start("login", NULL, &myauthconv, &pamh)) == PAM_SUCCESS &&
    (ret = pam_authenticate(pamh, 0)) == PAM_SUCCESS &&
    (ret = pam_acct_mgmt(pamh, 0)) == PAM_SUCCESS;

    pam_end(pamh,ret);
  }

  if(authenticated)
```

```
    return 1;    // Authenticated
  else
    return -1;   // Not
}
```

The function auth_conv() is the callback function, or conversation function, which PAM will call when we call pam_authenticate() in our pam_authenticate_user() function. We walk the array of responses that we must provide, and copy the user-name and password that were provided as the optional appdata_ptr argument into the responses where appropriate.

```
int auth_conv(int num_msg,const struct pam_message **msg,

     struct pam_response **response, void *appdata_ptr) {
  struct pam_response *reply_with = NULL;
  int num_replies;
  struct auth_struct *user_data;
  user_data = (struct auth_struct *) appdata_ptr;

  if(num_msg <= 0)
    return PAM_CONV_ERR;

  reply_with = (struct pam_response *)calloc(num_msg, sizeof(struct pam_response));

  if(reply_with == NULL)
    return PAM_SYSTEM_ERR;

  for(num_replies = 0; num_replies < num_msg; num_replies++)
  {
    if(msg[num_replies]->msg_style == PAM_PROMPT_ECHO_OFF)
    {
      reply_with[num_replies].resp_retcode = PAM_SUCCESS;
      reply_with[num_replies].resp = strdup(user_data->password);
    }
    else if(msg[num_replies]->msg_style == PAM_PROMPT_ECHO_ON)
    {
      reply_with[num_replies].resp_retcode = PAM_SUCCESS;
      reply_with[num_replies].resp = strdup(user_data->username);
    }
    else
    {
      free(reply_with);
      return PAM_CONV_ERR;
    }
```

```
    }
    *response = reply_with;
    return PAM_SUCCESS;
}
```

We implement a unique wrapper function called get_connection() for our server. This function, upon being called for the first time, will set up the BIO sockets for listening and prepare to accept incoming connections, and then return the first incoming connection as a new SSL pointer. Subsequent calls will return subsequent connections, such that repeated calls result in returning each connection as it comes in, since it blocks until a connection is available. This wrapper allows us to drop it in a for loop later and handle connections as they arrive on an individual basis.

```
SSL *get_connection(char *port) {
    SSL *my_ssl = NULL;
    static SSL_CTX *my_ssl_ctx = NULL;
    static SSL_METHOD *my_ssl_method = NULL;
    static BIO *server_bio = NULL;
    BIO *client_bio = NULL;

    if (port && !server_bio) {
        my_ssl_method = TLSv1_server_method();
        if ((my_ssl_ctx = SSL_CTX_new(my_ssl_method)) == NULL) {
            report_error_q("Unable to setup context.",__FILE__,__LINE__,0);
        }
        SSL_CTX_use_certificate_file(my_ssl_ctx,"server.pem",SSL_FILETYPE_PEM);
        SSL_CTX_use_PrivateKey_file(my_ssl_ctx,"server.pem",SSL_FILETYPE_PEM);
        if (!SSL_CTX_check_private_key(my_ssl_ctx)) {
            report_error_q("Private key does not match certificate",
            __FILE__,__LINE__,0);
        }
        if ((server_bio = BIO_new_accept(port)) == NULL) {
            report_error_q(ERR_error_string(ERR_get_error(),NULL),
            __FILE__,__LINE__,0);
        }
        if (BIO_do_accept(server_bio) <= 0) {
            report_error_q(ERR_error_string(ERR_get_error(),NULL),
            __FILE__,__LINE__,0);
        }
    }

    if (port == NULL) {
        SSL_CTX_free(my_ssl_ctx);
```

```
        BIO_free(server_bio);
    } else {
        if (BIO_do_accept(server_bio) <= 0) {
            report_error_q(ERR_error_string(ERR_get_error(),NULL),
            __FILE__,__LINE__,0);
        }
        client_bio = BIO_pop(server_bio);
        if ((my_ssl = SSL_new(my_ssl_ctx)) == NULL) {
            report_error_q(ERR_error_string(ERR_get_error(),NULL),
            __FILE__,__LINE__,0);
        }
        SSL_set_bio(my_ssl,client_bio,client_bio);
        if (SSL_accept(my_ssl) <= 0) {
            report_error_q(ERR_error_string(ERR_get_error(),NULL),
            __FILE__,__LINE__,0);
        }
    }


    return my_ssl;
}
```

The `child_process()` function is actually where the server performs its duties. It is this function that each child process is directed to after forking. The `switch()` statement determines what action the client has requested, and the two cases `REQUEST_KEY_AUTH` and `REQUEST_PASS_AUTH` are handled in a complementary manner to the client (when the client is to write, the server reads, and vice versa).

```
void child_process(SSL *my_ssl) {
    char *username = NULL, *password = NULL,*key_file = NULL;
    RSA *users_key = NULL;
    int authenticated = 0;
    int string_size = 0;
    unsigned int signed_size = 0;
    byte_t *signed_buffer = NULL;

    w_memory_init();

    switch (ssl_read_uint(my_ssl)) {
    case SSL_ERROR:

report_error_q(ERR_error_string(ERR_get_error(),NULL),__FILE__,__LINE__,0);
        break;
    case REQUEST_KEY_AUTH:
```

```
        username = ssl_read_string(my_ssl,1024);
        string_size = strlen(username) +
          strlen(network_get_ip_address(my_ssl)) + 10;
        key_file = w_malloc(string_size);
        snprintf(key_file,string_size,"%s.%s.pub",username,
          network_get_ip_address(my_ssl));
        users_key = key_read_pub(key_file);
        w_free(key_file);
        signed_size = ssl_read_uint(my_ssl);
        signed_buffer = (byte_t *)w_malloc(signed_size);
        if(ssl_read_bytes(my_ssl,signed_buffer,signed_size) != 0)
            report_error_q("Error reading signed data from client",
          __FILE__,__LINE__,0);
        if(key_verify_signature(users_key,signed_buffer,signed_size,
         username,strlen(username)) == 0) {
            ssl_write_uint(my_ssl,SERVER_AUTH_SUCCESS);
            printf("(%s) User %s authenticated via
                PKI\n",network_get_ip_address(my_ssl),username);
        } else {
            ssl_write_uint(my_ssl,SERVER_AUTH_FAILURE);
            printf("(%s) User %s failed via PKI\n",
                network_get_ip_address(my_ssl),username);
        }
        break;
    case REQUEST_PASS_AUTH:
        username = ssl_read_string(my_ssl,1024);
        password = ssl_read_string(my_ssl,1024);
        authenticated = pam_authenticate_user(username,password);
        printf("(%s) User %s %s via PAM\n",network_get_ip_address(my_ssl),
          username,authenticated ? "authenticated" : "failed");
        if(authenticated) {
            ssl_write_uint(my_ssl,SERVER_AUTH_SUCCESS);
            users_key = key_net_read_pub(my_ssl);
            string_size = strlen(username) +
              strlen(network_get_ip_address(my_ssl)) + 10;
            key_file = w_malloc(string_size);
            snprintf(key_file,string_size,"%s.%s.pub",username,
              network_get_ip_address(my_ssl));
            key_write_pub(users_key,key_file);
            w_free(key_file);
        } else {
            ssl_write_uint(my_ssl,SERVER_AUTH_FAILURE);
        }
```

```
            break;
    }

    if(users_key) {
        key_destroy_key(users_key);
    }

    SSL_shutdown(my_ssl);
    SSL_free(my_ssl);
    exit(EXIT_SUCCESS);
}
```

Because our server is designed to fork, the majority of the work is actually performed in the child_process() function, and our main() function is quite short and to the point. We first check our arguments, using the first argument as the port number to listen on, and then go into an infinite loop. Within the loop, we retrieve a connection and fork, and immediately after the child process begins it uses the daemon() system call to ensure that it does not become defunct and force the parent process to wait for it. This allows the parent process to continue on to the next connection almost immediately. Each child process then enters the child_process() function and handles the connection appropriately.

```
int main(int argc, char *argv[]) {
    char *port = NULL;
    SSL *my_ssl = NULL;
    int my_pid = 0;

    if (argc != 2) {
        fprintf(stderr, "Usage: %s port\n",argv[0]);
        exit(EXIT_FAILURE);
    }

    openssl_init();
    port = argv[1];

    for (;;) {
        my_ssl = get_connection(port);
        my_pid = fork();

        if (my_pid == 0) {
            child_process(my_ssl);
            daemon(0,0);
        } else {
```

```
            waitpid(my_pid,NULL,0);
        }
    }
    return 0;
}
```

Running the Client and Server

With our implementation complete, we can now move on to running and using our client and server programs. First, we build all the code by running

```
make
```

within our top-level directory. Once it's built, we need to open two terminals. In one, we run the server as root (su – first if necessary), and in the other, we run the client as any valid user on the system.

> **NOTE** *The makefiles for this sample are included with the book's files, which are available for download from the Downloads area of the Apress website (*http://www.apress.com*).*

We run the server with

```
$ ./server/auth_server 9091
```

which will run the server and have it listen on port 9091. To run the server we must ensure there is a private key and certificate in the current directory named server.pem. These can be created using the methods discussed in Chapter 10. We can then run the client with

```
$ ./client/auth_client localhost 9091
```

The client should connect and prompt us for our password. Once we enter the password for the user who ran the client, the server should authenticate us and a PKI key should be traded. In the client's terminal, we should now be able to see the private key with

```
$ ls ~/.localhost.priv
```

Likewise, we should be able to see the public key in our current directory (where the server was run from) as [username].127.0.0.1.pub, where [username] is the name of the user who ran the client. If the same user runs the client again, the server should come back with success and we will not be prompted for our password, as authentication was done through the PKI verification process.

Analysis

With all the code in place, it's time to analyze our own code and look for weaknesses, things that we may want to change in the future, and so on. First we'll examine the result of running a tool such as Flawfinder on the source. Then we'll look at some things we can do with our code in the future to enhance its value.

Flawfinder Audit

We run the Flawfinder tool from the top-level directory with

```
$ flawfinder .
```

Flawfinder will then run recursively on that directory and examine all our source files automatically. The result of the run is something like the following:

```
Flawfinder version 1.24, (C) 2001-2003 David A. Wheeler.
Number of dangerous functions in C/C++ ruleset: 128
Examining ./client/auth_client.c
Examining ./client/auth_client.h
Examining ./common/common.h
Examining ./common/common.c
Examining ./server/auth_server.h
Examining ./server/auth_server.c
./client/auth_client.c:29:  [4] (buffer) sprintf:
  Does not check for buffer overflows. Use snprintf or vsnprintf.
./client/auth_client.c:154:  [2] (misc) fopen:
  Check when opening files - can an attacker redirect it (via symlinks),
  force the opening of special file type (e.g., device files), move
  things around to create a race condition, control its ancestors, or change
  its contents?.
./client/auth_client.c:213:  [2] (buffer) char:
  Statically-sized arrays can be overflowed. Perform bounds checking,
  use functions that limit length, or ensure that the size is larger than
  the maximum possible length.
```

```
...

...

...
Number of hits = 54
Number of Lines Analyzed = 1373 in 1.13 seconds (2172 lines/second)
Not every hit is necessarily a security vulnerability.
There may be other security vulnerabilities; review your code!
```

As the tag line says, not all the hits the tool finds are necessarily security holes, but it would be wise for us to check each to ensure proper usage and function. For instance, the first hit indicates that we used the sprintf() function rather than its safer alternative, snprintf(). If we look at the code itself, we see this:

```
host_port = w_malloc(strlen(host) + strlen(port) + 2);
sprintf(host_port,"%s:%s",host,port);
```

As a result of allocating space according to the length of the strings we later use as arguments to sprintf(), we are not at risk here. However, if we want to be extra safe, we could change the sprintf() call to snprintf() as follows:

```
snprintf(host_port,strlen(host) + strlen(port) + 1,"%s:%s",host,port);
```

This would appropriately avoid bounds overflow. Examination of the other hits reveals that they are also of the same quality. Valid warnings indicate where we may be unsafe, but examination reveals we have used things in a sane manner.

Future Improvements and Enhancements

There are places in particular situations where our example may fall short. Anytime you complete a project, you should review where and how it may be extended or enhanced to be more flexible, to be more appropriate, or to otherwise extend its own value.

Architecture Independence

Much of our example code relies on some assumptions about architecture. The functions ssl_read_uint() and ssl_write_uint() will not work if they are run where sizeof(unsigned integer) is different on each machine. It would be more flexible to send the smallest number of bytes possible to provide the necessary value and cast it up to the proper data type depending on architecture.

Likewise, the ssl_read_byte() and ssl_write_byte() functions make some assumptions about the basic data type that has a sizeof() == 1. On systems where the basic type char is more than a single byte, our server will not work correctly. Instead, the byte_t data type we defined in common.h should be changed to reflect a native data type that is a single byte in size. In commercial or large code bases, this is often done via scripts at compile time or through runtime examination of data types.

Process Model

While our 1:1 process/connection model is adequate for basic to moderate usage, it will not scale well. As the number of connections grows, so will the number of active processes using memory and system resources. A switch to a preforked setup would alleviate this in part by allowing for some control over the total number of processes in action at a time.

Additionally, our main process does not daemonize with a call to daemon(). It would be advisable to have our main process daemonize and change root to a protected directory. This way, we could protect potential path transversal attacks. As an offshoot of doing this, we could also look at redirecting our output on the server side from standard out to a logging utility such as syslog(). See the discussion of this in Chapter 7.

Avoiding Potential DDoS Attacks

The one area of security in which our example is lacking is protection from the potential of a DoS-style attack. All of our read functions, such as ssl_read_string(), are blocking, meaning that if a client was to connect and simply not send anything, a process would be started and stay around in a busy loop. If this happened enough within a small amount of time, it could exhaust system resources.

It is prudent to look at changing the design of our communication wrappers to include a timeout in some manner, although doing so with nonblocking SSL is probably the easiest. Information on using the SSL_read() and SSL_write() functions in a nonblocking manner is available in their respective man pages.

Additionally, when we perform a code review (a special thanks here to our book's excellent technical reviewer), other flaws may become apparent. For instance, in the function key_net_read_pub(), we first receive the size of the key from the network, and then allocate a buffer of that size. A malicious client could send us any value for that size and effectively cause us to allocate more memory than is reasonable or possible, causing our code to enter into undefined territory and thereby create some serious security concerns. It would be advisable to revise the code to include a sane limit for such allocation cases, either as a #define in the code, or as a configuration or compilation option.

Additional Security Concerns

As we mentioned in the last chapter, using a known sequence of data to verify a PKI key signature is not the safest of methods. Because our server and client examples operate over an already encrypted link, the risk of doing this is minimized. However, to increase the security and applicability of our examples, it is highly recommended that rather than using known data, the server would generate a random set of data that the client would then sign with the private key and send back. In this way, a man-in-the-middle attack or replay attack is less effective (if at all) in penetrating our security and masquerading as a particular user.

TIP *A replay attack involves an attacker recording the data sent to the server by the client and attempting to connect to the server and resend the same data in the hopes that the server will respond identically. When this attack is successful, the client can then impersonate a user whose session the attacker has recorded and potentially negate all of our security precautions.*

General Enhancement

The other place our server and client could be enhanced is in their abilities and protocol. It might be useful to add a method and protocol by which the client could have the server remove a public key or vice versa. We could also extend the PKI system to store both the private and public keys locally for the client, and reuse that key for access to other systems. Additionally, we could store the private keys in an encrypted manner by asking the user for a password each time (while still upholding our desire to not pass a password over the wire), which would allow the user to access the server without having to implicitly trust the root account on the client machine. Such enhancements greatly rely on the exact use of the system and how best to make the system interact with the user.

Summary

Our real-world example pulls together many of the ideas and topics we discussed in previous chapters. In this chapter, you saw how to put safe and secure programming practices into play, how to secure a communications channel, and how to authenticate users. We looked at the decisions that were required to design a program of real-world proportions, and we developed a protocol design of our own to solve the needs our program addresses. Combining all the techniques from this section and those from earlier in the text will result in extremely reliable, secure server and client implementations for whatever your needs may be.

APPENDIX

IPv6

IN CHAPTER 1, WE DISCUSSED the Internet Protocol (IP) and IP addressing. Each IP address is 32 bits long, with a network portion and a host portion. The 32-bit version of IP addressing traces back to RFC 760, circa 1980, and is known as *Internet Protocol version 4*, or IPv4.

When originally proposed, 32 bits seemed like plenty. There was no consensus that a 32-bit address space wouldn't be enough to handle the number of devices using a particular network. However, with the Internet explosion in the early 1990s, and along with it PDAs, cell phones, homes with several computers, laptops, businesses with a computer for every employee, and more servers than anyone cares to count, it soon became obvious to various groups that a 32-bit address space might not be enough. Contributing to the address shortage was the early practice of allocating huge address spaces to corporations and government entities, whether they needed that many addresses or not. Over time, many address spaces have been wasted. For example, a large company might have been assigned a Class A address space such as 10.0.0.0. A Class A address space has 16,777,214 hosts. Unless that organization had over 16 million network nodes, most of the address space would be wasted, since traffic for the entire space would be routed to the organization, making it impossible for a node outside the organization to use an address in that space.

A solution was needed to allow for the explosive growth of the Internet and the future scarcity of IP addresses. To increase the size of the address space, a new addressing scheme was proposed: *Internet Protocol version 6*, or IPv6. The IPv6 space is 128 bits, compared to 32 bits for IPv4. Described in RFC 2460, IPv6 offers several benefits over IPv4:

- *Expanded address space*: As just mentioned, IPv6 offers 128 bits instead of 32 bits.

- *Simplified header format*: IPv4-specific fields have been deleted or made optional.

- *Support for extensions and options*: Header changes allow for more efficient packet forwarding and more flexible limits on header field length.

- *Flow labeling*: Packets can be labeled as requiring special handling as requested by the sender.

- *Privacy and authentication features*: Data integrity, authentication, and other security capabilities are built in.

Like IPv4, IPv6 is a layer 3 protocol. For a refresher on layer 3, see the "Protocol Layer Models" section of Chapter 1 and Figure 1-8.

A full discussion about the IPv6 address space, the various address types (some of which are unused and exist only for research and experimentation purposes), IPv6 routing, and IPv6 subnetting is beyond the scope of this appendix. In this appendix, we present an overview of IPv6 addressing, how to determine if your Linux system is ready for IPv6 communications, how to use the IPv6 versions of the functions presented in Chapter 2, and we briefly cover some issues that you need to consider when porting an IPv4 application to IPv6.

IPv6 Addressing

IPv6 addresses are 128 bits long, or four times as large as the IPv4 address space. At 32 bits, the IPv4 address space is 2^{32}, or 4,294,967,296, possible addresses (a little over 4 billion). In contrast, the IPv6 address space is 2^{128}, or 340,282,366,920,938,463,463,374,607,431,768,211,456 (3.4×10^{38}) possible addresses. To put that into perspective, the IPv6 address space provides for approximately 6.5×10^{23} addresses for every square meter of the Earth's surface.

It's pretty difficult for humans to manage 3.4×10^{38} addresses, and each address would be a number with up to 39 digits, like this one:

340282366920938463463374607431768211455

Obviously, a different method is needed. If we take the number and represent it in hexadecimal instead, we can represent each number with 4 bits, knocking our address down to 32 characters:

0xffffffffffffffffffffffffffffffff

This still isn't very convenient. The designers of IPv6 chose a format that uses a colon (:) as a separator between each 16-bit block and removes the standard hexadecimal flag, 0x. That leaves eight 16-bit blocks:

ffff:ffff:ffff:ffff:ffff:ffff:ffff:ffff

A usable address, then, might look like this:

2ffe:ffff:0100:f232:0210:a4ff:fcd3:8188

That's still a bit unwieldy, so let's remove the leading zeros in each block:

`2ffe:ffff:100:f232:210:a4ff:fcd3:8188`

And still further, we can replace blocks containing only zeros with `::`. For example, an address of `2ffe:dede:0100:f101:0:0:0:1` can be written like this: `2ffe:dede:100:f101::1`. In IPv4, the localhost (or loopback) address is `127.0.0.1`. In IPv6, the same address would be `0000:0000:0000:0000:0000:0000:0000:0001` or simply `::1`. Also like IPv4, there are certain special addresses, such as the "any" address. In IPv4 format, this address would be `0.0.0.0`. In IPv6 format, it would be `0000:0000:0000:0000:0000:0000:0000:0000` or simply `::`.

There's even a way to create an IPv6 address out of a given IPv4 address. These addresses are known as *6to4 addresses*. Let's look at an example, using a reserved Class C address, with a subnet of `/24`: `192.168.10.1/24`. We want to convert this IPv4 address into a compatible IPv6 address using the 6to4 method defined in RFC 3056.

> **NOTE** *Converting an IPv4 address into an IPv6 address is not the same as assigning an IPv6 address. Converting an address from one format to another is typically only useful in a* tunneling *situation, where you don't have an IPv6 network, but you have IPv6 applications at each endpoint. For example, you could connect two IPv6 networks using a pre-existing IPv4 network without having to convert the IPv4 network to IPv6. For more information on this, consult RFC 3056.*

First, all such addresses begin with `2002`. The next 32 bits are the IPv4 address, in hexadecimal format. So far, our example IPv4 address in IPv6 format looks like this:

`2002:c0a8:0a01`

The `c0a8` is equal to the `192.168` portion of our IPv4 address, and `0a01` is `10.1`. The next 16 bits are for our subnet identifier, and the remaining 64 bits denote the interface ID. We stated earlier that our subnet was a `/24`, or a subnet mask of `255.255.255.0`. By default, we have a single IPv6 interface, so our final IPv6-formatted IPv4 address looks like this:

`2002:c0a8:0a01:24:0000:0000:0000:0001`

which can also be written as

`2002:c0a8:0a01:24::1`

Remember, the 2002 portion of the address flags a particular IPv6 address type, denoting an embedded IPv4 address, also known as a 6to4 address.

IPv6 and Linux

Before you can use IPv6 on your Linux system, you must determine if your system is IPv6-capable and, if it is capable, if it is ready for IPv6 communications. Modern Linux kernels (2.4.*x* and up) include IPv6 support, but your system may not have it enabled. If possible, avoid 2.2.*x* kernels, as their IPv6 implementations are no longer current. The kernel support for IPv6 is a module, which can be loaded on demand or loaded on startup automatically. To determine if your system is ready for IPv6, check for the existence of if_inet6 in /proc/net:

```
[user@host projects]$ test -f /proc/net/if_inet6 && echo "Ready for IPv6"
```

If you don't see the "ready" message, you'll need to load the IPv6 kernel module. Use the modprobe command to do this:

```
[user@host projects]$ modprobe ipv6
```

Assuming you didn't receive an error message, check your system again:

```
[user@host projects]$ test -f /proc/net/if_inet6 && echo "Ready for IPv6"
Ready for IPv6
[user@host projects]$
```

You can also check your IPv6 status using /sbin/lsmod, like so:

```
[user@host projects]$ /sbin/lsmod |grep ipv6
```

which, if your system is ready to go, should give you output that looks like this:

```
ipv6                  160768  -1
```

Remember that if you just used modprobe to load the IPv6 module, the next time you reboot your system, the module won't be loaded. This will cause problems for any IPv6 applications you have set to run as services, and it will prevent you from working with IPv6 until you load the module again. You can tell your system to load the IPv6 module automatically, on demand, by modifying /etc/modules.conf and adding the following line to it:

```
alias net-pf-10 ipv6
```

With this addition to the modules.conf file, your system will load the IPv6 module the first time an application requires it and keep it loaded until a reboot. After a reboot, it will stay unloaded until needed again.

Now that we've loaded the IPv6 module, let's check back with our earlier discussion on IPv6 addressing. We said that the IPv6 equivalent of the IPv4 localhost address of 127.0.0.1 was 0000:0000:0000:0000:0000:0000:0000:0001 or simply ::1. Since this is true, we should be able to use a utility like /bin/ping to ping our own system using the IPv6 version. Let's try it:

```
[user@host projects]$ ping ::1
ping: unknown host ::1
[user@host projects]$
```

Unless something deeper is wrong, it looks like ping doesn't support our IPv6 addressing scheme. That's because, like our own applications, the typical network tools included with a distribution only support IPv4, as is the case with ping. To work with IPv6, we need to use the IPv6 versions of the tools. Typically, the IPv6-enabled versions of network tools (and functions) simply append the number 6 to their name. For example, while we would use ping for IPv4, we would use ping6 for IPv6. With that in mind, let's try our experiment again, this time using ping6:

```
[user@host projects]$ ping6 -c 5 ::1
PING ::1(::1) 56 data bytes
64 bytes from ::1: icmp_seq=1 ttl=64 time=0.034 ms
64 bytes from ::1: icmp_seq=2 ttl=64 time=0.031 ms
64 bytes from ::1: icmp_seq=3 ttl=64 time=0.029 ms
64 bytes from ::1: icmp_seq=4 ttl=64 time=0.026 ms
64 bytes from ::1: icmp_seq=5 ttl=64 time=0.026 ms

--- ::1 ping statistics ---
5 packets transmitted, 5 received, 0% packet loss, time 3996ms
rtt min/avg/max/mdev = 0.026/0.029/0.034/0.004 ms
[user@host projects]$
```

That looks much better! This output shows that our system is ready to send and receive IPv6 traffic on its local interface, known as ::1.

Porting to IPv6

In Chapter 2, we presented the socket and network support functions used when developing network-enabled applications. As you've already seen in the preceding ping experiment, incorporating support for IPv6 into applications isn't transparent. If you don't explicitly implement IPv6 in your applications, they will only support IPv4. As the use of IPv6 continues to grow, it will probably end up the default at some point in the future, but for now the default is IPv4. If you want IPv6, you have to take special steps when developing your applications.

The main issues you need to consider when using IPv6 are as follows:

- Supporting the larger IPv6 address space in your socket address structures

- Handling name-to-address and address-to-name conversions in a manner that works for both IPv4 and IPv6

- Supporting the larger IPv6 address in user interface properties such as text boxes

You don't need to be concerned with changing the flow of your applications. Whether you use IPv4 or IPv6, the logical flow of socket applications, as shown in Figure 2-1 in Chapter 2, is the same. Moreover, you don't need to use different function calls for the foundation functions like socket(), bind(), accept(), and listen(). These functions support both IPv4 and IPv6, using the socket address structures to determine which address space is being used. For example, referring back to the "Socket Constants" section of Chapter 2, you see the following, from /usr/include/bits/socket.h:

```
#define PF_INET6        10      /* IP version 6.  */
#define AF_INET6        PF_INET6
```

As you can see, we can easily instruct our socket() function to use IPv6 by changing the address family, like this:

```
/* create a streaming IPv4 socket   */
V4Socket = socket(PF_INET, SOCK_STREAM, IPPROTO_TCP);

/* create a streaming IPv6 socket   */
V6Socket = socket(PF_INET6, SOCK_STREAM, IPPROTO_TCP);
```

Once we start using the PF_INET6 address family, the only thing left to do is handle the larger IPv6 address. Our original IPv4 addresses were handled by the sockaddr_in structure, and as you might guess by now, IPv6 addresses are handled by a structure called sockaddr_in6, which looks like this:

```
struct sockaddr_in6 {
    sa_family_t sin6_family;     /* AF_INET6 */
```

```
    in_port_t sin6_port;        /* Transport layer port # */
    uint32_t sin6_flowinfo;     /* IPv6 flow information */
    struct in6_addr sin6_addr;  /* IPv6 address */
    uint32_t sin6_scope_id;     /* IPv6 scope-id */
};
```

Once we've switched to the PF_INET6 address family and the new sockaddr_in6 structure, we're just about finished porting to IPv6. A few minor issues remain, such as handling the differences when using the gethostbyname() and gethostbyaddr() functions with IPv6, which we will discuss later as we go through our examples.

IPv6 Server

Let's take a look at the simple TCP server that we discussed in Chapter 2. It was originally set up to use IPv4; here, we port it to IPv6. We start out with our standard declarations and setup as shown originally, but this time we use sockaddr_in6:

```
#include <stdio.h>
#include <sys/types.h>
#include <sys/socket.h>
#include <netdb.h>

const char APRESSMESSAGE[] = "APRESS - For Professionals, By Professionals!\n";

int main(int argc, char *argv[]) {

    int simpleSocket = 0;
    int simplePort = 0;
    int returnStatus = 0;
    struct sockaddr_in6 simpleServer;
```

Next, we do our check for the right number of arguments, and if everything is OK, we go ahead and get a socket descriptor. Note that we make another change for IPv6, this time using the PF_INET6 address family in our socket() call.

```
    if (2 != argc) {

        fprintf(stderr, "Usage: %s <port>\n", argv[0]);
        exit(1);

    }
```

```
simpleSocket = socket(PF_INET6, SOCK_STREAM, IPPROTO_TCP);

if (simpleSocket == -1) {

    fprintf(stderr, "Could not create a socket!\n");
    exit(1);

}
else {
    fprintf(stderr, "Socket created!\n");
}
```

We continue with our server by retrieving the port number to use for receiving client connections and setting up our new IPv6 address structure.

```
/* retrieve the port number for listening */
simplePort = atoi(argv[1]);

/* set up the address structure */
/* use INADDR_ANY to bind to all local addresses  */
bzero(&simpleServer, sizeof(simpleServer));
simpleServer.sin_family = PF_INET6;
simpleServer.sin_port = htons(simplePort);
```

Unlike our IPv4 server, we have to use a special function to convert the string representation of our address to the binary representation that the sockaddr_in6 structure will use. Remember that localhost in IPv6 format is ::1.

```
inet_pton(PF_INET6, "::1", &(simpleServer.sin6_addr));
```

Once our address and port are set up, we bind to the socket and continue into our primary processing loop.

```
/*  bind to the address and port with our socket  */
returnStatus = bind(simpleSocket,
                    (struct sockaddr *)&simpleServer,
                    sizeof(simpleServer));

if (returnStatus == 0) {
    fprintf(stderr, "Bind completed!\n");
}
else {
    fprintf(stderr, "Could not bind to address!\n");
```

```
            close(simpleSocket);
            exit(1);
        }

        /* let's listen on the socket for connections        */
        returnStatus = listen(simpleSocket, 5);

        if (returnStatus == -1) {
            fprintf(stderr, "Cannot listen on socket!\n");
            close(simpleSocket);
            exit(1);
        }

        while (1)

        {

            struct sockaddr_in6 clientName = { 0 };
            int simpleChildSocket = 0;
            int clientNameLength = sizeof(clientName);

            /* wait here */

            simpleChildSocket = accept(simpleSocket,
                                       (struct sockaddr *)&clientName,
                                       &clientNameLength);

            if (simpleChildSocket == -1) {
                fprintf(stderr, "Cannot accept connections!\n");
                close(simpleSocket);
                exit(1);
            }

            /* handle the new connection request  */
            /* write out our message to the client */
            write(simpleChildSocket, APRESSMESSAGE, strlen(APRESSMESSAGE));
            close(simpleChildSocket);

        }

        close(simpleSocket);
        return 0;


}
```

As you can see, we've made very few changes. We change to using the PF_INET6 address family in our call to socket(), and we change our address structures to use the IPv6 versions instead of the IPv4 versions. Other than that, the code is the same as our IPv4 server from Chapter 2.

To run our IPv6 server, compile it, and then run it using a port number as the only argument. You should see output similar to this:

```
[user@host projects]$ cc -o ip6Server ip6Server.c
[user@host projects]$ ./ip6Server 9999
Socket created.
Bind completed!
```

To stop the server, use Ctrl+C. Once we port the client from Chapter 2 to IPv6, we'll be able to run them together and make our connection.

IPv6 Client

Like our server, our simple TCP client also needs to be ported to IPv6 to match. We start out with the same setup as the original IPv4 version, changing our address structure to the IPv6 version.

```c
#include <stdio.h>
#include <sys/types.h>
#include <sys/socket.h>
#include <netdb.h>

int main(int argc, char *argv[]) {

    int simpleSocket = 0;
    int simplePort = 0;
    int returnStatus = 0;
    char buffer[256] = "";
    struct sockaddr_in6 simpleServer;

    if (3 != argc) {

        fprintf(stderr, "Usage: %s <server> <port>\n", argv[0]);
        exit(1);

    }
```

For our call to socket(), we use the PF_INET6 address family and then continue with our setup of the sockaddr_in6 structure.

```
/* create a streaming socket      */
simpleSocket = socket(PF_INET6, SOCK_STREAM, IPPROTO_TCP);

if (simpleSocket == -1) {

    fprintf(stderr, "Could not create a socket!\n");
    exit(1);

}
else {
        fprintf(stderr, "Socket created!\n");
}

/* retrieve the port number for connecting */
simplePort = atoi(argv[2]);

/* set up the address structure */
/* use the IP address argument for the server address  */
bzero(&simpleServer, sizeof(simpleServer));
simpleServer.sin_family = PF_INET6;
```

We use the same conversion function as our server to handle our address.

```
inet_pton(PF_INET6, argv[1], &(simpleServer.sin6_addr));

simpleServer.sin_port = htons(simplePort);

/*  connect to the address and port with our socket  */
returnStatus = connect(simpleSocket,
                    (struct sockaddr *)&simpleServer,
                    sizeof(simpleServer));

if (returnStatus == 0) {
        fprintf(stderr, "Connect successful!\n");
}
else {
    fprintf(stderr, "Could not connect to address!\n");
    close(simpleSocket);
    exit(1);
}
```

```
/* get the message from the server    */
returnStatus = read(simpleSocket, buffer, sizeof(buffer));

if ( returnStatus > 0 ) {
    printf("%d: %s", returnStatus, buffer);
} else {
    fprintf(stderr, "Return Status = %d \n", returnStatus);
}

close(simpleSocket);
return 0;

}
```

Once we do our setup and have our socket, the rest of the client code is the same as the IPv4 version in Chapter 2.

To run our IPv6 client, compile it, and then run it using the IPv6 version of the localhost address, as well as the port number you used when starting the server. You should see output similar to this:

```
[user@host projects]$ cc -o ip6Client ip6Client.c
[user@host projects]$ ./ip6Client ::1 9999
Socket created!
Connect successful!
46: APRESS - For Professionals, By Professionals!
[user@host projects]$
```

Porting existing applications to IPv6 is not difficult. Once the address family is changed and the appropriate address structure is used, the normal rules and processes for TCP connections apply.

Address Conversion Functions

Several of the functions explained in Chapter 2 included informational and resolution functions such as getservbyname(), getservbyport(), and gethostbyname(). An application can use these functions to get information about the connection or service in question. This information can be used at runtime to set application parameters such as which port to use for connections or what IP address resolves to a particular host name. With IPv6, many of these functions have been consolidated into two new resolution functions: getnameinfo() and getaddrinfo().

getnameinfo()

This function is used for protocol-independent resolution of addresses to names. As shown in Figure A-1, it combines the functionality of gethostbyaddr() and getservbyport().

IPv6	IPv4
getnameinfo()	getservbyname()
	getservbyport()
	getpeername()

Figure A-1. The getnameinfo() function

getnameinfo() takes a number of parameters, like a pointer to a sockaddr structure and pointers to buffers that can hold the values returned by the function.

```
int getnameinfo(const struct sockaddr *sa, socklen_t salen,
                char *host, size_t hostlen,
                char *serv, size_t servlen, int flags);
```

When called, a host name or service name is not required and can be replaced by NULL, but one of them must be provided. The flags argument can be used to modify the values returned by a successful cal to getnameinfo(), such as returning only the host name portion of a fully-qualified domain name (FQDN).

getaddrinfo()

This function is used for protocol-independent resolution of names to addresses. It is the reverse of getnameinfo(). As shown in Figure A-2, it combines the functionality of several functions such as getservbyname() and gethostbyname().

IPv6	IPv4
getaddrinfo()	getservbyname()
	gethostbyname()

Figure A-2. The getaddrinfo() function

getaddrinfo() is thread-safe and takes a number of parameters, such as a pointer to a sockaddr structure. If the call to getaddrinfo() completes successfully, it creates one or more socket address structures that can be used by connect() and bind(). Since getaddrinfo() is protocol independent, it can be used for both IPv4 and IPv6 communications.

```
int getaddrinfo(const char *node, const char *service,
                const struct addrinfo *hints,
                struct addrinfo **res);
```

getaddrinfo() has two companion functions, freeaddrinfo() and gai_strerro().

```
void freeaddrinfo(struct addrinfo *res);
const char *gai_strerror(int errcode);
```

The freeaddrinfo() function is used to free up the addrinfo structure when your application is done with it. For reporting errors, getaddrinfo() uses its own error function called gai_strerror() instead of the typical perror().

Future Enhancements

Back in Chapter 2, we discussed the sockaddr_in structure. This structure supports IPv4, but not IPv6. As we noted in the previous two sections, the IPv6 version of the structure is known as sockaddr_in6 and looks like this:

```
struct sockaddr_in6 {
    sa_family_t sin6_family;     /* AF_INET6 */
    in_port_t sin6_port;         /* Transport layer port # */
    uint32_t sin6_flowinfo;      /* IPv6 flow information */
    struct in6_addr sin6_addr;   /* IPv6 address */
    uint32_t sin6_scope_id;      /* IPv6 scope-id */
};
```

At first glance, the easiest thing to do to port an application to IPv6 would be to change the code to use sockaddr_in6 instead of sockaddr_in, as we did with our IPv4 client and server earlier in this section. But what happens, then, if you want to use IPv4 as well as IPv6? By switching the structures, you end up splitting your application into an IPv4 version and an IPv6 version. This is workable, but it isn't the optimal solution. Fortunately, there's a better way. Instead of trying to determine which structure to use when, and instead of maintaining two versions of the same application, you can use a special structure specifically designed for portability, the sockaddr_storage structure:

```
/* Structure large enough to hold any socket address (with the historical
   exception of AF_UNIX).  We reserve 128 bytes.  */
#if ULONG_MAX > 0xffffffff
# define __ss_aligntype __uint64_t
#else
# define __ss_aligntype __uint32_t
#endif
#define _SS_SIZE        128
#define _SS_PADSIZE     (_SS_SIZE - (2 * sizeof (__ss_aligntype)))

struct sockaddr_storage
  {
    __SOCKADDR_COMMON (ss_);     /* Address family, etc.  */
    __ss_aligntype __ss_align;   /* Force desired alignment.  */
    char __ss_padding[_SS_PADSIZE];
  };
```

The sockaddr_storage structure uses 128 bytes and is designed to be large enough to hold any socket address. By using this new structure, you can hide the particulars of whether the address space is IPv4 or IPv6, while still allowing the application to use either. By using sockaddr_storage along with the IPv4-compatible functions getnameinfo() and getaddrinfo(), you can create applications that are ready for either IPv4 or IPv6.

Let's tweak our IPv6 client so that it can handle either an IPv4 or an IPv6 connection. The changes are fairly simple. We start out with our standard declarations.

```
#include <stdio.h>
#include <sys/types.h>
#include <sys/socket.h>
#include <netdb.h>

int main(int argc, char *argv[]) {

    int simpleSocket = 0;
    int simplePort = 0;
    int returnStatus = 0;
    char buffer[256] = "";
```

The next thing we need to do is declare our `addrinfo` structure, because this version of our client must handle either an IPv4 address or IPv6 address. We set up our structure like this:

```
struct addrinfo hints, *res;

bzero(&hints, sizeof(struct addrinfo));
hints.ai_family = PF_UNSPEC;
hints.ai_socktype = SOCK_STREAM;
```

We use two `addrinfo` structures. Of special note here is the use of `PF_UNSPEC` to set `ai_family` in the first structure. This is a special constant that means the address family is unspecified. The first structure, called `hints`, is used to set our protocol preferences. The second `addrinfo` structure, called `res`, is used to contain a linked list of all the possible addresses on this host. This is used because a given host can have more than one IP address, whether the IP version is 4 or 6. For our purposes, we're using only localhost.

Next, we do a standard arguments check, and then we populate our `addrinfo` structure using the `getaddrinfo()` function we've already discussed. For the arguments to `getaddrinfo()`, we use the server's IP address and the server's port number from our command line, and we pass it pointers to our `addrinfo` structure.

```
if (3 != argc) {

    fprintf(stderr, "Usage: %s <server> <port>\n", argv[0]);
    exit(1);

}

/* setup the address structure */
returnStatus = getaddrinfo(argv[1], argv[2], &hints, &res);

if(returnStatus) {

  fprintf(stderr, "getaddrinfo: %s\n", gai_strerror(returnStatus));
    exit(1);

}
```

As noted previously, we need to remember to use `getaddrinfo()`'s special error function, `gai_strerror()`, instead of the typical `perror()`. Our next step is to create our socket. This is a change from our earlier client code, because instead

of using our command-line arguments directly, we use the values from our
addrinfo structure that were filled in by getaddrinfo().

```
/* create the socket      */
simpleSocket = socket(res->ai_family, res->ai_socktype, res->ai_protocol);

if (simpleSocket == -1) {

    fprintf(stderr, "Could not create a socket!\n");
    exit(1);

}
else {
        fprintf(stderr, "Socket created!\n");
}
```

Next, we take our socket and make our connection to the server. As before,
we use the values in our addrinfo structure.

```
/*  connect to the address and port with our socket  */
returnStatus = connect(simpleSocket, res->ai_addr, res->ai_addrlen);

if (returnStatus == 0) {
        fprintf(stderr, "Connect successful!\n");
}
else {
    fprintf(stderr, "Could not connect to address!\n");
    close(simpleSocket);
    exit(1);
}
```

Then we read the message from the server, just as we did in our earlier client
examples.

```
/* get the message from the server   */
returnStatus = read(simpleSocket, buffer, sizeof(buffer));

if ( returnStatus > 0 ) {
    printf("%d: %s", returnStatus, buffer);
} else {
    fprintf(stderr, "Return Status = %d \n", returnStatus);
}
```

Finally, we close our socket and clean up, remembering to use getaddrinfo()'s companion function, freeaddrinfo(), to clean up our structure.

```
close(simpleSocket);
freeaddrinfo(res);
return 0;

}
```

That is all that's needed to handle either IPv4 or IPv6 addresses. You can test your multiaddress client using the IPv4 server from Chapter 2, and the IPv6 server from this appendix. For example, take the server example from Chapter 2 and start it on port 8888. Take the IPv6 server from this appendix and start it on port 9999. Using the new multiaddress client, we can run a test like this:

```
[user@host projects]$ cc -o multiClient multiClient.c
[user@host projects]$./multiClient 127.0.0.1 8888
Socket created!
Connect successful!
46: APRESS - For Professionals, By Professionals!
[user@host projects]$ ./multiClient ::1 9999
Socket created!
Connect successful!
46: APRESS - For Professionals, By Professionals!
[user@host projects]$
```

In the tests just shown, we make our first connection using the IPv4-style 127.0.0.1 (localhost), while our second connection is done using the IPv6-style ::1. As you can see, using the same version of our client and our addrinfo structure, we're able to connect to either an IPv4 server or an IPv6 server.

Summary

IPv6 is the next-stage IP addressing scheme. Using four times as many bits (128) as the current standard, IPv6 offers nearly limitless growth as well as advanced features such as improved routing, authentication and privacy features, and the ability to extend header information to take advantage of future needs. IPv6 addresses are backward compatible with IPv4 addresses.

Porting an existing IPv4 application to use IPv6 is not difficult, but a developer should remember some key points when doing the port:

- Each system running the application needs to support IPv6, and the IPv6 support must be enabled.

- The user interfaces for the application must accommodate the larger address values that are possible with IPv6.

- Using `getaddrinfo()` and `getnameinfo()` can provide name and address conversions for both IPv4 and IPv6 without being specific to either.

- If it's using IPv4 and IPv6, the application should accommodate both and use a portable structure for storing address and port information.

Index

Symbols and Numbers

@ (at sign) prefix, 216, 219, 223
: (colon), in IPv6 addresses, 342
6to4 addresses, 343

A

accept() function, 53–54, 76–77, 249
AcctSync project, 279
acknowledgment number, 30–31
active servers, 139–140
active sockets, 42
address conversion functions, 352–354
address family constants, 44–45
addresses, 8–17
    broadcast, 10, 14
    Ethernet, 8–10
    Internet Protocol, 12–17
    IPv6, 342–344
    loopback, 14–15
    MAC, 10
    multicast, 10
addrinfo structures, 356–357
Advanced Research Projects Agency
    (ARPA), 41
ai_family constant, 356
Apache Project, 128
Apache Web Server, 114, 128
appdata_ptr argument, 329
application programming interface
    (API), 44
application protocols, 87, 137–153
    binary vs. ASCII, 158
    client commands and, 142–146
    design considerations for, 138–142,
        155–172
    established vs. custom, 157–158
    example of using, 149–150
    registration of, 150–153
    server messages and, 146–149
    TCP vs. UDP, 155–157

applications
    case studies, 185–227, 301–339
    chat, 142–150, 185–227
    debugging, 173–177, 178–179
    PAM-aware, 266–268
    secure, 301–339
    See also client-server applications
architecture
    client-server, 99–135, 158–161
    forking server, 110
    multiplexing server, 104
    multiprocess server, 110
    multithreaded server, 120
    prethreaded server, 124
    process pool, 115
    three-tier, 159–161
    two-tier, 158–159
architecture independence, 336–337
arguments
    backlog, 52, 75
    socket function, 46
ASCII protocol
    binary protocol vs., 158
    message format, 138–139
ASP (Active Server Pages), 89
asymmetric key cryptography, 236–237
asynchronous transfer mode (ATM), 6
at sign (@) prefix, 216, 219, 223
atomic requests, 86
attacks, 281–282
    denial of service, 281–282, 337–338
    exploitation, 282
    information retrieval, 281
    man-in-the-middle, 236–237
    network mapping, 281
    replay, 338
auth_client.c file, 318–327
auth_client.h file, 318
auth_conv() function, 329
authentication, 261–279
    custom protocols and, 141
    old scenario of, 261–262

forums.apress.com

JOIN THE APRESS FORUMS AND BE PART OF OUR COMMUNITY. You'll find discussions that cover topics of interest to IT professionals, programmers, and enthusiasts just like you. If you post a query to one of our forums, you can expect that some of the best minds in the business—especially Apress authors, who all write with *The Expert's Voice*™—will chime in to help you. Why not aim to become one of our most valuable participants (MVPs) and win cool stuff? Here's a sampling of what you'll find:

DATABASES
Data drives everything.

Share information, exchange ideas, and discuss any database programming or administration issues.

INTERNET TECHNOLOGIES AND NETWORKING
Try living without plumbing (and eventually IPv6).

Talk about networking topics including protocols, design, administration, wireless, wired, storage, backup, certifications, trends, and new technologies.

JAVA
We've come a long way from the old Oak tree.

Hang out and discuss Java in whatever flavor you choose: J2SE, J2EE, J2ME, Jakarta, and so on.

MAC OS X
All about the Zen of OS X.

OS X is both the present and the future for Mac apps. Make suggestions, offer up ideas, or boast about your new hardware.

OPEN SOURCE
Source code is good; understanding (open) source is better.

Discuss open source technologies and related topics such as PHP, MySQL, Linux, Perl, Apache, Python, and more.

PROGRAMMING/BUSINESS
Unfortunately, it is.

Talk about the Apress line of books that cover software methodology, best practices, and how programmers interact with the "suits."

WEB DEVELOPMENT/DESIGN
Ugly doesn't cut it anymore, and CGI is absurd.

Help is in sight for your site. Find design solutions for your projects and get ideas for building an interactive Web site.

SECURITY
Lots of bad guys out there—the good guys need help.

Discuss computer and network security issues here. Just don't let anyone else know the answers!

TECHNOLOGY IN ACTION
Cool things. Fun things.

It's after hours. It's time to play. Whether you're into LEGO® MINDSTORMS™ or turning an old PC into a DVR, this is where technology turns into fun.

WINDOWS
No defenestration here.

Ask questions about all aspects of Windows programming, get help on Microsoft technologies covered in Apress books, or provide feedback on any Apress Windows book.

HOW TO PARTICIPATE:
Go to the Apress Forums site at **http://forums.apress.com/**.
Click the New User link.